Number	Statistic	Formula	Page
(10.5)	Y intercept	$a = \bar{Y} - b\bar{X}$	206
(10.6)	Slope of regression line	$b = \dfrac{\Sigma XY - (\Sigma X)(\Sigma Y)/n}{\Sigma X^2 - (\Sigma X)^2/n}$	206
(10.12)	Variance of Y "unexplained" by X	$s_{Y|X}^2 = \dfrac{1}{n-2}(\Sigma y^2 - b\Sigma xy)$	211
(10.13)	Variance for Y intercept	$s_a{}^2 = s_{Y|X}^2 \left(\dfrac{1}{n} + \dfrac{\bar{X}^2}{\Sigma x^2}\right)$	212
(10.14)	Variance for the slope of a regression line	$s_b{}^2 = \dfrac{s_{Y|X}^2}{\Sigma x^2}$	212
(10.17)	Student's t for the slope of a regression line	$t = \dfrac{b - B}{s_b}$	213
(10.18)	Student's t for Y intercept	$t = \dfrac{a - A}{s_a}$	214
(10.28)	Coefficient of linear correlation	$r = \dfrac{\Sigma XY - n\bar{X}\bar{Y}}{\sqrt{(\Sigma X^2 - n\bar{X}^2)(\Sigma Y^2 - n\bar{Y}^2)}}$	217
(10.30)	Student's t for coefficient of linear correlation (when $H_0: \rho = 0$)	$t = r\sqrt{\dfrac{n-2}{1-r^2}}$	218
(11.26)	Newman-Keuls test	$q_r = \dfrac{\bar{Y}_j - \bar{Y}_i}{\sqrt{MSW/n}}$	243
(12.1)	The χ^2 test for one-dimensional table	$\chi^2 = \displaystyle\sum_{i=1}^{K} \dfrac{(f_o - f_e)^2}{f_e}$	259
(12.2)	The χ^2 test for two-dimensional table	$\chi^2 = \displaystyle\sum_{r=1}^{r}\sum_{c=1}^{c} \dfrac{(f_o - f_e)^2}{f_e}$	262
(12.10)	The rank order correlation coefficient	$r_{rho} = 1 - \dfrac{6\displaystyle\sum_{i=1}^{n} D_i{}^2}{n(n^2 - 1)}$	268

Statistics for Physical Education, Health, and Recreation

Statistics for Physical Education, Health, and Recreation

CHARLES O. DOTSON
University of Maryland

DON R. KIRKENDALL
University of Kentucky

Harper & Row, Publishers
NEW YORK, EVANSTON, SAN FRANCISCO, LONDON

Sponsoring Editor: Joe Ingram
Project Editor: Ralph Cato
Designer: Jared Pratt
Production Supervisor: Stefania J. Taflinska

Statistics for Physical Education, Health, and Recreation

Library of Congress Cataloging in Publication Data

Dotson, Charles O
  Statistics for physical education, health, and
recreation.

  Bibliography: p.
  1. Physical education and training—Statistical
methods. I. Kirkendall, Don R., joint author.
II. Title. [DNLM: 1. Physical education and
training—Statistics. HA29 D725s]
GV436.D67   613.7′01′82   74-2669
ISBN 0-06-041687-4

Contents

Preface

A study of statistics has become essential to the preparation of professionals in physical education and related disciplines. *Statistics for Physical Education, Health, and Recreation* is intended as a first-course text for both the newer undergraduate classes as well as the more traditionally graduate levels.

Many features of this text should be particularly helpful to the first-course student, whether he be undergraduate or graduate. Some of these features are not commonly found in introductory texts. First, the authors have endeavored to keep all examples and exercises *relevant*—specifically pertaining to one or more of the fields of physical education, recreation, and health. The authors believe this strategy will avoid the presentation of statistics in a vacuum, an often-mentioned obstacle to learning the subject that, among other factors, may markedly deteriorate student interest in the course. Second, the *conceptual approach* is utilized in the initial presentation of all materials, and topics are included that are necessary for an introductory understanding as well as for any future study of statistics, either formally or on one's own. Third, the very important concept of inference is introduced *early* in the text and emphasized throughout. Little distinction is made between descriptive and inferential statistics; as a result, probability concepts should be seen by the student as an integral part of statistics. Further, probability concepts associated with continuous variables are presented by *example and logic* rather than through the calculus. The treatment of most topics is rather exhaustive *when* the material presented promises to contribute to the understanding of important concepts. Again, where a formal mathematical proof *would ordinarily* require more student background than a second course in high school algebra could provide, statistical formulas are illustrated *by example* instead. Through this method, students should develop an appreciation for the underlying concepts *that might not occur* if they are told to accept something on face value. Some instances of this strategy are the presentation of concepts involving unbiased estimators and the central limit theorem.

The authors believe the following specific innovations of presentation and organization will be especially helpful to beginning students. In Chapter 2, a procedure for involving the student with *the use of a computer* is suggested. Data are stored and, throughout the remainder of the text, exercises are provided that are specifically designed to be solved using the computer.

Chapter 4 introduces the *relationships* among parameters, statistics, populations, and samples, a strategy that should provide a preliminary basis for the study of probability and its resulting applications.

Procedures for estimating needed sample sizes in various hypothesis tests are presented in Chapter 9, as part of the attempt throughout the text to *bring the theoretical and practical aspects of statistics into accord.*

It should be noted that considerable material on probability has been included in Chapters 5 and 6. Although this may constitute a more comprehensive coverage of probability than many instructors feel is necessary, the text is organized such that an instructor may conveniently omit those portions of Chapters 5 and 6 that he deems inappropriate to his own methods and schedule. The authors nevertheless think he should have the *option* of an in-depth treatment of probability theory. The redundancy that occurs between Chapter 4 and Chapters 5 and 6 is intentional in order that portions of the latter chapters may be more easily omitted from a particular course.

The statistical tables provided in Appendix B and, particularly, the shortened versions of the normal and *F*-tables—easily accessible on the back endpapers—should prove invaluable. In addition, the presentation of key text formulas for quick reference on the front endpapers should also be of value. Appendix A provides a practical review of basic mathematical and algebraic operations for those students who require it, and Appendix C consists of a comprehensive index to statistical notation that may be utilized for both familiarization and review.

The sincere desire of the authors is that *Statistics for Physical Education, Health, and Recreation* will allow the instructor to present statistical concepts in a manner such that students will understand them, be able to apply them, and be adequately prepared to pursue advanced topics, whether with guidance or on their own.

There are numerous people to whom the authors are deeply grateful. We are indebted to Virgil Anderson of the Department of Statistics at Purdue University for the time and effort he gave to our own training in statistics. We are grateful to G. Alan Stull, William J. Stanley, and D. Laine Santa Maria for permission to use some of their statistics exercises and computer programs, and for their critical reading of the manuscript. The authors also wish to thank Russ Wilkins, editor for Harper & Row, who was willing to pursue a somewhat different project and was sincere about making a contribution to the profession.

Special thanks are also due to Lana Gibbons, Karen Haller, Gail Lovings, and Becky Renfro for their excellent secretarial assistance in preparing the manuscript. Finally, but hardly least, the authors are indebted to their wives, Japalene and Gloria, and their children, Dwayne, Chris, Randy, and Melissa, who stood by them in this endeavor and made it all seem worthwhile.

Charles O. Dotson
Don R. Kirkendall

Statistics for Physical Education, Health, and Recreation

1

Introduction to Statistics

1.1 INTRODUCTION

The pronouns "you" and "we" are used frequently throughout this text. Rather than accept these terms as simply grammatical conveniences, let us identify whom the authors have in mind when using these pronouns.

This text is written with the student of physical education, health, and/or recreation in mind. This student ("you") may be either an undergraduate or a graduate who is enrolled in his first statistics course. "You" also refers to the professionally dedicated student who desires to better himself in order to make a greater contribution to his students and, consequently, to his profession. Finally, "you" refers to the true student, the individual who is willing to *think* and who is endowed with the perseverance necessary to "stick with it" when the going gets a little tough. "You" does not include the person who throws up his hands in disgust and quits the first, second, third, etc. time he comes up against something new and sometimes a little difficult. The material in this text is geared for you and your background; however, there will be times when the material will seem difficult or even inappropriate. You must not give up at these times if you are to benefit from the study of statistics.

When the authors say "we" they refer to a team that includes you, your instructor, and the authors of this text. The team's goal is to provide you with maximum knowledge and understanding of concepts in basic statistics. As with any team effort, success depends on the contributions made by each member. The authors have tried to write the text with concept acquisition as the main goal. Your instructor will certainly make every effort to clarify those concepts that need further explanation. That leaves you as the other member of this team and the team's success or failure rests heavily on your shoulders since learning is an active rather than a passive activity.

1.2 WHY STUDY STATISTICS?

Although you have now begun to read your statistics book, you are still likely to wonder why the study of statistics is necessary for a student of physical education, health, or recreation. The answer to this question will become more apparent as you acquire a greater knowledge and understanding of statistics. Until you are familiar with the subject, however, you may need some rationale for making your study.

One reason for studying statistics is that it will help you in working with statistical data related to your students. Very often, simply knowing a score will tell you very little. For example, if you only know that a student has scored 68 on a tennis skills test, you may have difficulty evaluating his performance; in other words, the significance of this score may be unknown. The application of statistical tools may provide greater insight into the meaning of this score. Therefore, one of our first purposes in studying statistics is to add meaning to numbers or scores which might otherwise be difficult to interpret. As an extension of this purpose, we as teachers often wish to describe not only an individual but a group of individuals with respect to a measured characteristic. For example, we may wish to compare the physical fitness of our current students with the fitness level of our previous years' classes. Again, knowledge of statistics can provide the necessary tools for making this comparison. At other times we may want to say something about a total group after having observed phenomena on only a portion of the individuals in that group. For example, suppose we want to know how our ninth-grade students compare with national norms on a standardized drug knowledge test. If we only have 50–100 ninth-grade students, it is a simple matter to administer the test to the students and make comparisons with the norms. However, if we have a large number of ninth-graders, say 1000 or more, we might prefer to use a portion of these students, say 100, as representatives of our entire group. This would allow us to answer our question without spending the extra time or money to test all of our students. With an understanding of statistics the necessary tools to do this are provided.

There are other kinds of questions that can be better answered with an understanding of statistics. However, the most important reason for studying statistics is probably that an understanding of statistical concepts opens the doors to professional literature. It is the obligation of professionals in any field to be apprised of the most current knowledge available in that field. In order to accomplish this, professionals must be able to read and understand current research literature.

An analogy from the medical field may suffice to illustrate this point. It is very doubtful that any of us would patronize a medical doctor if we thought he was unaware of the very latest advances in the medical profession or if we suspected that he was unable to read his professional literature. By the same token, should parents or the teaching profession expect any less from a teacher of physical education and/or health or from a practitioner in recreation? Certainly not. Hence, the need arises for the professional in physical education, health, or recreation education to keep abreast of the newest developments in the profession by being able to read and interpret relevant research findings. This is possible only if he has some understanding of basic statistical concepts.

1.3 WHAT IS STATISTICS?

There are those who conceive of statistics as a group of neatly arranged tables and figures filled with numerals and symbols. Others think of statistics as a collection of vital facts such as " Kentucky hit 50% of its shots and made seven errors in the first half" or " 36–24–36." The above are certainly examples of statistics, but they do not give much insight into what statistics is as a discipline. Thus, let us first try to find out what statistics is when we consider it as a field of study.

For the purposes of this text, you should think of statistics as *the study of certain tools which make it possible to systematically describe, investigate, and interpret phenomena in a discipline.* This not only involves the collection of data but also the analysis, interpretation, and presentation of it. If we think of statistics in this way, it does not become an end in itself—just as anatomy, physiology, psychology, sociology, etc. are not ends in themselves for a physical educator, but rather helpful tools to aid the teacher of physical education in accomplishing professional goals. It is with such intent that this text was written, namely to provide future and present physical educators, health educators, and recreators with tools that will aid them in becoming more competent professionals.

REASONING IN STATISTICS

In studying physical education, health, and recreation, or for that matter in any endeavor to increase knowledge, one must frequently reach conclusions on the basis of incomplete information; if it were necessary to attain complete information before reaching a conclusion, there would not be much time left for progress. Drawing conclusions from something less than complete information is commonly referred to as *inductive reasoning*. Induction is the process of generalization, of drawing conclusions after observing a specific set of instances. This kind of reasoning is usually contrasted with the opposite process, *deductive reasoning*, where one proceeds from generally accepted laws or statements to specific situations or cases. Deductive reasoning allows us to formulate specific hypotheses from rather broad generalizations or theories; this is a necessity in the research process. Inductive reasoning allows us to reverse this procedure and make generalizations (inferences) after determining the truth of a specific hypothesis.

Sometimes the beginning statistics student has trouble accepting the inductive techniques utilized in statistics. However, if you think about it, you will realize that inductive reasoning is used by all of us throughout our lives. For example, after a small child touches a hot stove burner a few times, he makes the generalization that all stove burners will burn his hand. It is not necessary or possible for him to touch all burners before making such a conclusion. If we buy a bag of peanuts and the first few taken from the bag are rotten, we are likely to conclude that most of the peanuts in the package are rotten. We would generally not taste all of them before reaching this conclusion. So, the inductive process is not something that defies "common sense."

Traditionally, the study of statistics has been divided into two main branches, descriptive and inferential statistics. Descriptive statistics has generally been thought to be confined to the deductive process while inferential statistics has been thought to deal only in the inductive process. Many recent statistics texts do not categorize the study of statistics in this way, but assume that all study of statistics is inferential. Although this text tends toward this latter view, a slight distinction between descriptive and inferential statistics is made. However, the position will be taken that inductive as well as deductive reasoning may at times apply to descriptive statistics.

DESCRIPTIVE STATISTICS

There are times when a teacher, or any person involved with people, wishes to describe an entire group, not just a few individuals belonging to the group. This desire to describe, of course, could apply to any set of observations, whether they be observations of people or objects. The area of descriptive statistics involves the description of a group (set) of individuals or things by means of graphic, tabular, or numerical devices. This description may take one of the following forms:

1. Determining the frequency with which various values occur. *Example 1:* There are 15 girls and 21 boys in the afternoon health education class. *Example 2:* There are four boys in the ninth grade who are over 72 in. tall, 12 between the heights of 68 and 72 in., 10 between the heights of 64 and 68 in., and three who are less than 64 in. tall. Generally, a graphic representation, table, and/or figure enhances the comprehension of this type of description.
2. Determining a typical or usual value. *Example:* The typical or most frequently occurring family size in the United States is 4.
3. Determining the amount of variability in a set of scores or observations. *Example:* The number of chins performed by a group of students ranged from 0 to 16.
4. Determining the degree of relationship existing between two or more observations from a group of individuals or objects. *Example:* The grades obtained by students in kinesiology may be related to the grades they receive in anatomy.

The examples above for various types of descriptive statistics could be inductive. This concept may be illustrated by referring back to point two. In this case, we could have used a subset of the total United States population to determine the most frequently occurring family size in the United States. In the same way, referring back to point four, we might have used the grades of only 50–100 students to test the hypothesized relationship between grades in kinesiology and anatomy. The same type of approach could be used with the other examples. In other words, we may often describe the characteristics of a group after having observed the characteristic(s) of only a few members of that group.

INFERENTIAL STATISTICS

Any time we make inferences or conclusions on the basis of incomplete information we take a risk that we may be wrong. In the example cited earlier involving the package of peanuts, there is the possibility that we could be wrong in concluding that the bag of peanuts was rotten. With inferential statistics the reliability of our conclusions may be evaluated objectively in terms of probability statements. Inferential statistics allows us to make conclusions, but lets us know the risk (probability of being wrong) involved in making them. For this reason, the theory of probability plays a fundamental role in the understanding and application of inferential statistics.

Inferential statistics always involves: (1) the establishment of a hypothesis, (2) the collection of data from a subgroup of the group to be studied, and (3) the rejection or acceptance of the hypothesis based on the results obtained from the subgroup and an awareness of the probability (stated as a percentage) that this hypothesis might be wrong. For example, suppose we wish to know if the part method of teaching soccer (instruction consisting only of funda-mentals) is as effective as teaching soccer via the "whole" method (instruc-tion consisting of playing the game). We would first establish a hypothesis, usually in a form expressing no difference between the methods.

Hypothesis: There is no difference in soccer skill achieved between students who are taught by the "part" method and those who are taught by the "whole" method.

Since it is impossible for us to use all students to try this hypothesis, we might form two subgroups of our students and assign a different teaching method to each subgroup. At the conclusion of the soccer unit, we would administer a skills test and compare the averages of the scores of the two subgroups. Obviously, we would not expect the averages to be exactly the same. But through the application of inferential statistics, we could determine whether or not the difference between the two subgroups is larger than could be reasonably expected by chance, and based on this finding we could draw the appropriate conclusion.

The second and third chapters of this text are primarily concerned with descriptive statistics. Chapter 4 provides a further explanation of the prin-ciples involved in inferential statistics and extends the application of inductive reasoning to descriptive and inferential statistics. Chapters 5, 6, and 7 present the probability concepts necessary in the application of inferential statistics. The remainder of the text is concerned with inferential statistics procedures.

MISUSE OF STATISTICS

Sometimes people raise an eyebrow when the word "statistics" is used and immediately anticipate some devious statement. People have even referred to "lying" statistics. Statistics, of course, are inanimate objects and can never lie. But just as a slick-tongued con man can distort facts with rhetoric, the unscrupulous individual with a knowledge of statistics can also distort truth. Since it is not the purpose of this text to present knowledge in the misuse of statistics, little time will be spent in describing such procedures. Rather, we hope that through your understanding of the concepts involved in the application of statistics, you will be able to detect the misuse of statistics and avoid the same yourself.

1.4 HELPFUL HINTS IN STUDYING STATISTICS

Before leaving this introductory chapter, the authors feel obligated to suggest a few procedures that helped them as students and later on helped their classes with the study of statistics.

1. Read all material slowly and read it more than once. Reading and understanding statistics is not like reading a novel. It requires extreme concentration and usually repetition.
2. Attempt to keep up in your daily work. Statistics is not an assorted array of lateral facts. Rather, it is vertical in nature in that each new concept is based on previously presented concepts. Thus, if one allows things to slide, a "snowball effect" will take place.
3. Work through the examples given and then work assigned problems. Hopefully, you may learn from the practice provided by the examples.
4. Most important, don't give up!

Studying statistics is analogous to learning a new sports skill. Do you remember the first time you gripped a golf club how uncomfortable many of the "proper" grips felt? As you played more, you discovered that at least one of these basic grips wasn't so bad after all. So it is with the study of statistics. You need to work with it for a while before you feel comfortable with it. The more you are exposed to the concepts within, the clearer they will become.

Finally, a couple of devices included throughout the text which are intended to aid you in the pursuit of understanding statistics deserve mention. All the examples given throughout the text are realistic ones which are either directly related to the fields of physical education, health, and recreation or are from areas generally considered to be common knowledge. Exercises are presented after major sections of the chapter under study, rather than at the end when numerous concepts may have "piled up." However, additional exercises are presented at the end of each chapter in order to allow the student to integrate the various concepts contained in any chapter.

GOOD LUCK!

Exercises

1. Give an example where you have used the inductive process, the deductive process.
2. Give two specific situations where you, as a professional, will need to describe some group.
3. Describe an "experiment" which will require the application of some inferential technique.
4. Review the articles in the last three issues of *Research Quarterly*. How many articles presented research with no application of statistics?

2

Data Organization, Representation, and Storage

2.1 INTRODUCTION

To know something about an individual or an object, it is imperative to observe and record some characteristic pertaining to that object or person. For example, to know how well someone plays tennis, we must observe that person performing skills related to tennis. The phenomenon we observe is referred to as a *variable*. In our example the variable involved would be tennis skill. In general, *a variable is anything that may take on different values from person to person, object to object, or time to time.*

Observations can be made with varying degrees of sophistication. The crudest kind of observation is expressed as a simple qualitative description. For example, we could say that Player A plays tennis well while Player B is a poor tennis player. This kind of observation is not precise and is nondescriptive. No one would know exactly what we mean by good or poor. Therefore, we try to make observations that can be recorded in numerical scores. A numerical score is referred to as a *measurement* resulting from observation and generally reflects the extent to which an individual or object possesses a particular characteristic. One single numerical score obtained through observation is referred to as a *datum*. We are generally familiar with the plural of datum, namely *data*, which refers to a group of numerical scores or measurements. The terms measurements, data, and observations are used interchangeably in everyday as well as in statistical and scientific language. In this text, and generally in statistical writings, these terms in their plural form refer to a group of numerical scores.

It is necessary to distinguish the difference between *discrete* and *continuous* variables. A discrete variable must have a countable or finite number of possible units, but a continuous variable may take on an unlimited number of intermediate values. For example, we can count the exact number of situps performed by an individual or we can record the number of points a player scores in a basketball game. These are discrete variables. Examples of continuous variables are time, height, weight, and skill in a sport.

Even when we have continuous variables, our measurement of these variables is discrete. In scoring gymnastics, it is possible to have scores ranging from 0.1 to 10.0 in 0.1 increments, indicating a discrete scale. The phenomenon, gymnastics skill, is a continuous variable, but our scale of measurement is discrete. This will be the case with all continuous variables since we are limited in the precision of our measuring instruments. The degree to which continuous phenomena are continuous is determined by the accuracy of our measuring devices.

2.2 DATA ORGANIZATION

An unorganized group of scores contains a definite amount of information. Our interest is in organizing and representing these scores so that their information is relayed and interpreted to others.

10

FREQUENCY DISTRIBUTIONS

Suppose that we have measured weights, to the nearest pound, for each girl in our sixth-grade physical education class. The weights for these girls (56 of them) are recorded in Table 2.1.

We call this array of weights a distribution of weights—in general, any collection or array of measurements is referred to as a *distribution*. Such an unorganized distribution makes it difficult to describe or interpret data. To extract relevant information from this distribution, we must devise an organizational scheme. Our first thought might be to list the scores from highest to lowest and record the *frequency* of occurrence for each score. This organized array is called a *frequency distribution*. The frequency distribution of data on weights of sixth-grade girls is presented in Table 2.2.

TABLE 2.1

Weights of Sixth-Grade Girls, Measurements to Nearest Pound

97	104	99	93	94	97	98	103
98	97	99	97	98	95	94	96
100	96	97	98	100	101	95	101
98	97	100	97	97	97	96	99
96	95	99	103	92	97	99	97
92	101	95	95	96	94	90	93
100	93	98	96	100	99	97	98

TABLE 2.2

Frequency Distribution of Weights of 56 Sixth-Grade Girls

Weight (lb)	Tally	Frequency
104	/	1
103	/ /	2
102		0
101	/ / / /	4
100	/ / / /	4
99	LHT /	6
98	LHT / / /	8
97	LHT LHT / /	12
96	LHT /	6
95	/ / / /	4
94	/ / /	3
93	/ / /	3
92	/ /	2
91		0
90	/	1
	Total	56

Table 2.2 should facilitate the interpretation of our weight data. For example, we can tell that more girls weigh 97 pounds than any other weight and that very few of the girls' weights are at the high or low end of the distribution.

There are several other descriptions that can be readily derived from Table 2.2. The primary descriptions usually determined are the *relative frequency, percent of frequency, cumulative frequency, cumulative relative frequency,* and *cumulative frequency percent.* These are presented in Table 2.3 for the data on weights of sixth-grade girls.

Note that the "weight" column is denoted as the "midpoint." This is done to reiterate that the discrete scores we record are being used to measure a continuous variable. While weight is a continuous variable, the measurements recorded are in discrete units of one pound. For example, the six weights which we recorded as 99 are actually weights ranging from 98.500... to 99.499..., but we only recorded them to the nearest pound, that is, 99. In other words, any weight equal to or greater than 98.5 and less than 99.5 was recorded as 99. To acquaint you with the usual way of expressing this statement, we have to introduce a few "shorthand" notations. The symbol " $>$ " is read "greater than" and " $<$ " is read "less than." When we wish to write "equal to or greater than," we combine the equal sign ("$=$") with the greater than symbol (" $>$ ") and write " $\geq$ "; this is read "equal to or greater than." Likewise, the symbol " $\leq$ " is read "equal to or less than." Thus, we could express the concept of a continuous scale in our example above

TABLE 2.3

Relative Frequency, Percent of Frequency, Cumulative Frequency, Cumulative Relative Frequency, and Cumulative Frequency Percent of Weights of Sixth-Grade Girls

Weight (lb) Midpoint	Frequency	Relative Frequency	Percent of Frequency	Cumulative Frequency	Cumulative Relative Frequency	Cumulative Frequency Percent
104	1	0.02	2	56	1.00	100
103	2	0.04	4	55	0.98	98
102	0	0	0	53	0.94	94
101	4	0.07	7	53	0.94	94
100	4	0.07	7	49	0.87	87
99	6	0.11	11	45	0.80	80
98	8	0.14	14	39	0.69	69
97	12	0.21	21	31	0.55	55
96	6	0.11	11	19	0.34	34
95	4	0.07	7	13	0.23	23
94	3	0.05	5	9	0.16	16
93	3	0.05	5	6	0.11	11
92	2	0.04	4	3	0.06	6
91	0	0	0	1	0.02	2
90	1	0.02	2	1	0.02	2
Totals	56	1.00	100			

by saying that any weight W will be recorded as 99 if $W \geqslant 98.5$ and $W < 99.5$. The $W < 99.5$ could be rewritten, without a change in meaning, as $99.5 > W$. Therefore, for more compactness and clarity we would write that W will be recorded as 99 if $98.5 \leqslant W < 99.5$. This is read " W is equal to or greater than 98.5 and less than 99.5." You will find this little "shorthand" technique quite useful in your study of statistics.

The *relative frequency* of any score is determined by dividing the frequency of that score by the total number of observations. For example, in Table 2.3 the weight of 94 has the relative frequency of $3/56 = 0.05$. A percent of frequency is obtained by multiplying the relative frequency by 100. These provide additional meaning to our scores. We can now state, for example, that 0.11, or 11%, of the girls had recorded weights of 96 pounds, or we could more appropriately state that 11 percent of the girls weigh between 95.5 and 96.5.

Additionally, we can look at any interval of scores and talk about the percentage of girls having weights in that interval. For example, 0.57, or 57%, of our girls had weights $\geqslant 95.5$ but < 99.5. The 0.57, or 57%, was obtained by adding the relative frequencies or percentages for the individual weights of 96, 97, 98, and 99—that is, $0.11 + 0.21 + 0.14 + 0.11 = 0.57$, or 57%.

The *cumulative frequency*, *cumulative relative frequency*, and *cumulative frequency percent* are common descriptions involving intervals. The cumulative frequency of a score is the accumulated frequency of scores for all values $\leqslant$ the given score. For example, the cumulative frequency of 6 recorded for 93 is obtained by adding the frequencies $3 + 2 + 0 + 1$ corresponding to the weights 93, 92, 91, and 90. This means that there were six recorded scores of 93 or less. The cumulative relative frequency of a score is the cumulative frequency for that score divided by the total number of scores. For instance, using this column we would state that $49/57$, or 0.86, of the girls had recorded weights of 100 or less. By multiplying a cumulative relative frequency by 100, one can obtain the cumulative frequency percent or the percentile rank of that score. *Percentile ranks* are commonly understood by lay persons and, therefore, are frequently useful. Specifically, the *percentile rank of any given score is a number representing the percent of scores in a group that are equal to or less than that given score*. From Table 2.3 again, the percentile rank of the score 92 is 6, the percentile rank of 97 is 55, and the percentile rank of 100 is 87. The counterpart to the percentile rank is the *percentile*, where the *percentile is defined as the score at or below which a given percent of the cases lie*. From Table 2.3, the sixth percentile is 92, the 55th percentile is 97, and the 87th percentile is 100. These are usually written as $P_{06} = 92$, $P_{55} = 97$, and $P_{87} = 100$. In each of these, the score of interest is the percentile and the cumulative frequency percent is the percentile rank.

We will often want a particular percentile, say P_{10} or P_{95}. To find these in any set of data, we first find the cumulative frequency corresponding to the desired percentile. For P_{10}, we take $(0.10 \times n)$, where n is the total number of scores. In our example, we find that $0.10 \times 56 = 5.6$ (or when rounded to a whole number, 6) is the cumulative frequency corresponding to P_{10}. To find P_{10}, we next count 5.6 scores up from the low end of our distribution and find (from Table 2.3) that the fifth and sixth scores recorded are 93. Thus, $P_{10} = 93$, since 10% of the girls had recorded weights $\leqslant 93$. Similarly, for P_{95}, we find $0.95 \times 56 = 53.2$. Counting 53.2 scores up from the bottom, we find that the 53rd score recorded was 101, while the 54th score was 103. We could use 101 as our P_{95}. While this is recommended for use in practical applications, there are those who would argue that to be more accurate, we would record $P_{95} = 101 + (0.2 \times 2) = 101 + 0.4 = 101.4$. In other words, we have found the 53.2 score on a scale we assume to be continuous. Again, it is recommended that in finding percentiles we round off to a whole number the cumulative frequency corresponding to the desired percentile.

GROUPED FREQUENCY DISTRIBUTIONS

Many basic statistics books devote considerable attention to the collapsing of collected data into more compact forms. Although this practice is useful for a pictorial description, it will only be briefly presented here, and then not used for the remainder of the text.

Collapsing data is really an extension of the interval concept presented in the last section. In our current example of sixth-grade girls' weights, we could group our data into intervals of five and assume that all the scores in any given interval are equal to the midpoint. Table 2.4 shows the results obtained by using this procedure.

This table is referred to as a *grouped frequency distribution*. If we were to use this grouped frequency distribution, we would assume that 6 girls had weights of 91, 33 had weights of 96, 16 weighed 101 pounds, and one weighed 106 pounds. Notice that we have grouped a few weights in each interval; for example, the bottom interval includes all weights between 88.5 and 93.5. Obviously, when we use this method we lose a great amount of precision in measurement. Therefore, this procedure is recommended only as a means of providing a compact, comprehensive picture of data. If additional calcula-

TABLE 2.4

Grouped Frequency Distribution of Weights of 56 Sixth-Grade Girls

Weight Interval	Midpoint	Frequency
104–108	106	1
99–103	101	16
94–98	96	33
89–93	91	6

TABLE 2.5

Relative and Cumulative Frequency Percents of Grouped Frequency Distribution of Weights

Weight Interval	Midpoint	Frequency	Relative Frequency	Percent of Frequency	Cumulative Frequency	Percentiles
104–108	106	1	0.02	2	56	100
99–103	101	16	0.28	28	55	98
94–98	96	33	0.59	59	39	70
89–93	91	6	0.11	11	6	11
Totals		56	1.00	100		

tions are to be performed on data, then we recommend using the actual measurements that were recorded in order to avoid the loss of information that results from grouping.

It should be pointed out that the determination of relative frequencies, percent of frequencies, cumulative frequencies, and percentiles can also be recorded in grouped frequency distributions. Relative frequencies, frequency percents, cumulative frequencies, and percentiles for the grouped frequency distribution in Table 2.4 are presented in Table 2.5.

Exercises

1. Determine which of the following are continuous and which are discrete.
   a. skill in basketball
   b. temperature
   c. situps
   d. strength
   e. postage required on a letter
   f. sex
   g. sports knowledge
   h. state of residence
   i. actual height
   j. recorded height
   k. results of a coin flip
2. Express each of the following statements in verbal form and indicate whether each is true or false.
   a. $2 < 3$
   b. $16 < 14$
   c. $-2 > 0$
   d. $-5 < -3$
   e. $4 \leqslant 4$
   f. $4 \geqslant 4$
   g. $-6 > 4$
   h. $8 > -12$

3. a. Complete the following table:

Scores Attained on the Dyer Wallboard Test* by 153 College Students

Score	Frequency	Relative Frequency	Percent of Frequency	Cumulative Frequency	Cumulative Frequency Percent
30	1	___	___	___	___
29	0	___	___	___	___
28	2	___	___	___	___
27	5	___	___	___	___
26	9	___	___	___	___
25	7	___	___	___	___
24	13	___	___	___	___
23	16	___	___	___	___
22	18	___	___	___	___
21	20	___	___	___	___
20	16	___	___	___	___
19	7	___	___	___	___
18	12	___	___	___	___
17	14	___	___	___	___
16	6	___	___	___	___
15	3	___	___	___	___
14	0	___	___	___	___
13	2	___	___	___	___
12	1	___	___	___	___
11	0	___	___	___	___
10	1	___	___	___	___

* The Dyer Wallboard Test is used as a measure of the skill in the forehand and backhand drives in tennis.

  b. Explain what each of the columns above represents.
  c. Determine each quartile and give a verbal interpretation for each: (i) P_{25}, (ii) P_{50}, (iii) P_{75}.
  d. For each of the following numbers find the percentile rank and explain what this means: (i) 15, (ii) 22, (iii) 28.

4. The results from standardized written tests given in measurement and evaluation classes for the past three semesters are listed below.

Examination Scores of 107 Measurement and Evaluation Students

66	62	56	68	68	45
54	50	52	60	51	37
46	47	47	56	57	63
43	36	32	53	53	59
71	64	29	49	47	52
58	60	63	42	38	56
55	56	60	22	41	47
50	53	57	44	27	36
49	48	52	50	62	62
43	39	49	58	59	58
68	68	41	62	55	55
61	58	26	63	53	51
55	56	62	59	48	47
41	69	43	60	57	55
50	62	54	60	64	57
53	52	46	51	55	62
58	55	57	62	59	58
51	46	50	51	58	

a. Construct a frequency distribution.
b. Find the percentile rank for: (i) 60, (ii) 72, (iii) 45.
c. Find the percentiles: (i) P_{20}, (ii) P_{30}, and (iii) P_{87}.

5. Given the following scores attained by 80 students on the Vanderhoof Golf Drive Test:

24	21	21	36	25
23	42	18	34	34
9	37	43	38	33
31	25	8	36	37
16	24	19	36	35
16	13	20	12	15
21	23	27	12	15
26	25	18	27	24
26	32	27	28	23
19	22	20	34	31
35	22	30	32	29
33	14	26	30	29
40	39	25	21	26
29	17	25	25	24
28	38	34	23	25
23	20	25	13	23

a. Construct a frequency distribution giving the relative frequencies, relative frequency percents, cumulative frequencies, and cumulative frequency percents.
b. Find P_{10}, P_{17}, P_{65}, and P_{95} from the distribution of scores above.
c. Find the percentile ranks of the following scores: (i) 45, (ii) 24, (iii) 19, (iv) 14.

6. a. Construct a grouped frequency distribution like the one given in Table 2.5 for the examination scores in Exercise 4. Use the intervals 21–27, 28–34, 35–41, 42–48, 49–55, 56–62, 63–69, 70–76.
    b. If we assume a continuous scale, what values are included in each interval? Use $>$, $<$, and $=$ to express your answer.
7. Using the intervals 9–12, 13–16, 17–20, 21–24, 25–28, etc., construct a complete grouped frequency distribution from the golf skill test scores in Exercise 5.

2.3 GRAPHIC REPRESENTATION

The organization and description procedures presented thus far may help one to interpret data. However, a graphical representation of data may provide an even clearer "picture." Graphs or pictographs based on the organization and descriptions presented in the previous section usually make the major characteristics of the data so obvious that even the lay individual will grasp their meaning. The most common graphical representations, histograms, polygons, and ogives, will be described here; other forms of graphic presentation, such as bar graphs and pictographs, are simply adaptations of these.

HISTOGRAM

A histogram is a graphic picture of a frequency distribution. Rectangles or bars are erected to represent the frequency for some particular score or interval. Suppose we have found the number of chins six boys can do to be 2, 3, 4, 5, 5, 7. The frequency distribution in this case would be quite simple. We could represent these scores graphically as shown in Figure 2.1.

We represent each observation or frequency by an equal unit of area. This is a histogram. Of course, we generally have considerably more data than what we have presented here.

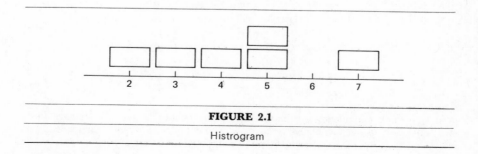

FIGURE 2.1

Histrogram

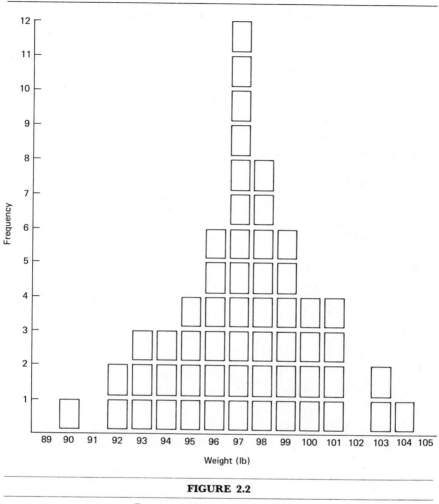

FIGURE 2.2

Frequency histogram for weights

A frequency distribution of 56 weights was presented earlier in Table 2.2 and is represented graphically in Figure 2.2. We can see that this picture or histogram greatly enhances our view of the distribution of scores.

Generally, the histogram is presented without the divisions between the rectangles that represent each individual score. Instead, a scale of frequencies is presented on the left and a bar is erected to the appropriate height (Figure 2.3). It is important to notice that each observation is still represented by an equal amount of area. Note also that in all histograms, we use the intervals

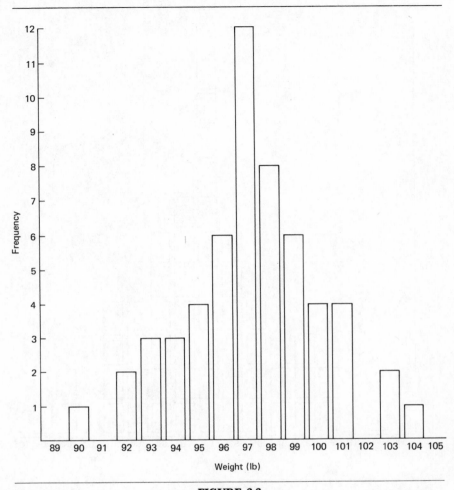

FIGURE 2.3

Frequency histrogram for weights

which were previously discussed in connection with continuous variables. For example, for the scores recorded as 99, the bar goes from 98.5 to 99.5.

A histogram is also useful in presenting relative frequencies. Using the relative frequencies from the weights example (Table 2.2), we have constructed the histogram in Figure 2.4. You can see that we have simply changed the scale on the left-hand side. The areas remain the same as in the frequency histogram.

Grouped frequency distributions are most appropriately presented in

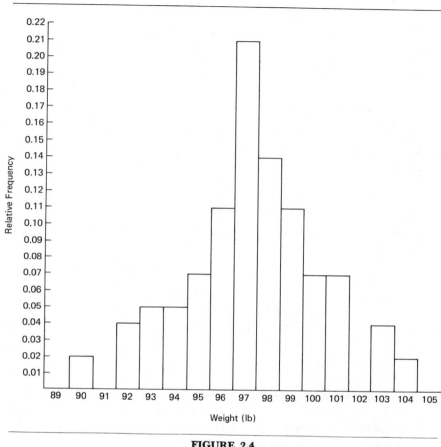

FIGURE 2.4

Relative frequency histrogram for weights

histograms. For example, the grouped frequency distribution of Table 2.5 can be represented by the histogram in Figure 2.5.

FREQUENCY POLYGON

Another graphic method for the presentation of a frequency distribution is the frequency polygon; this is constructed by simply connecting with straight lines the midpoints of the tops of the bars of a histogram. A polygon is superimposed over the histogram on the left side of Figure 2.6. The frequency polygon by itself is presented on the right side of Figure 2.6. Obviously, it is not necessary to construct a histogram prior to the construction of a polygon.

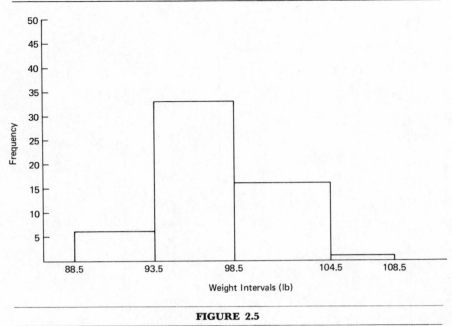

FIGURE 2.5

Grouped frequency histrogram

The frequency distribution for this polygon is the same as that used previously in the histogram examples. Note that a zero frequency is added at each end of the polygon so that the polygon does not appear to float. The frequency polygon is exactly like the histogram in that frequency is represented by the area under portions of the polygon rather than by the height of the various points that have been plotted.

The polygon is preferable to the histogram when two or more frequency distributions are compared, because the frequency polygons may provide a clearer pictorial comparison than either the actual distributions or the derived histograms.

The frequency polygon is often smoothed out until it is a smooth curve rather than a jagged polygon. Of course, when we construct a polygon based on data collected from a larger number of people or objects and when our measurements become more and more precise (approaching continuous data), our polygon comes close to being a smooth curve. The frequency polygon in Figure 2.6 is smoothed out in Figure 2.7.

As with the histogram, the polygon or its smoothed curve can be used with grouped frequency distributions and can also be used to represent relative as well as absolute frequencies.

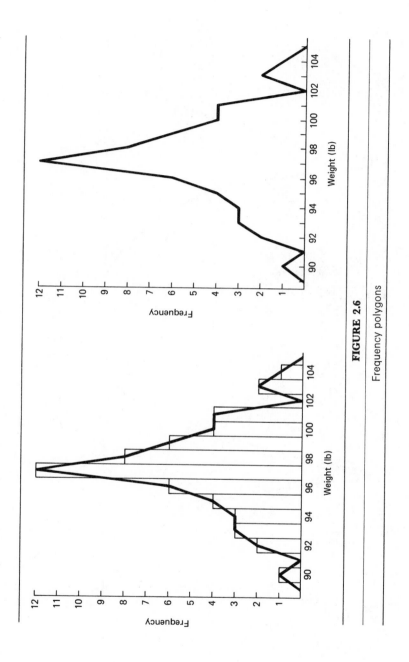

FIGURE 2.6

Frequency polygons

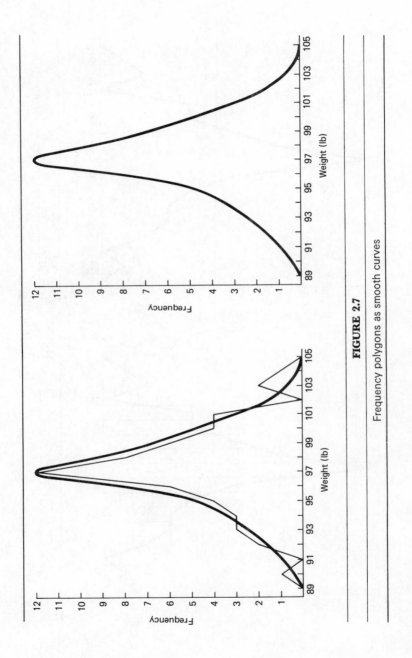

FIGURE 2.7

Frequency polygons as smooth curves

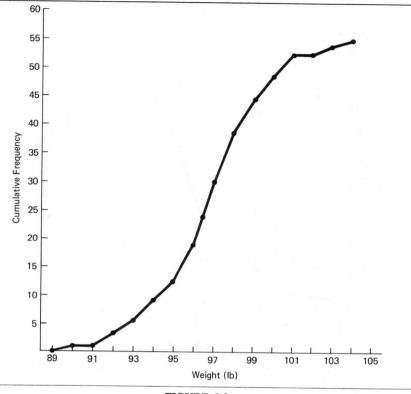

FIGURE 2.8

Cumulative frequency polygons

OGIVE

A cumulative frequency distribution may be conveniently presented by means of a cumulative distribution polygon, usually called an *ogive* (ō-gīve). To construct the cumulative distribution polygon, or ogive, we must connect by line segments the points that were plotted for the cumulative frequency histogram.

The ogive for the cumulative frequency distribution of girls' weights is presented in Figure 2.8.

We could easily have the percentiles on our ordinate scale instead of the cumulative frequencies. Such a polygon is presented in Figure 2.9. When percents are used, this graph becomes a very handy device for estimating percentiles and/or percentile ranks. For example, we can estimate $P_{90} = 101$, $P_{60} = 97.5$, $P_{50} = 97$.

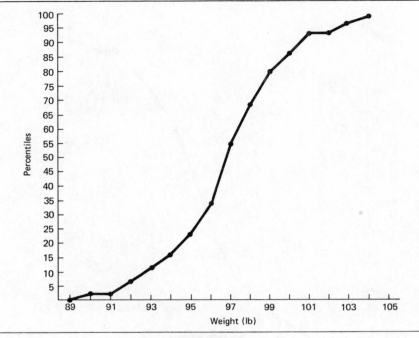

FIGURE 2.9

Cumulative frequency polygons for percentiles

Exercises

8. For the following soccer dribbling test scores (in seconds) construct a:
   a. histogram for frequencies
   b. histogram for relative frequencies
   c. frequency polygon for frequencies
   d. frequency polygon for relative frequencies
   e. ogive for cumulative frequencies
   f. ogive for cumulative percents

   Soccer Dribbling Scores, in Seconds, for Fifteen Students

12	20	16
18	28	12
15	20	16
27	28	16
12	27	15

9. From the following frequency distribution of chinning scores for junior high students construct a:
   a. histogram for frequencies
   b. histogram for relative frequencies
   c. frequency polygon for frequencies
   d. frequency polygon for relative frequencies
   e. ogive for cumulative frequencies
   f. ogive for cumulative percents

Chinning Scores for Junior High School Students

Number of Chins	Frequency
0	7
1	11
2	10
3	12
4	10
5	12
6	10
7	8
8	6
9	6
10	3
11	0
12	2
13	1
14	1
15	1
16	1

10. By using the ogive in 9(f), estimate:
    a. P_{10}
    b. P_{17}
    c. P_{75}
    d. P_{90}
11. Using the ogive in 9(f), estimate the percentile rank of:
    a. 5
    b. 2
    c. 9
    d. 13
12–13. From the frequency and grouped frequency distributions you obtained in Exercises 4 and 6 of this chapter, construct a:
    a. histogram for frequencies
    b. histogram for relative frequencies
    c. frequency polygon for frequencies
    d. frequency polygon for relative frequencies
    e. ogive for cumulative frequencies
    f. ogive for cumulative percents

2.4 DATA STORAGE

Since the early 1950s, we have seen an ever increasing advance in the development and use of computers. Some have even coined the present time as being the "computer age." In the earlier stages of this development, computers were thought to be toys for those few scientists who had failed to outgrow their childish tendencies. This belief is no longer existent. All of us now come into contact, either directly or indirectly, with computers. They are a real part of our lives.

Computers may cause us headaches at times, such as when they are responsible for 60-year-old ladies being called up for the draft, but it would be virtually impossible for us to live at our present level or pace if we did not have computers since they do save us a great deal of time. Computers are used in almost all areas of employment, including teaching. Not only does the university professor rely on the computer to help him with his research, but there is increasing use of the computer by elementary and secondary school administrators and teachers. Therefore, it seems imperative that the teacher who is trained for the future should have some exposure to the use of computer facilities. Statistics is one area of study that readily provides a meaningful introduction to computers. However, the use of computers is by no means limited to the field of statistics.

It is not the intent of this text to train you to be a computer programmer or operator. We have presented the material in this section to introduce you to the computer, and, hopefully, to motivate you to use the computer at your institution for working problems throughout the remainder of the text. In following that intent, we have included problems in each of the succeeding chapters that are pinpointed for computer application. The computer applications are not intended to replace the traditional routes for working problems. Rather, they are intended to save the reader time in the application of statistics once he has understood the basic concepts. It is our belief that such understanding will be facilitated by the student's working through some problems by hand.

DATA CARDS

The first step in learning to use a computer is to find out how to record or store data. Anytime we have large quantities of data, we need to have some compact, organized form of storing that data until it is needed. The most convenient way for the novice to store data is by placing it on data cards. This is also the usual method for transmitting data to the computer. A more economical and compact method of storage is the computer tape. However, since tape systems vary from computer to computer and since tapes are necessary only when tremendous masses of data are being stored, only data cards will be discussed here. We assume that you will inquire about taping at your institution if your future work should call for it.

A data card is presented in Figure 2.10.*

FIGURE 2.10

Data punch card

As you can see, a data card has 80 identical columns, each with 10 rows numbered 0, 1, 2, ..., 8, 9. Our problem is to be able to record our data on such cards in a consistent and meaningful way. We do this by punching holes in the card. To the computer, the punched holes in the card are the only important features. The computer is not affected by the color of the card, by the clipping of the upper right corner, by whether the card has square or round corners, or by what is printed on the card. These features are useful only for manual handling and identification.

Suppose we have recorded the following data for five college students:

	Sex	Age (months)	Height (in.)	Weight (lb)	Russell–Lange Volleyball Serve Test	Situps
Bob	M	265	68.5	164.0	49	85
Karen	F	256	63.0	98.0	31	46
Jim	M	260	73.0	185.5	37	98
Judy	F	245	65.5	106.5	28	83
Lee	F	242	70.0	176.0	30	59

All important information is converted to numerical data. Thus, each student will need to be assigned a number and will then be referred to by his/her number instead of by name. Let us assign the numeral 1 to Bob, 2 to Karen, 3 to Jim, 4 to Judy, and 5 to Lee. We also need to identify each student according to sex. Therefore, we can let 1 represent male and 2 represent

* Some computer manufacturers use a different layout for their punched cards. However, translating machines do exist which read cards punched in one system and from them produce cards punched for the other system. Check with your institution's computing center for details.

female. Since the rest of our information on these students is already numerical we may now represent all the information on our students by the following:

Student No.	Sex	Age	Height	Weight	R.–L. test	Situps
01	1	265	68.5	164.0	49	85
02	2	256	63.0	98.0	31	46
03	1	260	73.0	185.5	37	98
04	2	245	65.5	106.5	28	83
05	2	242	70.0	176.0	30	59

Obviously, without the information at the top of each column and our knowledge from the above discussion, the numbers we have would be meaningless. Converting all our information to a numerical form is referred to as *coding our data*. Without the code we never know what we have.

We are now ready to place our numerical data on data cards. We will do this by using a machine to make punches on the cards. This machine is set up on the same order as a typewriter. There will be one card for each student since data from only one student will be punched on a card. If the amount of data on each student required it, there could be more than one card per student.

The data information will be assigned to specific columns on the data card. For our example, let us assign a student's identification number to columns 1 and 2, assuming that we might have 10 or more students. Of course, if we had 100 or more students, we would need to devote three or more columns. This principle is applied throughout, namely that at least as many columns must be assigned for a variable as there are digits in the largest value of the variable.

Continuing our discussion, let us assign the sex identification to column 5; age to columns 8, 9, and 10; height to columns 13, 14, and 15; weight to columns 18, 19, 20, and 21; Russell-Lange Volleyball serving skills test scores to columns 24 and 25; and the number of situps to columns 28 and 29. The number of spaces between variables is completely arbitrary; spaces are used for convenience only. We can have any number of spaces or no spaces between the variables. The punched card for Bob (student 1) would look like this:

Karen's card would look like this:

Note that no decimals were punched on the cards. Many computer systems will not accept decimals on punched cards. You will learn how to identify the decimals in the scores shortly. Almost all computing centers have "worksheets" which make it convenient to read data and place them on cards. An example of such a worksheet with the data from our five students is shown in Figure 2.11. All data are placed on such a worksheet before the data cards are punched.

DATA FORMAT CARD

Now that our data are placed on cards, we need a way to identify the form in which the data appear on the cards in order to relate the arrangement of our data to the computer. A punched data card is used for this purpose and is usually called a *data format card*.

The number of digits that are required to record a score may be thought of as a *field*. In our illustration, the student's identification number required a field of 2, sex a field of 1, age and height fields of 3 each, and so on. The student's number and sex were all whole numbers, while height and weight each contained a decimal. We represent the fields for the various scores as follows:

Student No.	F2.0	which reads:	a field of 2 with no decimals
Sex	F1.0	—	a field of 1 with no decimals
Age	F3.0	—	a field of 3 with no decimals
Height	F3.1	—	a field of 3 with 1 decimal
Weight	F4.1	—	a field of 4 with 1 decimal
R.-L. test	F2.0	—	a field of 2 with no decimals
Situps	F2.0	—	a field of 2 with no decimals

If we have all whole number fields in our data, it is sometimes permissible to replace the F with an I, standing for integer. If we were to use only our student number and sex above, we would have I2 for student number and

IBM — FORTRAN Coding Form — GX28-7327-6 U/M 050** Printed in U.S.A.

PROGRAM | PROGRAMMER | DATE | PUNCHING INSTRUCTIONS: GRAPHIC / PUNCH | PAGE OF | CARD ELECTRO NUMBER*

STATEMENT NUMBER (1–5) | CONT. (6) | FORTRAN STATEMENT (7–72) | IDENTIFICATION SEQUENCE (73–80)

STUDENT NUMBER	SEX	AGE (MOS.) (XXX)	HEIGHT (INS.) (XX.X)	WEIGHT (LBS.) (XXX.X)	R.L.-V.B. (XX)	SITUPS (XX)	
01	1	265	685	1640	49	85	BOB
02	2	256	630	980	31	46	KAREN
03	1	260	730	1855	37	98	TIM
04	2	245	655	1065	28	83	JUDY
05	2	242	700	1760	30	59	LEE

*A standard card form, IBM electro 888157, is available for punching statements from this form

**Number of forms per pad may vary slightly

FIGURE 2.11
Data worksheet

I1 for sex. However, we cannot mix the two notations and if any decimals exist, we must use the field notation F for all data. Since we have data with decimals in our problem we will need to adhere entirely to the F notation. Our data were put in a form with spaces in between each score. In order to instruct the computer to skip columns, we use X. For example, 6X would tell the computer to skip 6 columns when reading our data cards. Also, a comma is placed between each message to the computer. Referring back to our worksheet, we note that the format statement for our data would be as follows:

(F2.0, 2X, F1.0, 2X, F3.0, 2X, F3.1, 2X, F4.1, 2X, F2.0, 2X, F2.0)

Note that the format statement is enclosed by parentheses. This is the procedure set up by most computer systems.

Our format statement above can be written more compactly if we eliminate the 2X between each field—that is, there is no change if instead of thinking of male as just being 1, we think of it as 001. Thus, we could think of sex as being a field of 3 with no decimals, or F3.0. Similarly, Jim's weight is the same if we think of it as 00185.5 instead of just 185.5. Thereby, weight could be represented by F6.1—a field of six with one decimal place. Our shortened format statement then would appear as:

(F2.0, F3.0, F5.0, F5.1, F6.1, F4.0, F4.0)

Another shorthand procedure permits us to combine adjacent fields that are identical into one statement. Since our last two fields are identical, i.e., F4.0, we could identify them as 2F4.0 and our further shortened statement would be:

(F2.0, F3.0, F5.0, F5.1, F6.1, 2F4.0)

We can often tell the computer to do calculations without giving it identification data. When this is the case, we can easily use our format card to tell the computer to ignore that information. If in our present problem, we want the computer to ignore the student's identification number and sex, then we eliminate the first five columns of the card and write:

(5X, F5.0, F5.1, F6.1, 2F4.0)

CONTROL CARDS

Up to this point, we have outlined the procedures for storing data on cards. Two other kinds of cards are needed in order to actually use the computer— *job control* cards and *program control* cards. These are the cards that actually permit the entrance of data into the computer and tell the machine what to do with the data. Since the number and form of messages differ greatly from one computing center to another, it would be impossible to outline any general procedures for these operations. Rather, it will be necessary for you to consult with your institution's computing center. Most centers already have statistical programs available and they are outlined quite clearly and simply so that with minimal practice you will be able to use the computing facilities. Possibly the most widely used set of statistical programs is the BMD series from the Health Sciences Computing Facility, BMD: Biomedical Computer Programs, University of California, Los Angeles.

After you have become familiar with some of the specifics of your institution's computing facility—such as worksheets and special formats—it is advisable for you to store or record the data given in the exercise immediately following this section. These data will be used for computer calculations throughout the text. You will also need to acquaint yourself with the use of some of the hardware at your computing center—namely the keypunch machine, card sorter, duplicator, and printer. This will facilitate your work throughout this text and hopefully throughout your career.

Exercise

14. Using the data on 96 high school students given on the following pages:

   a. Place the data on worksheets obtained from your computing center using the following code:

      Columns 1 & 2—Subject number
      Columns 3 & 4—Grade in school
      Column 5—Sex
      Column 6—Hand dominance
      Columns 7, 8, & 9—Age
      Columns 10, 11, & 12—Height
      Columns 13, 14, & 15—Weight
      Columns 16, 17, & 18—50-yd dash
      Columns 19, 20, & 21—1000-yd run
      Columns 22, 23, & 24—Long jump
      Columns 25, 26, & 27—Situps
      Columns 71–80—Name of student

   b. Punch data cards for these data.
   c. Punch a format statement card identifying all numeric information on the cards.
   d. Punch a format statement card which omits subject number, grade in school, sex, hand dominance, and weight.
   e. Make three copies of the data cards by use of the reproducer.
   f. Sort one copy of the cards by sex (column).
   g. Sort the second copy by hand dominance.
   h. Sort the third copy by grade in school.

Name	Subject Number	Grade in School	Sex Male–1 Female–2	Hand Dominance Right–1 Left–2	Age (months)	Height (nearest $\frac{1}{2}$ in.)	Weight (lb)	Time for 50-yd Dash (nearest $\frac{1}{10}$ sec)	Time for 1000-yd. Run (sec)	Standing Long Jump (in.)	Situps
Larry	01	9	1	2	175	57.5	87	6.7	221	76	70
Douglas	02	9	1	1	182	64.0	114	7.2	221	73	50
Ronnie	03	9	1	1	176	68.5	141	7.0	283	80	28
William	04	9	1	1	176	60.5	183	6.8	202	84	30
William	05	9	1	1	168	68.0	140	8.0	239	58	50
Mike	06	9	1	1	175	65.0	134	6.5	209	98	25
William	07	9	1	1	176	68.0	150	7.9	295	65	30
Alfred	08	9	1	1	177	67.0	139	7.0	206	71	60
Victor	09	9	1	1	177	65.0	136	7.2	210	76	80
Tim	10	9	1	1	188	66.5	131	7.0	212	87	80
Danny	11	9	1	1	175	70.0	128	7.2	213	80	90
Ricky	12	9	1	1	177	64.0	128	9.2	309	54	20
Johnny	13	9	1	1	175	69.5	127	6.9	217	68	80
Michael	14	9	1	1	179	71.0	139	7.2	263	78	76
Robert	15	9	1	1	173	63.5	94	8.0	275	60	50
Steve	16	9	1	1	171	63.5	181	7.3	236	72	65
Glenn	17	9	1	1	180	67.0	137	6.5	214	94	50
Carl	18	9	1	1	182	68.0	156	7.3	274	71	18
Steve	19	9	1	1	176	66.0	114	6.9	220	94	28
Sandra	20	9	2	1	175	64.0	171	8.4	290	58	10
Pamela	21	9	2	1	181	63.0	124	10.5	591	46	15
Michele	22	9	2	1	176	61.0	116	8.2	379	72	30
Letitia	23	9	2	1	178	63.0	125	7.6	387	72	50
Jo Anna	24	9	2	1	172	60.0	102	9.1	450	60	50
Joan	25	9	2	1	182	65.0	112	7.1	324	75	15
Sandy	26	9	2	1	174	66.5	113	7.5	269	76	50
Colette	27	9	2	1	175	63.0	118	7.9	326	65	40
Mary	28	9	2	1	181	64.0	103	7.8	314	64	50
Kay	29	9	2	2	181	64.0	137	7.8	315	68	65
Debbie	30	9	2	1	175	65.0	117	14.6	645	34	16
Judy	31	9	2	1	172	66.0	129	8.4	323	63	42

Continued

Name	Subject Number	Grade in School	Sex Male—1 Female—2	Hand Dominance Right—1 Left—2	Age (months)	Height (nearest ½ in.)	Weight (lb)	Time for 50-yd dash (nearest $\frac{1}{10}$ sec)	Time for 1000-yd. Run (sec)	Standing Long Jump (in.)	Situps
Joyce	32	9	2		185	63.0	107	7.6	342	75	50
Diane	33	9	2		175	66.0	182	8.3	343	71	37
Lois	34	9	2		173	64.5	116	7.9	387	70	15
Terry	35	9	2		176	63.0	136	7.3	294	85	50
Cecelia	36	9	2		173	64.0	117	8.7	321	58	25
Patricia	37	9	2		174	63.5	126	8.9	305	49	11
Kaye	38	9	2	2	181	61.5	87	8.0	336	70	50
David	39	10	1		186	69.0	144	7.0	255	80	50
Jesse	40	10	1	2	189	68.0	113	6.6	197	87	50
Roosevelt	41	10	1	2	190	68.5	129	6.6	307	93	100
Huey	42	10	1	1	187	67.5	128	8.2	255	82	25
Gary	43	10	1	1	185	68.5	136	6.6	187	84	101
Larry	44	10	1	1	187	74.0	200	6.2	183	85	25
Larry	45	10	1	1	187	67.0	127	6.6	306	86	25
Tom	46	10	1	1	194	62.0	134	6.6	189	88	25
Paul	47	10	1	1	193	74.0	211	6.6	234	84	25
John	48	10	1	1	190	72.5	154	6.7	225	88	100
George	49	10	1	1	193	67.0	159	6.6	209	90	60
Larry	50	10	1	1	190	64.0	114	7.0	227	78	25
Thomas	51	10	1	1	192	72.5	142	6.6	227	100	25
William	52	10	1	1	195	67.0	150	7.2	228	73	50
Randall	53	10	1	1	189	60.5	113	8.5	308	56	25
Delbert	54	10	1	1	185	59.5	121	7.7	198	70	52
Tim	55	10	1	1	184	63.5	101	7.0	219	84	25
Chinita	56	10	1	1	187	63.0	119	7.2	251	72	100
Gloria	57	10	1	1	190	65.0	153	8.4	395	58	43
Vernesser	58	10	2	1	190	68.0	189	7.4	326	72	41
Sandy	59	10	2	1	201	64.0	147	7.7	314	51	75
Lyndia	60	10	2	1	195	64.0	124	7.5	314	78	100
Elaine	61	10	2	1	188	65.0	137	7.3	253	80	101
Ophelia	62	10	2	1	184	65.0	102	11.8	387	56	45
Connie	63	10	2	1	185	65.0	129	8.7	368	60	50

Name											
Dianna	64	10	2	2	180	63.0	120	8.6	354	65	56
Carol	65	10	2	1	189	59.0	114	8.0	385	50	20
Delaine	66	10	2	1	191	63.0	125	7.7	374	71	55
Terry	67	10	2	2	174	63.0	117	7.4	333	73	55
Judy	68	10	2	1	189	65.5	123	7.6	380	66	57
Becky	69	10	2	2	187	61.0	96	7.2	266	65	60
Wanda	70	10	2	2	185	61.0	131	7.5	323	82	53
Peggy	71	10	1	2	195	60.5	115	7.2	308	77	63
Harold	72	11	1	1	206	73.0	152	6.8	211	94	100
Roderick	73	11	1	1	205	68.0	138	6.5	232	79	75
Gary	74	11	1	1	200	67.0	185	6.7	196	87	51
Michael	75	11	1	2	197	67.7	157	7.0	242	81	25
Vincent	76	11	1	1	203	76.0	155	6.5	204	98	103
Danny	77	11	1	1	205	70.0	169	6.6	198	94	100
Gary	78	11	1	1	208	73.5	148	6.3	243	90	59
Howard	79	11	1	1	199	69.5	154	6.4	208	84	100
George	80	11	1	1	208	69.0	136	7.2	243	76	62
Danny	81	11	1	1	205	67.0	133	6.5	305	105	50
Melvin	82	11	1	1	200	66.0	136	7.1	225	90	36
Michael	83	11	1	1	206	73.0	146	7.0	325	88	25
Earl	84	11	1	1	189	72.5	143	6.7	182	93	74
Catherine	85	11	2	1	203	67.0	124	7.1	240	75	50
Mary	86	11	2	2	199	65.0	124	6.9	313	61	50
Yolanda	87	11	2	1	196	65.0	133	7.5	249	79	50
Ruth	88	11	2	1	206	65.5	155	9.3	377	49	70
Althea	89	11	2	1	199	61.0	113	7.3	257	65	50
Diane	90	11	2	1	204	64.0	126	8.0	379	55	31
Karen	91	11	2	1	200	61.0	121	7.4	452	65	30
Aritha	92	11	2	1	197	65.0	115	8.4	337	59	22
Sharon	93	11	2	1	197	64.0	128	7.9	386	66	30
Esther	94	11	2	1	203	62.0	152	8.0	500	72	50
Arletta	95	11	2	1	196	67.0	168	7.2	420	84	50
Cindy	96	11	2	1	203	62.0	146	8.3	442	72	40

3

The Summarization of Data

3.1 INTRODUCTION

To describe or summarize the character of a group or distribution of numerical scores, we need some way to indicate particular features of the distribution. In the last chapter, we saw how tabulations (frequency distributions, relative frequency, etc.) and pictures or graphs (histograms, polygons, etc.) can be used to describe and summarize our data. Although these methods are useful in some situations, they do not allow us to make a concise presentation or to apply most statistical methods. We need to be able to describe a distribution of scores by means of certain numerical measures. This can be accomplished if we perform certain arithmetical operations on our data. The most common descriptive measures are ones of central tendency or value and dispersion or scatter.

3.2 MEASURES OF CENTRAL TENDENCY

When working with any set of data, we can usually notice a clustering or centering that occurs some place in the distribution of scores. This " clustering " is a phenomenon referred to as *central tendency*; it seems to imply that there should be some typical score which describes this distribution. Connotations frequently implied by the phrase "central tendency" include *average, typical, normal,* and *common*. While these terms may help you to comprehend the idea of central tendency, none of them precisely describe what central tendency means. Three commonly used measures of central tendency that are precisely defined are the *mean, median,* and *mode*.

THE MEAN

The *arithmetic average,* or the *mean, is the sum of all the observations or scores in a distribution divided by the number of observations.* This is a central tendency measure that is familiar to all of us. If we have four students who perform 5, 4, 2, and 7 chins, we find the average of these to be

$$\frac{5+4+2+7}{4} = \frac{18}{4} = 4.5 \text{ chins}$$

If we note an observation symbolically by an X, then we would denote the mean by $\bar{X}$, read as " X-bar." In our example, $\bar{X} = 4.5$. (It should be noted that although the mean is 4.5, it is not possible for anyone to do 4.5 chins.)

It will facilitate future discussions, particularly those involving a large number of scores or observations, if we have a shorthand method of representing $\bar{X}$ instead of having to use a lengthy sentence to explain how to find the mean. Suppose, in general, that we let X_1 be the symbol representing the value of our first observation, X_2 the symbol representing the second value,

X_3 the symbol representing the third value, and so on. If we have five observations or scores, X_1, X_2, X_3, X_4, X_5, then we shall have

$$\bar{X} = \frac{X_1 + X_2 + X_3 + X_4 + X_5}{5} \tag{3.1}$$

If there are 50 observations, then

$$\bar{X} = \frac{X_1 + X_2 + X_3 + \cdots + X_{50}}{50} \tag{3.2}$$

This notation, of course, could be extended indefinitely.

We can make our definition of the mean even more compact and convenient if we adopt a symbol, $\sum$ (Greek letter capital sigma), to indicate "the sum of" something. This symbol will always tell us to add some group of numbers. For example, with five observations we would write

$$\bar{X} = \frac{X_1 + X_2 + X_3 + X_4 + X_5}{5}$$

$$= \frac{\sum\limits_{i=1}^{5} X_i}{5} \tag{3.3}$$

The $\sum\limits_{i=1}^{5} X_i$ is read as "the sum of the five observations X_1 through X_5.

Thus, $\sum\limits_{i=1}^{50} X_i$ would mean "the sum of the 50 observations X_1 through X_{50}.

One other procedure will complete our "shorthand" notation for the mean. It would save time and confusion to have an expression for defining the mean concisely and clearly. If we allow n to generally denote the number of observations that we have, then

$$\bar{X} = \frac{X_1 + X_2 + X_3 + \cdots + X_n}{n}$$

$$= \frac{\sum\limits_{i=1}^{n} X_i}{n} \tag{3.4}$$

and we have accomplished our goal of having a convenient and concise formula that applies to all situations.

The mean is the center of the distribution of scores in the sense that it is the center of gravity. If we think of each score's distance from the center of a bar as being weight, then the mean will act as the fulcrum of a balance scale. From our earlier chin scores of 2, 4, 5, and 7, which had an $\bar{X} = 4.5$, we can see on the balance scale in Figure 3.1 that the weight on each side of the fulcrum is exactly the same. We can demonstrate this center of gravity concept by taking two steps. First we subtract the mean from each score to

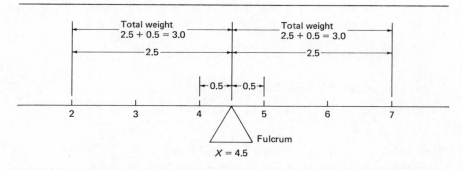

FIGURE 3.1

The mean as a balancing point

determine the differences, or distances, from the mean. Then we add these distances from the mean, as shown below.

$$
\begin{aligned}
\sum_{i=1}^{4} (X_i - \bar{X}) &= (X_1 - \bar{X}) + (X_2 - \bar{X}) + (X_3 - \bar{X}) + (X_4 - \bar{X}) \\
&= (5 - 4.5) + (4 - 4.5) + (2 - 4.5) + (7 - 4.5) \\
&= 0.5 + (-0.5) + (-2.5) + 2.5 \\
&= 0
\end{aligned}
\tag{3.5}
$$

In general,

$$
\sum_{i=1}^{n} (X_i - \bar{X}) = 0
\tag{3.6}
$$

since

$$
\sum_{i=1}^{n} (X_i - \bar{X}) = \sum_{i=1}^{n} X_i - \sum_{i=1}^{n} \bar{X}
$$

$$
= \sum_{i=1}^{n} X_i - n\bar{X}
$$

But,

$$
\bar{X} = \frac{\sum_{i=1}^{n} X_i}{n}
$$

and

$$
\sum_{i=1}^{n} X_i - n\bar{X} = \sum_{i=1}^{n} X_i - \frac{\not{n} \sum_{i=1}^{n} X_i}{\not{n}} = 0
$$

Therefore, *the sum of the deviations about the mean is zero in any distribution.*

THE MEDIAN

Another measure that describes the "center" of a distribution of scores is the *median*. *The median, denoted by Mdn, for a set of values or scores is the middle point or that point which divides the distribution of scores in half*. In other words, if we have an ordered array of *n* scores, the median is the $(n + 1)/2$ score in that array. If we have an ordered array of the number of chins performed by 11 students as 1, 3, 3, 4, 4, 5, 7, 9, 12, 15, and 17, then the median is the $(11 + 1)/2 = 6$th (sixth) score from either end. Thus, our median is equal to 5. This satisfies our definition since there are an equal number of scores (5) on each side of this point. For the six ordered scores 7, 11, 13, 16, 18, 19, the median will be the $(6 + 1)/2 = 3.5$th score. Since we do not have a 3.5th score, we take the midpoint between the third and fourth score, or 14.5, to be our median. This again satisfies our definition since there are three scores on each side of this point.

THE MODE

The last central tendency measure to be considered is the *mode*. This is denoted by M_0 and defined as *the most frequently occurring score*. For a distribution of 3, 6, 7, 7, 7, 8, 8, 9, 10, the mode would be 7 since it occurs the most frequently (three times). It is possible to have more than one mode for a distribution. For the scores 5, 5, 6, 8, 9, 9, 19, 21, there would be two modes, namely 5 and 9, since each of them occurs twice. We would then say that the distribution is bimodal. If there were three modes, we would say it was trimodal, and so on. It is also possible for a distribution to be without a mode. For example, if we had a distribution of 12, 13, 15, 20, 22, 24, 25, we would conclude that a mode does not exist.

The mode is not a particularly useful measure of central tendency because it is not reliable and because there is a possibility that it may not even exist.

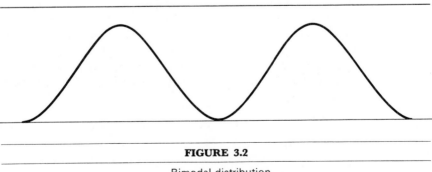

FIGURE 3.2

Bimodal distribution

The only time it might be of use is with a bi- or trimodal distribution such as that shown in Figure 3.2. In this case, the multiple modes might possibly describe the distribution more adequately than the mean or median. Unfortunately, the mode is sometimes used as a "quick" means of determining central tendency. This might not be too bad if its use were only temporary, but because the mode is easy to find it is sometimes erroneously used as a substitute for the mean or median.

THE CHOICE OF CENTRAL TENDENCY MEASURES

We have already essentially eliminated the use of the mode. Thus, the discussion here will be limited to the appropriate uses of the mean and median. The mean is most commonly employed in reporting data because of its arithmetical basis. If we have the mean of the same variable for two different groups, we can combine the two means and derive a combined average. For example, if we have the mean on a standardized test from this year's statistics class of 20 students and last year's class of 30 students (this year's mean, $\bar{X}_1 = 60$, last year's, $\bar{X}_2 = 70$), then

$$\frac{20(60) + 30(70)}{50} = \frac{1200 + 2100}{50} = 66$$

would be the composite mean for the two classes. In general, if we have two groups of size n_1 and n_2, with respective means of $\bar{X}_1$ and $\bar{X}_2$, the mean for the entire group of $n_1 + n_2$ individuals or objects is equal to $(n_1 \bar{X}_1 + n_2 \bar{X}_2)/(n_1 + n_2)$. This may, of course, be logically extended to any number of groups. However, this application is not meaningful with the median since the median is not arithmetically based.

Since the mean does take into account every score in the distribution, it is sometimes unduly affected by a few extreme scores and may give a distorted picture of the distribution of scores. For example, with the chinning scores of 4, 6, 6, 8, we have an $\bar{X} = 6$ and a median of 6. If we had another individual added to the group who did 36 chins, then our scores would be 4, 6, 6, 8, 36 and our $\bar{X}$ would be 12—a shift of 6, although our median would remain at 6. Thus, if we have a small number of scores and a few of them are extreme, the median may provide a more realistic description of the distribution than will the mean. Throughout most of this text we will use the mean as our central tendency measure. In Chapter 8 we provide stronger justifications for this use.

If the distribution of our data is symmetrical (exactly the same on each side) and unimodal, the mean, median, and mode will be identical. But, as a distribution becomes more skewed (asymmetrical), the differences between the various measures of central tendency become greater.

Exercises

1. For the following group of situp scores, find the $\bar{X}$, *Mdn*, and M_0 and write an interpretation of each.

50, 55, 20, 22, 35, 41, 20, 16, 35

2. The following scores on a standardized test were obtained for physical education orientation classes for three semesters.

Fall Semester '71	Spring Semester '72	Fall Semester '72
56	45	70
50	66	30
57	38	44
55	52	50
58	50	55
62	49	60
59	73	30
71	60	40
38	60	65
41	34	50
63	55	50
45	60	58
47	53	45
68	45	45
52	60	50
49	33	60
50		62
50		43
		50
		43
		51

a. Find the mean, median, and mode for each year's class.
b. Find the mean for the entire group of 55 students by two different methods. Are the means obtained by these methods the same?

3. The average golf score reported by a player for a handicap tournament is 78. The player informs us that he doesn't remember how many rounds of golf he played to establish this average but he does recall that his total strokes were 702. Determine how many rounds of golf he played.

3.3 MEASURES OF VARIATION

Although the measures presented in the previous section serve to describe the important characteristic of central tendency, by themselves they do not adequately describe a distribution. It is possible for distributions to have the same mean and/or median, and yet be very different in their appearance. This is dramatically demonstrated by the graphs in Figure 3.3. In this

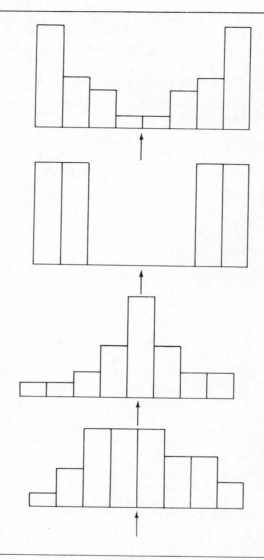

FIGURE 3.3

Different distributions with equal means

figure, we note that although the distributions have precisely the same mean, there is considerable difference in the spread of their scores. Thus, it is important for us to have some measure(s) that describes the scatter or variation of scores. The measures of variation to be discussed are the *variance, standard deviation, coefficient of variation,* and *range.*

THE VARIANCE AND STANDARD DEVIATION

Any good measure of variation should be large when the scores are spread out and small when they are grouped closely together. At first glance, we might think that the sum of deviations about the mean

$$\sum_{i=1}^{n}(X_i - \bar{X})$$

would be a good candidate to accomplish this purpose. However, as was shown previously, this measure will always be equal to zero.

This shortcoming can be eliminated by squaring each of the deviations before they are added.

$$\sum_{i=1}^{n}(X_i - \bar{X})^2 \tag{3.7}$$

This expression is read "the sum of the squared deviations about the mean." As the number of observations increases, this measure of variation becomes larger. Since this is undesirable, the sum of the squared deviations about the mean is divided by a number that is one less than the total number of observations.* This is called the *variance*, and is represented symbolically by s^2.

$$s^2 = \frac{\sum_{i=1}^{n}(X_i - \bar{X})^2}{n-1}$$

$$= \frac{(X_1 - \bar{X})^2 + (X_2 - \bar{X})^2 + \cdots + (X_n - \bar{X})^2}{n-1} \tag{3.8}$$

The standard deviation is defined as the positive square root of the variance. It is thus represented by

$$s = \sqrt{\frac{\sum_{i=1}^{n}(X_i - \bar{X})^2}{n-1}} \tag{3.9}$$

It should be rather clear that the variance and standard deviation provide a measure of dispersion or scatter. If all values in our distribution are exactly the same, the variance and standard deviation will be zero. If the scores or observations are all very close together, these measures of variation will be smaller than when the scores are greatly scattered. To illustrate this important characteristic, we have presented three examples below.

---

* You will note that we obtained the variance by dividing by $n-1$ rather than n. Many texts introduce s^2 with n in the denominator; however, the authors chose to use $n-1$ since division by $n-1$ is necessary in order to use s^2 in many of the statistical methods throughout the remainder of the text. We hope that this practice will avoid confusion for the beginning student. This will be discussed further in Chapter 4.

Example 1   Given the scores 18, 18, 18, 19, 19, 20, 21,

$$\bar{X} = 19$$

$$s^2 = \frac{(-1)^2 + (-1)^2 + (-1)^2 + 0^2 + 0^2 + (1)^2 + (2)^2}{6} = \frac{8}{6} = 1.33$$

$$s = \sqrt{1.33} = 1.15$$

Example 2   Given the scores 11, 13, 16, 19, 22, 25, 27,

$$\bar{X} = 19$$
$$s^2 = 36.33$$
$$s = 6.03$$

Example 3   Given the scores 2, 5, 10, 17, 26, 33, 40,

$$\bar{X} = 19$$
$$s^2 = 209.33$$
$$s = 14.47$$

Each Example has seven scores and the same mean, but we see the scores in Example 2 are more scattered, or spread out, than the scores in Example 1, and the scores in Example 3 are considerably more scattered than the scores in Example 2 or 1. As a result, our variances and standard deviations reflect this same order of scatter.

Obviously, if we are working with a great number of scores or observations, finding the deviation of each score from the mean and then squaring it will become laborious. Therefore, we use algebraically equivalent formulae for s^2 and s that are generally simpler to use for computations when a desk calculator is available.*

$$s^2 = \frac{\sum X_i^2 - [(\sum X_i)^2/n]}{n-1} \tag{3.10}$$

and

$$s = \sqrt{\frac{\sum X_i^2 - [(\sum X_i)^2/n]}{n-1}}$$

For example, if we have the numbers 2, 4, 6, and 8, with $\bar{X} = 5$, the variance using mean deviations is

$$s^2 = \frac{(-3)^2 + (-1)^2 + (1)^2 + (3)^2}{3} = \frac{20}{3}$$

* Note that instead of continuing to use $\sum\limits_{i=1}^{n}$ we will simply use $\sum$ from now on.

Using our newly derived formula,

$$s^2 = \frac{(2^2 + 4^2 + 6^2 + 8^2) - [(20)^2/4]}{3}$$

$$= \frac{120 - 100}{3}$$

$$= \frac{20}{3}$$

We shall use the variance as our measure of dispersion in further calculations throughout the text. However, as a descriptive measure, the standard deviation is generally reported in lieu of the variance. This is because the standard deviation is expressed in the same units as the original scores or observations, while the variance is expressed in the squares of these units. We can think of the standard deviation as being a "kind of average" deviation between the mean and the scores in the distribution.

Finally, neither the variance nor the standard deviation has a clear physical world interpretation similar to the "center of gravity" explanation of the mean. Thus, this is one of the places where you are asked to accept the measures as useful since they do accomplish the purposes of a measure of dispersion.

COEFFICIENT OF VARIATION

The variance and standard deviation are absolute, rather than relative, measures of variation. These measures will generally provide us with the information we will need for the computations discussed throughout the remainder of this text. However, if we want to compare the relative variations of two or more variables that have different units of measurement, we need measures of variation that are independent of the unit of measure. The *coefficient of variation*, or *relative standard deviation*, is such a measure.

Denoted by C, the coefficient of variation is the ratio of the standard deviation to the mean.

$$C = \frac{s}{\bar{X}} \tag{3.11}$$

This measure is usually given as a percentage which is obtained by multiplying C by 100. The coefficient of variation allows us to compare the dispersion of data that have different means and/or different measurement units.

Suppose for tenth-grade boys we have scores on two items of the AAHPER Youth Fitness test: the 50-yard dash and softball throw for distance. If the means and standard deviations for the variables are

50-yard dash $\bar{X}_1 = 6.6$ sec

$s_1 = 0.8$ sec

Softball throw $\bar{X}_2 = 185$ ft

$s_2 = 15$ ft

we would be hard pressed to determine which set of scores is dispersed or scattered the most since one is in terms of seconds and the other is in terms of feet. If we were to make a guess on the basis of the standard deviations, we would probably guess that more variability exists in the softball throw than in the 50-yard dash. This would, of course, be only a guess. When computing the coefficients of variation, we find

$$C_1 = \frac{0.8}{6.6}$$

$$= 0.12 \quad (\text{or } 12\%)$$

for the 50-yard dash scores and

$$C_2 = \frac{15}{185}$$

$$= 0.08 \quad (\text{or } 8\%)$$

for the softball throw for distance. Now we see that the variation among the dash scores is actually greater than among the softball throw scores. This comparison is valid and meaningful since the effect of the units of measurement have been removed.

THE RANGE AND SEMI-INTERQUARTILE RANGE

A rather crude measure of variation is the *range*, which is *the difference between the largest and smallest scores in a distribution.* If in a set of test scores the highest score attained was 97 and the lowest was 26, the range would be $97 - 26 = 71$.

The range can be a useful indicator of variation when just a few observations have been made. The range, however, has all the disadvantages of the median plus the range becomes less and less reliable as the number of observations increases and it is unduly affected by extreme scores. Thus, it is appropriate to put the range in the same category as the mode.

On some occasions the shortcomings of the range are overcome by the use of the *semi-interquartile range*, which is defined as one-half the difference between the 75th and 25th percentiles, $(P_{75} - P_{25})/2$. Although extreme scores do not affect this measure as much as they affect the range, the semi-interquartile range is still generally unacceptable and will not be used in succeeding operations.

3.4   UNIFORM CHANGES: THEIR EFFECT ON CENTRAL TENDENCY AND VARIATION

In working with data, we sometimes find it necessary and/or convenient to add a constant to or subtract a constant from each observation or to multiply or divide each observation by a constant. Let us see how these various operations affect the mean, variance, and standard deviation. For illustrative purposes, suppose we have the following five observations: 10, 12, 16, 22, and 24. The mean, variance, and standard deviation for these five scores are

$$\bar{X} = \frac{84}{5} = 16.8$$

$$s^2 = \frac{1560 - [(84)^2/5]}{4} = 37.2$$

and

$$s = \sqrt{37.2}$$
$$= 6.10$$

If we add 5 to each score, we have 15, 17, 21, 27, and 29. The new $\bar{X} = \frac{109}{5}$ = 21.8,

$$s^2 = \frac{2525 - [(109)^2/5]}{4}$$

$$= 37.2$$

and

$$s = 6.10$$

We see that the mean is increased by 5, but the variance and standard deviation remain unchanged. Subtraction, of course, will reduce the mean.

Thus, adding a constant to or subtracting* a constant from each score or observation

---

* To show this algebraically, since

$$\bar{X} = \frac{\sum X}{n}$$

$$= \frac{X_1 + X_2 + \cdots + X_n}{n}$$

then adding a constant C to each observation, we have

$$\frac{(X_1 + C) + (X_2 + C) + \cdots + (X_n + C)}{n} = \frac{\sum X_i + \sum C}{n}$$

$$= \frac{\sum X_i + nC}{n}$$

$$= \frac{\sum X_i}{n} + \frac{\cancel{n}C}{\cancel{n}}$$

$$= \bar{X} + C$$

and

$$\text{new } s^2 = \frac{\sum [(X_i + C) - (\bar{X} + C)]^2}{n - 1}$$

$$= \frac{\sum [X_i + \cancel{C} - \bar{X} - \cancel{C}]}{n - 1}$$

$$= \frac{\sum (X_i - \bar{X})^2}{n - 1} = s^2$$

which is the original variance.

in a distribution respectively increases or decreases by that constant amount the mean of the distribution, but has no effect on the variance or standard deviation.

If we multiply the original observations (10, 12, 16, 22, and 24) by the constant 2, the new scores will be 20, 24, 32, 44, and 48. The mean, variance, and standard deviation are

$$\bar{X} = \frac{168}{5}$$

$$= 33.6$$

$$= 2 \times 16.8$$

$$s^2 = \frac{6240 - [(168)^2/5]}{4}$$

$$= 148.8$$

$$= 4 \times 37.2$$

and

$$s = 12.20$$

$$= 2 \times 6.1$$

We now see that the new mean is equal to two times the original mean, the new variance is four times the original variance, and the new standard deviation is two times the original standard deviation. The converse would be true had we divided instead of multiplied. *Thus, multiplying (or dividing)* each score or observation in a distribution by a constant will multiply (or divide) the mean by the same constant, will multiply (or divide) the variance by the square of that constant, and will multiply (or divide) the standard deviation by that constant.*

A special application of these procedures is commonly made when we find particular kinds of scores called *standard scores*. First, a special constant, namely $\bar{X}$, is subtracted from each observation in the distribution so that we have

$$X_1 - \bar{X}, X_2 - \bar{X}, \ldots, X_n - \bar{X}$$

Thus, the new mean is $\bar{X} - \bar{X} = 0$ while our variance and standard deviation remain the same. Next, each of these new scores is divided by another special constant, namely s, the standard deviation. The new set of numbers is

$$\frac{X_1 - \bar{X}}{s}, \frac{X_2 - \bar{X}}{s}, \ldots, \frac{X_n - \bar{X}}{s}$$

* To show this algebraically,

$$\text{New mean} = \frac{\sum CX_i}{n} = \frac{C \sum X_i}{n} = C\bar{X}$$

$$\text{New variance} = \frac{\sum (CX_i - C\bar{X})^2}{n-1} = \frac{\sum C^2 (X_i - \bar{X})^2}{n-1} = \frac{C^2 \sum (X_i - \bar{X})^2}{n-1} = C^2 s^2$$

$$\text{New standard deviation} = \sqrt{C^2 s^2} = Cs$$

The new mean will still be zero, since $s \cdot 0 = 0$. However, the new variance is $s^2/s^2 = 1$ and the standard deviation is $\sqrt{1} = 1$. Scores transformed in this way are *standard scores* and are often referred to as *Z-scores* (scores with mean 0 and variance 1). This standardization of scores

$$Z_i = \frac{X_i - \bar{X}}{s} \tag{3.12}$$

allows a comparison to be made across various items of performance for the same individual. For example, if we know that John put the shot 32 feet, ran the 100 in 11.8 seconds, and scored 75 on a written test, there would be no way of comparing his performances. If we standardize each of his scores and find that his respective Z-scores are shot put $Z = -0.4$, 100-yard dash $Z = 0.1$, and written test $Z = 0.6$, we will know that he did best on the written test, followed by the 100-yard dash, and shot put. In addition, we can average his Z-scores [average $Z = (-0.4 + 0.1 + 0.6)/3 = 0.1$], which is impossible to do with the scores in their original form. Since working with negative numbers and decimals may be undesirable, we can take one further step to transform Z-scores to more "convenient" scales. For example, if a mean of 50 and a standard deviation of 10 are desired, we multiply each of our standard Z-scores by 10 and add 50 to each of them. Such standardized scores are referred to as *T-scores*. They can be calculated as follows:

$$T\text{-score}_{(i)} = 50 + 10Z_i = 50 + \frac{10(X_i - \bar{X})}{s} \tag{3.13}$$

Other common standardizations are:

1. Mean of 50 and standard deviation of 16.67, called 6-σ scores.

$$6\text{-}\sigma = 50 + \frac{16.67(X_i - \bar{X})}{s} \tag{3.14}$$

2. Mean of 500 and standard deviation of 100. Graduate Record Exam scores are of this form:

$$\text{GRE score}_{(i)} = 500 + \frac{100(X_i - \bar{X})}{s}$$

3. Mean of 5 and standard deviation of 2, called *stannines*.

$$\text{Stannine score}_{(i)} = 5 + \frac{2(X_i - \bar{X})}{s} \tag{3.15}$$

Exercises

4. Find the range, variance, standard deviation, and coefficient of variation for the situp scores of Exercise 1 of this chapter and write an interpretation of each.
5. a. Find the variance, standard deviation, coefficient of variation, range, and semi-interquartile range for each of the groups in Exercise 2.
   b. Which group had the most variability?
   c. How did you determine the answer for b?

6. Add 5 to each of the scores in Exercise 1 and find the new mean, median, mode, range, variance, standard deviation, and coefficient of variation. How do each of these compare with those found earlier?

7. The following are scores for John on three different events:

    Chins: 7
    Shot put: 36 ft
    40-yard dash: 7.6 sec

    The means and standard deviations for the respective items are chins $\bar{X} = 5, s = 1.5$; shot put $\bar{X} = 37, s = 8$; and 40-yard dash $\bar{X} = 7.0, s = 0.5$.
    a. Compared to the group, in which event did John do best? Second best? (Hint: Change each score to a standard score. Be careful on the dash though—a large score indicates slowness.)
    b. How would you assess John's overall performance?

8. Convert John's scores to the following standard scores:
    a. Z-scores
    b. T-scores
    c. 6-σ scores
    d. Mean of 500, $s = 100$

In Exercises 9–13, compute the $\bar{X}$, s^2, s, median, coefficient of variation, and range for the data given in the indicated exercises of Chapter 2.

9. Exercise 4 of Chapter 2.
10. Exercise 5 of Chapter 2.
11. Exercise 6 of Chapter 2.
12. Exercise 8 of Chapter 2.
13. Exercise 9 of Chapter 2.
14. Rank Exercises 9–13 according to the variability of their data.

COMPUTER APPLICATIONS

In the exercises below, you will need a prepared computer program at your institution or the one given following these exercises for finding the $\bar{X}$, s^2, and s.

15. From the fitness data recorded in Chapter 2, Exercise 14, use the computer to find the $\bar{X}$, s^2, and s for each of the following for the total group.
    a. Age in months
    b. Height
    c. Weight
    d. 50-yard dash
    e. 1000-yard run/walk
    f. Standing long jump
    g. Situps
16. From the fitness data recorded in Chapter 2, Exercise 14, use the computer to find the $\bar{X}$, s^2, and s for each of the following for boys. Then do the same for girls.
    a. Age in months
    b. Height
    c. Weight
    d. 50-yard dash
    e. 1000-yard run/walk
    f. Standing long jump
    g. Situps
17. Repeat 15 and 16 first for left-handed students and then for right-handed students.
18. Repeat the above for each of the three grades.

FORTRAN IV PROGRAM
Mean, Variance, and Standard Deviation

Col. 7   72
↓   ↓

```
      READ (5,100) N                                                    1
      SUMX = 0.0                                                        2
      SUMXSQ = 0.0                                                      3
      DO 50 J = 1, N                                                    4
      READ (5,101) X                                                   5
      SUMX = SUMX + X                                                   6
   50 SUMXSQ = SUMXSQ + X**2                                            7
      S = N                                                             8
      XBAR = SUMX/S                                                     9
      VAR = (SUMXSQ - (S*XBAR**2))/(S-1)                              10
      SD = SQRT(VAR)                                                   11
      WRITE (6,102) XBAR, VAR, SD                                      12
  100 FORMAT (I2)                                                      13
  101 FORMAT (6X,F3.0)                                                 14
  102 FORMAT (' ','MEAN =',F10.3,'VAR =',F10.3,'SD =',F7.3)            15
      STOP                                                             16
      END                                                              17
```

Above is a very simple computer program. It is written in FORTRAN IV language. We will briefly explain each statement to familiarize you with the types of instructions that a computer requires. This discussion is not to be considered detailed.

All computer programs consist, basically, of three kinds of instructions: input, arithmetic, and output. When keypunching computer programs, you must remember that statements describing instructions to the computer must appear in columns 7–72. Columns 1–5 are used for cross referencing within the program. For example, the first card in the program above instructs the card reader (which is identified by the number 5) to read the sample size N appearing on the first card immediately following the last statement card of the program. The card reader is instructed to read the value of N according to the format given in statement 100. The second and third program cards instruct the computer to reserve two storage locations in memory, name them SUMX and SUMXSQ, respectively, and "clear" the two locations in a manner that is similar to the clearing procedure followed with a dual memory desk calculator. The fourth card instructs the computer to set J equal to one, execute all operations down to and including statement 50, then set J equal to two and repeat the process. This process (called a Do loop) continues until J has been set equal to N. The "process" the computer is instructed to complete is exactly the accumulation process you follow when calculating $\sum X$ and $\sum X^2$ simultaneously on a desk calculator. First, the card reader is instructed to read the value of X on the first data card according to the format given by statement 101. Then, the value of X is added to the value currently stored in the storage location that was previously named SUMX. Next, the value of X is squared and added to the value currently stored in the storage location previously named SUMXSQ. By repeating the process for each of the remaining data cards, we obtain $\sum X$ and $\sum X^2$ stored as SUMX and SUMXSQ, respectively.

The eighth through the eleventh cards instruct the computer to calculate the mean, variance, and standard deviation and store them as XBAR, VAR, and SD, respectively. Finally, the twelfth program card instructs the printer (identified by the number 6) to type the values of XBAR, VAR, and SD on output paper according to the format given in statement 102. This completes the operations required of the computer, and accordingly the last two cards of the program instruct the computer to stop execution of the program.

The following sequence of cards is required to prepare the above program for your institution's computer center.

1. System cards (Check with your institution's computer center for details.)
2. Program cards (Note that the card reader and printer may be assigned numerals other than those given here. Check with your computer center.)
3. Sample size card (keypunched according to format statement 100)
4. Data cards (keypunched according to format statement 101)
5. Job termination card (Check with your computer center for details.)

As a final note, it should be observed that the format given in statement 101 identifies the variable age recorded on the fitness data cards you were requested to keypunch as an exercise in Chapter 2. The format statement may be changed to compute $\bar{X}$, s^2, and s for other variables of interest. For example, the format statement (15X,F3.1) is required for the variable of 50-yard dash.

4

Populations, Samples, Parameters, and Statistics

4.1 INTRODUCTION

The definition of the four nouns in the title of this chapter and their relationship to one another provide the basis for the study of statistics.

As mentioned in Chapter 1, we can seldom make observations on all the objects or persons we desire to study or describe. For example, suppose we live in a town of 20,000 (call it Wonder City) that has 3000 residents between the ages of 16 and 21. We wish to determine the physical condition of the persons in this age group by finding the mean value of maximum oxygen uptake, $\dot{V}O_{2max}$. It would be an overwhelming, if not impossible, task to measure $\dot{V}O_{2max}$ on all 3000. We would likely take a carefully selected subgroup of youths, say 100, measure their $\dot{V}O_{2max}$, find the mean value, and infer that this mean value would be a good estimate of the mean for the total group. In making such an inference, we know that there is a chance that we might be in error. You have undoubtedly recognized, and correctly so, that this is an exercise in the inductive process outlined in Chapter 1.

In this example, the group on which we wish information (youth in our city between 16 and 21 years of age) is the *population. A population, which is sometimes referred to as a universe, is defined as a set of individuals (or objects) with some common characteristic(s) that is (are) considered for a particular purpose.* The population is always defined by the experimenter or inquirer either directly by choice or indirectly by what is done; the former is preferred. We may want our population to be quite large or relatively small. There is no such thing as *the* population for all situations, but instead there is a population for each particular situation that arises. Often our population will contain an uncountable or infinite number of individuals or objects. Most of the procedures presented in the rest of this text will assume the existence of a very large or infinite population.

The present example defines the population as the 3000 youths between the ages of 16 and 21 in Wonder City. We have decided that the individuals in the population should have two characteristics in common—residence in Wonder City and age between 16 and 21. We could have defined our population to be much larger—say, all youth in our state—or much smaller, such as those youths who attend one particular school within Wonder City.

Once a population has been defined, it is our purpose to determine specific characteristics about that population. *The name given to any measurable characteristic of a population or universe is a parameter.* In other words, *parameters* are constant values that are used to describe populations. In the Wonder City example, we have already discussed two characteristics (age and residence). We did not, however, provide a *measure* of these characteristics. If we knew or determined the mean age of our population, or determined the exact number of those youths in Wonder City, these would be examples of parameters. The main parameter of interest in this example is the mean value of maximum oxygen uptake, $\dot{V}O_{2max}$, for the 3000 youths. Other likely population parameters of interest would be the variance and standard deviation of maximum oxygen uptake.

Whenever it is feasible to determine population parameters, we will want to do so. As stated previously, this is seldom possible in terms of time or financial expenditure, and we would therefore select a subset of our population, determine the desired characteristic on this subset, and infer this characteristic back to the population. *Any subset of a population is a sample.* *Any measurable characteristic of a sample is called a "statistic."* Therefore, a *statistic* is to a *sample* as a *parameter* is to a *population*.

Suppose in the present example we select 100 youths from our population and determine their mean oxygen uptake. Our *sample* is the 100 youths and the mean value determined is a *statistic*. We might have also found other statistics, such as the variance and standard deviation of $\dot{V}O_{2max}$, for the sample. We use statistics of the sample as estimates of the parameters of the population. This inductive procedure is summarized by the following diagram:

We define a population, select a sample from that population, determine statistics of interest for that sample, and use these statistics as estimates of parameters for the population. This is without doubt the most important concept to be introduced in this text since it is the very essence of inferential statistics.

The parameters and statistics of interest in this chapter are the mean, variance, and standard deviation. We will denote the mean of a population by the Greek letter μ (mu), the variance of the population by σ^2 (sigma squared), and the population standard deviation by σ. The corresponding sample statistics for the mean, variance, and standard deviation will be denoted, respectively, as $\bar{X}$ (or any Arabic letter with a bar over the top), s^2, and s. Thus, $\bar{X}$ is used as an estimate of μ, s^2 as an estimate of σ^2, and s as an estimate of σ.

4.2 SELECTION OF SAMPLES

Until now we have not paid attention to how we select a sample. The method of choosing the sample will determine the sample's usefulness. If we do not select our sample by precise rules, we may be limited in our ability to make inferences to the intended population. Sampling procedures may be classified in one of two main categories—*systematic* or *random*.

In a systematic sample, some specific system is used to select the individuals or objects to be included in the sample. For example, if we select every tenth student from an alphabetical list, then we are creating a systematic sample. There are times when a systematic sample will best give us the sample needed. There are procedures for utilizing this kind of sample in appropriate situations; however, since nearly all theoretical development of statistical methods is based on the concept of randomness and since this is an introductory text, we will concern ourselves almost exclusively with random samples.

In a random sample, by definition, every individual or object in the population has an equal chance of being selected. For this condition to be rigidly met, every individual or object chosen must be returned to the population before another individual or object is selected. This is referred to as *sampling with replacement.* With this procedure, a person or object can be chosen twice in the same sample. If our population is of infinite size or quite large in relation to the size of our sample, this is unlikely to occur. In practice, with a large population, we seldom use sampling with replacement because it makes no practical difference, and because it is impossible or impractical to carry out. Unless otherwise noted, it will be assumed throughout the remainder of the text that our population is large enough so that selecting our sample without replacement has no practical effect on the results of our calculations.

The concept of a random sample is relatively simple to understand. Obtaining such a sample is not always so simple. If we are able to list all the individuals or objects in a population, then it is not very difficult to select a sample by writing names on pieces of paper, mixing the pieces in a hat, and drawing out names, or by using random numbers generated from a random number table or a random number selection computer program. But if we are unable to identify all the members of the population, sampling becomes a real problem. There are sampling techniques that can be used in these situations, but such procedures require a substantial background (entire texts have been devoted to this subject). Therefore, we shall assume for the purposes of this text that a random sample has been obtained from the population of interest. However, it is important, even at this stage in the study of statistics, to realize that it is necessary to *select* a sample if we plan to infer characteristics to any group larger than the sample itself.

4.3 SAMPLING DISTRIBUTIONS

When a sample is selected, we should realize that it is only one of several possible samples. Suppose that we were able to identify from some population all possible samples of a particular size. If we determine the mean and variance for *each* of those samples, we know that these statistics will not be the same for all the samples. We would thus have a *distribution of means* and a *distribution of variances.* These distributions are usually called *sampling distributions*; so we have a *sampling distribution of the means* and a *sampling distribution of the variances.* Although it is grammatically incorrect, the singular forms of "means" and "variances" are traditionally used in the two terms; this gives us: *sampling distribution of the mean* and *sampling distribution of the variance.*

We shall sometimes use this traditional terminology, but it will greatly enhance your understanding of the underlying concept if you continue to realize that these terms do refer to the distributions of the means and variances from all possible samples of a particular size. To illustrate more clearly the concept of a sampling distribution, let us take a rather simple example and find the sampling distributions for the mean and variance. Keep in mind that this procedure would generally be impossible and that the example has been created only for illustrative purposes.

Suppose we have a population of six students and we record their abdominal skinfold measures (to the nearest millimeter). The measurements recorded for the six students are $X_1 = 6$, $X_2 = 9$, $X_3 = 10$, $X_4 = 12$, $X_5 = 13$, and $X_6 = 16$. If we decide to take samples of size $n = 2$, then there are 36 different samples possible. These samples of size $n = 2$ are presented in Table 4.1. Note that since our population is small in relation to our sample size, we include as possible those samples that were drawn with replacement. Thus a person may be in the same sample more than once and more than one sample may be composed of the same pair of scores.

Presented in successive columns of Table 4.1 are the mean, variance, and standard deviation for each of the 36 samples. Thus, we have a sampling distribution of the means, a sampling distribution of the variances, and a sampling distribution of the standard deviations for sample size $n = 2$. We have found the mean of each of the sampling distributions. The mean of the sample means is 11. When we calculate the mean of the population,

$$\mu = \frac{6 + 9 + 10 + 12 + 13 + 16}{6}$$

$$= \frac{66}{6}$$

$$= 11 \tag{4.1}$$

we notice that it is exactly the same as the mean of the sample $\bar{X}$'s, $\mu_{\bar{X}}$. Likewise, when we calculate the variance of our population,*

$$\sigma^2 = \sum_{i=1}^{N} \frac{(X_i - \mu)^2}{N}$$

$$= \frac{6^2 + 9^2 + 10^2 + 12^2 + 13^2 + 16^2 - [(66)^2/6]}{6}$$

$$= \frac{60}{6}$$

$$= 10 \tag{4.2}$$

---

* When we speak of a population size, we use N, while for the size of a sample we use n.

TABLE 4.1

All Possible Samples of Size $n = 2$ with Calculated Means, Variances, and Standard Deviations[a]

Samples	$\bar{X}$'s	s^2's	s's
6, 6	6	0	0
6, 9	7.5	4.5	2.12
6, 10	8	8	2.83
6, 12	9	18	4.24
6, 13	9.5	25.5	4.95
6, 16	11	50	7.07
9, 6	7.5	4.5	2.12
9, 9	9	0	0
9, 10	9.5	.5	.71
9, 12	10.5	4.5	2.12
9, 13	11	8	2.83
9, 16	12.5	24.5	4.95
10, 6	8	8	2.83
10, 9	9.5	.5	.71
10, 10	10	0	0
10, 12	11	2	1.41
10, 13	11.5	4.5	2.12
10, 16	13	18	4.24
12, 6	9	18	4.24
12, 9	10.5	4.5	2.12
12, 10	11	2	1.41
12, 12	12	0	0
12, 13	12.5	.5	.71
12, 16	14	8	2.83
13, 6	9.5	24.5	4.95
13, 9	11	8	2.83
13, 10	11.5	4.5	2.12
13, 12	12.5	.5	.71
13, 13	13	0	0
13, 16	14.5	4.5	2.12
16, 6	11	50	7.07
16, 9	12.5	24.5	4.95
16, 10	13	18	4.24
16, 12	14	8	2.83
16, 13	14.5	4.5	2.12
16, 16	16	0	0
Totals	396	360	90.50

[a] Population values are $X_1 = 6$, $X_2 = 9$, $X_3 = 10$, $X_4 = 12$, $X_5 = 13$, $X_6 = 16$.

The mean of each sample found by taking $\bar{X} = \dfrac{\sum\limits_{i=1}^{n} X_i}{n}$

we see that it is exactly the same as the mean of the sample s^2's, μ_{s2}. In the calculation of the population variance σ^2, we use

$$\sigma^2 = \frac{\sum_{i=1}^{N} (X_i - \mu)^2}{N}$$

The squared deviations are divided by N instead of by $N-1$. This is the appropriate formula for the calculation of the *population variance* and this is why the variance is sometimes referred to as the *mean-square deviation*. The mean of sample variances is equal to the population variance if and only if we divide the squared deviations in each *sample* by one less than the *sample size* $(n-1)$, and divide by N in the population. You can now see that in all of our work in Chapter 3 we assumed that we were working with a sample rather than a population. Anytime we are working with a population, though, the population formula is to be used.

Any statistic whose sampling distribution has as its mean the parameter of the population, that statistic is said to be an *unbiased estimate* of the parameter. Therefore, $\bar{X}$ is an unbiased estimate of μ, and s^2 is an unbiased estimate of σ^2. The mean of the sampling distribution of standard deviations, μ_s, found to be 2.51 in our example, is *not equal* to the standard deviation of the population, $\sigma = \sqrt{10} = 3.16$; thus the sample standard deviation, s, is a *biased estimate* of the population standard deviation, σ.

The variance of the sample means, $\sigma_{\bar{X}}^2$, in Table 4.1 was also calculated and found to be 5. We can also find $\sigma_{\bar{X}}^2$ by simply dividing σ^2 by the size of each of our samples.

$$\sigma_{\bar{X}}^2 = \frac{\sigma^2}{n} \tag{4.3}$$

The variance of each sample found by taking $s^2 = \dfrac{\sum_{i=1}^{n} (X_i - \bar{X})^2}{n-1}$

There are 36 samples, thus:

Mean of $\bar{X}$'s $= \mu_{\bar{X}} = \dfrac{396}{36} = 11$

Variance of $\bar{X}$'s $= \sigma_{\bar{X}}^2 = \dfrac{4536 - (396)2/36}{36} = \dfrac{180}{36} = 5$

Standard Deviation of $\bar{X}$'s $= \sigma_{\bar{X}} = \sqrt{5} = 2.24$

Mean of s^2's $= \mu_{s2} = \dfrac{360}{36} = 10$

Mean of s's $= \mu_s = \dfrac{90.50}{36} = 2.51$

In our example, $\sigma_X{}^2 = {}^{10}\!/_2 = 5$; therefore, the standard deviation of the sampling distribution of means is $\sigma_{\bar{X}} = \sigma/\sqrt{n}$, which gives us

$$\sigma_{\bar{X}} = \frac{2.24}{\sqrt{2}}$$

$$= 1.58$$

This standard deviation of the sampling distribution of means is referred to as the *standard error of the mean.*

Often when we want an estimate of $\sigma_{\bar{X}}{}^2$, we have only one sample and do *not* know the population variance. In these cases, we must use s^2 and find

$$s_{\bar{X}}{}^2 = \frac{s^2}{n} \tag{4.4}$$

This is an unbiased estimate of $\sigma_{\bar{X}}{}^2$ in most situations and therefore justifies its use. You will be asked to verify this fact for the skinfold example in one of the exercises at the end of the chapter. The estimate we use for the standard error of the mean is

$$s_{\bar{X}} = \frac{s}{\sqrt{n}} \tag{4.5}$$

As you might suspect, this is a biased estimate of $\sigma_{\bar{X}}$.

We can now see that sample statistics are used as estimates of population parameters. As is clearly illustrated in Table 4.1, with any given sample there is a chance or risk that we will be in error when using statistics as estimates of parameters. The size of this risk can only be determined by the application of probability concepts. Thus, the next two chapters will introduce the necessary concepts in probability and we shall then be ready to apply these concepts to various estimation procedures.

It is strongly advised that you review this chapter before going on, because a considerable number of vitally important concepts have been introduced. If you do not have a fundamental grasp of these concepts, the remainder of the text will not be meaningful.

Exercises

1. Give examples in health, physical education, or recreation of a population, sample, parameter, and statistic.
2. Given that the mean and variance of weights for a population of high school girls is $\mu = 110$, $\sigma^2 = 16$, find the variance and standard error of sample means when the size of the sample is:
   a. $n = 9$
   b. $n = 16$
   c. $n = 64$
   d. $n = 100$

3. a. From Exercise 2, what happens to the variance and standard error of sample means as the size of the samples gets larger?
   b. Why would this logically occur?
4. If the numbers 1, 2, and 3 are our population:
   a. Find μ, σ^2, and σ, and $\sigma_{\bar{x}}^2$ and $\sigma_{\bar{x}}$ for $n = 2$.
   b. Find all possible samples of size $n = 2$ (replacement sampling).
   c. Find the $\bar{X}$, s^2, and s for each sample.
   d. Find the mean of each of the statistics above and compare them with μ, σ^2, σ, and $\sigma_{\bar{x}}$.
5. For the example in Table 4.1, verify that $s_{\bar{x}}^2$ is an unbiased estimate of $\sigma_{\bar{x}}^2$ and that $s_{\bar{x}}$ is a biased estimate of $\sigma_{\bar{x}}$.

COMPUTER APPLICATIONS

In Exercises 6 through 15 assume that the data given in the indicated exercises of Chapter 3 constitute a random sample and find $s_{\bar{x}}^2$ and $s_{\bar{x}}$.

6. Exercise 4.
7. Exercise 5.
8. Exercise 9.
9. Exercise 10.
10. Exercise 11.
11. Exercise 12.
12. Exercise 14.
13. Exercise 15.
14. Exercise 16.
15. Exercise 17.

5

Fundamentals of Probability

5.1 INTRODUCTION

The previous chapters have dealt with appropriate techniques for reducing masses of data into convenient forms so that data may be easily described. The present chapter presents probability as a fundamental aspect of a scientific investigation.

A scientific investigation may be thought of as incorporating three concepts: an *experiment*, a *mathematical model*, and *probability*. We may describe an *experiment* as *any act yielding outcomes that can be repeated under given conditions*. Consequently, the throwing of one or more coins, the tossing of a die, or the drawing of a tennis ball from a bin are all examples of experiments. A *mathematical model* serves to aid the experimenter in the analysis of his experiment and *consists of all possible outcomes that may occur for the experiment*. The *probability of an event* associated with a set of possible outcomes serves as *the criterion for determining the reliability of conclusions drawn*.

The researcher in health, physical education, and recreation is interested in many experiments that are more serious than the ones described above. Theories of epidemics, epidemiological studies of degenerative diseases, characterization of the overload principle for cardiovascular endurance development, and a determination of the values of physical activity held by individuals are just a few examples that might be enumerated. In experiments of this type it is difficult to outline a complete set of possible outcomes. These situations consist of complicated combinations of events. We must resolve the problem of how to determine the probabilities associated with these events before we can answer the question of how reliable our conclusions are. The major part of this text is devoted to just this problem.

The above discussion may be summarized as follows:

If a proposed experiment can result in N equally likely and distinct outcomes, then an appropriate mathematical model for the experiment is a set of N possible outcomes with a probability of $1/N$ being associated with each.

Some simple experiments that may be conducted are illustrated in Table 5.1.

In each example we note that the experiment represents an act that can be repeated under the same conditions. But the same outcome may not result when the experiment is repeated—that is, the results may vary. How the outcomes may vary is determined from the experiment's mathematical model. We cannot know before the experiment is conducted which outcome will occur—that is, we cannot predict the outcome. The fact that the outcome cannot be predicted results from the element of chance. The likelihood of any one outcome, however, is given by its probability.

The foregoing provides a procedure for assigning probabilities to single distinct outcomes of an experiment. We may also be interested in the occurrence of one or more of a specified collection of outcomes. Such a collection is called an *event*. If A is an event, we shall write $P(A)$ for its probability.

TABLE 5.1

Simple Experiments and Their Mathematical Models

Experiment	MATHEMATICAL MODEL	
	Possible Outcomes	Probability
Coin toss	Head, Tail	½
Die toss	1, 2, 3, 4, 5, 6	⅙
Random selection of one individual from a group of 16	1, 2, ..., 16	1/16
Basketball player shoots one free throw	hit, miss	8/10
Two coins tossed simultaneously	HH, HT, TH, TT	¼

The general idea of the probability of an event may be expressed as follows:

If an experiment can result in any one of N equally likely and distinct outcomes, and if exactly m of these outcomes correspond to the event A, then the probability of event A is

$$P(A) = \frac{m}{N} \tag{5.1}$$

Some immediate consequences of this definition may be outlined. If an event A is certain to occur—that is, if all outcomes correspond to the event A, then

$$P(A) = 1 \tag{5.2}$$

If an event A is certain not to occur—that is, if no outcomes correspond to the event A, then

$$P(A) = 0 \tag{5.3}$$

It follows that

$$0 \leqslant P(A) \leqslant 1 \tag{5.4}$$

where the symbol $\leqslant$ means "equal to or less than." Also, if $\bar{A}$ is the event "A will not occur," then

$$P(\bar{A}) = 1 - P(A) \tag{5.5}$$

and

$$P(A) = 1 - P(\bar{A}) \tag{5.6}$$

Example 1 An infectious disease has a one-day infectious period, and after that day the patient is immune. Three hermits (A, B, and C) live on an island. If one has the disease he randomly visits another hermit for help during his infectious period. If the visited hermit has not had the disease, he catches it and is infectious the next day. Assume that one of the three hermits contacts the disease at random. What is the probability that the epidemic will run its course without hermit C contacting the disease?

SOLUTION   To establish a mathematical model for this experiment, we must first determine all the possible sequences (outcomes) that describe the progress the "epidemic" may take. Thinking about the infectious transmission sequence, we note that the following possibilities exist:

ABC	BAC	CAB
ACB	BCA	CBA
ABA	BAB	CAC
ACA	BCB	CBC

The first letter in each combination represents the hermit initially contacting the disease. The second letter represents the hermit visited by the first hermit during his infectious period, and the third represents the hermit in turn visited by the second hermit during his infectious period. Note that each of these sequences will stop the epidemic and one must be followed. In some cases the last hermit listed in the combination may contact the disease, but note that the remaining hermits are immune.

The mathematical model contains 12 possible outcomes, with a probability of $1/12$ associated with each. Only two sequences will result in hermit C not contacting the disease. These are ABA and BAB. Thus the probability of hermit C not getting the disease is

$$P(\bar{C}) = \frac{2}{12} = \frac{1}{6}$$

An alternative solution to the problem is to use Eq. (5.5)—that is,

$$P(\bar{C}) = 1 - P(C)$$

The probability that hermit C contacts the disease is

$$P(C) = \frac{10}{12}$$

Then

$$P(\bar{C}) = 1 - \frac{10}{12} = \frac{2}{12} = \frac{1}{6}$$

This experiment describes a simplified example of the mathematical theory of epidemics. It is obvious that in an epidemiological study of the magnitude involving, say, a flu epidemic in the United States, much more sophisticated procedures must be utilized to describe the progress of an epidemic in terms of numbers susceptible, infected, and immunized through time. In an elementary treatise on statistics, there is not space for a full study of such difficult problems. We attempt here to establish the basic principles of statistics that serve as the foundation for their study.

Exercises

1. Three teams finish in a three-way tie for the conference crown. The conference representative in a postseason tournament is to be determined by a simultaneous coin flip with the odd man declared the winner. Construct a mathematical model for the first flip of a coin. How many outcomes are favorable to the event "Team A will win the right to represent the conference"? What is its probability?
2. Construct a mathematical model for the sample means $(\bar{X}_i)$ listed in Table 4.1.
3. A pro shop has unmarked golf balls on sale. Included in the sale are 200 balls of 100 compression, 300 of 90 compression, and 500 of 80 compression. What is the probability that a golfer, selecting a ball at random, will:
   a. select a 100 compression ball.
   b. not select an 80 compression ball.
   c. select either an 80 or a 90 compression ball.
   d. at least get his money's worth if the sale price is $.95 and the balls are valued as follows: 100's valued at $1.25; 90's valued at $1.00; 80's valued at $.90.
   e. not get his money's worth using values given in (d).
4. One card is drawn from an ordinary 52-card bridge deck and one card is drawn from an ordinary 48-card pinochle deck. Find the following probabilities for each card.
   a. It is black.
   b. It is an honor card (i.e., 10, J, Q, K, or A).
   c. It is either an honor card or black.
   d. It is neither an honor card nor black.
5. A football bowl game ticket is to be given away as a door prize at a school function. Each of 400 individuals in attendance is given a number, 1 to 400. One of these numbers is to be selected at random and its holder awarded the game ticket. Find the probability that the winning ticket:
   a. has a numeral beginning with 3.
   b. has a numeral less than 100.
   c. is 345.

5.2 COMPOSITE EVENTS

By now it should be clear that events and only events have probabilities. It has been noted that an event is a collection of certain elementary events favorable to it and that the event occurs if one of these elementary events results during the performance of the experiment. This thought may be extended to include the notion that events may be described as certain combinations of other events.

We represent graphically the ideas underlying composite events and their probabilities by means of a simple dart game. Let A and B represent two dart boards, as presented in Figure 5.1.

The size of each dart board represents in a sense the probability that a thrown dart will hit that board. Since a single dart thrown at boards A and B in Figure 5.1(a) cannot possibly hit both boards simultaneously, A and B represent *mutually exclusive events*. We may state the following probability law for mutually exclusive events:

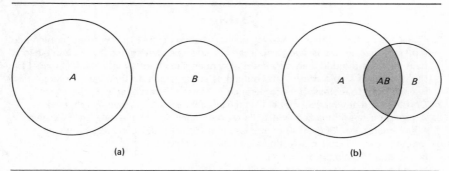

(a)   (b)

FIGURE 5.1

(a) Two mutually exclusive events. (b) Two nonmutually exclusive events.

If A and B are mutually exclusive events, then

$$P(A \text{ or } B) = P(A + B)$$
$$= P(A) + P(B) \tag{5.7}$$

A single dart thrown at dart boards A and B in Figure 5.1(b) may strike both A and B since the boards overlap. This implies that A and B are not mutually exclusive. The probability rule for *nonmutually exclusive events* is

$$P(A \text{ or } B) = P(A + B)$$
$$= P(A) + P(B) - P(AB) \tag{5.8}$$

The quantity, $P(AB)$, represents the probability that both A and B occur (e.g., the dart hits the intersection of dart boards A and B). Note that $P(A)$ and $P(B)$ each contain the probability $P(AB)$ and therefore $P(AB)$ is counted twice if Eq. (5.7) is used. Thus, Eq. (5.8) corrects for this double addition by subtracting $P(AB)$ from the right-hand side of Eq. (5.7), giving the probability for a nonmutually exclusive event.*

Example 2 A bin contains six white, four green, and three yellow tennis balls. What is the probability of selecting a green ball or a yellow ball if one ball is selected at random?

SOLUTION A single ball selected cannot be both yellow and green; thus, using Eq. (5.7) for mutually exclusive events, we get

$$P(G \text{ or } Y) = P(G + Y) = P(G) + P(Y)$$

$$= \frac{4}{13} + \frac{3}{13}$$

$$= \frac{7}{13}$$

* It might be noted that Eq. (5.7) is also a special case of Eq. (5.8) when $P(AB) = 0$.

Example 3 What is the probability of either of the events $E =$ "an even number of spots" or $M =$ "a multiple of 3" turning up from one die toss?

SOLUTION   Referring to the basic definition of an experiment, we note that the mathematical model contains 6 possible outcomes each with a probability of $\frac{1}{6}$. Outcomes favorable to event E are 2, 4, and 6. Similarly, outcomes favorable to event M are 3 and 6. We note, then, that the outcome 6 is common to both events, implying that both E and M may occur simultaneously; hence, E and M for this example are not mutually exclusive. We use Eq. (5.8), to get

$$P(E \text{ or } M) = P(E + M) = P(E) + P(M) - P(EM)$$
$$= \frac{3}{6} + \frac{2}{6} - \frac{1}{6}$$
$$= \frac{4}{6}$$
$$= \frac{2}{3}$$

Frequently, we may be given preliminary information concerning the occurrence of an event. The availability of this information often will influence the probability statements of interest. Figure 5.2 describes this idea using the dart game example. Figure 5.2(a) describes the event "dart board A is struck given that we know dart board B has been struck"; this is denoted $A|B$. The mathematical model for the event $A|B$ is based only on those possible outcomes favorable to the event B. In terms of our dart game, we eliminate that part of dart board A not common to B. Thus, the probability $P(A|B)$ is given by

$$P(A|B) = \frac{P(AB)}{P(B)} \qquad (5.9)$$

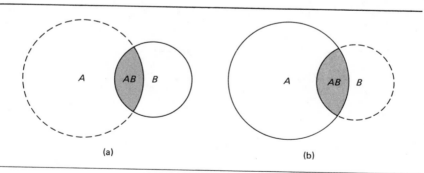

(a)   (b)

FIGURE 5.2

(a) Event $A|B$. (b) Event $B|A$.

Similarly, the probability for the event $B|A$, graphically defined in Figure 5.2(b), is

$$P(B|A) = \frac{P(AB)}{P(A)} \qquad (5.10)$$

Example 4 Suppose male and female students are distributed as follows:

	Freshmen (FR)	Sophomores (S)	Total
Males (M)	10	6	16
Females (F)	6	4	10
Totals	16	10	26

What is the probability of selecting a sophomore knowing that the student selected is a male?

SOLUTION The knowledge that a male was selected permits us to exclude all females from further analysis. Thus 6 sophomore males might be selected from a total of 16 males or

$$P(S|M) = \frac{6}{16}$$

$$= \frac{3}{8}$$

Using Eq. (5.9), we determine $P(M) = {}^{16}\!/_{26}$, $P(SM) = {}^{6}\!/_{26}$ and

$$P(S|M) = \frac{P(SM)}{P(M)}$$

$$= \frac{{}^{6}\!/_{26}}{{}^{16}\!/_{26}}$$

$$= \frac{(6)(26)}{(16)(26)}$$

$$= \frac{6}{16}$$

$$= \frac{3}{8}$$

Example 5 If we are told that a sophomore has been selected, what is the probability that the student is a female?

SOLUTION Using Eq. (5.10), we get

$$P(F|S) = \frac{P(FS)}{P(S)}$$

$$= \frac{4/26}{10/26}$$

$$= \frac{4}{10}$$

$$= \frac{2}{5}$$

The probability of a conditional event given by Eqs. (5.9) and (5.10) has the following immediate consequence: If A and B are any two events, then

$$P(AB) = P(A) \cdot P(B|A)$$
$$= P(B) \cdot P(A|B) \qquad (5.11)$$

Example 6 Suppose we randomly select 2 students without replacement from a class of 7 males and 3 females. What is the probability that both students selected will be females?

SOLUTION The probability that both will be females is the probability of selecting a female on the first selection multiplied by the probability of selecting a female on the second selection given that the student selected first was a female. That is, from Eq. (5.11),

$$P(F_1 F_2) = P(F_1)P(F_2|F_1)$$

$$= \frac{3}{10} \cdot \frac{2}{9}$$

$$= \frac{1}{15}$$

If the events A and B are such that the occurrence of one does not affect the probability of the occurrence of the other, then the two events are said to be *independent* and the probability of their simultaneous occurrence is

$$P(AB) = P(A) \cdot P(B) \qquad (5.12)$$

Example 7 Suppose we select one student from each of two classes. The first class contains 6 males and 4 females and the second class contains 4 males and 5 females. What is the probability that both students will be males? Both females? One female and one male?

SOLUTION The probability that both students selected are males is obtained by using Eq. (5.12) because the selection made from one class has no effect on the outcome when a student is selected from the second class. Then,

$$P(M_1M_2) = P(M_1)P(M_2)$$

$$= \frac{6}{10} \cdot \frac{4}{9}$$

$$= \frac{(2 \cdot 2)}{(5 \cdot 3)}$$

$$= \frac{4}{15}$$

Similarly, the probability that both students will be females is

$$P(F_1F_2) = P(F_1)P(F_2)$$

$$= \frac{4}{10} \cdot \frac{5}{9}$$

$$= \frac{2}{9}$$

If one male and one female are selected, we note that either of the following events may occur:

A. A male is selected from class 1 and a female from class 2.
B. A female is selected from class 1 and a male from class 2.

Thus, the event "one male and one female" consists of the combined event *A* or *B*. This gives

$$P(\text{one male and one female}) = P(M_1F_2 \text{ or } F_1M_2)$$

Now, the events M_1F_2 and F_2M_1 are mutually exclusive, permitting us to use Eq. (5.7). This gives

$$P(M_1F_2 \text{ or } F_1M_2) = P(M_1F_2 + F_1M_2) = P(M_1F_2) + P(F_1M_2)$$

Then, using Eq. (5.12), we get

$$P(M_1F_2) + P(F_1M_2) = [P(M_1) \cdot P(F_2)] + [P(F_1) \cdot P(M_2)]$$

$$= \left(\frac{6}{10} \cdot \frac{5}{9}\right) + \left(\frac{4}{10} \cdot \frac{4}{9}\right)$$

$$= \frac{30}{90} + \frac{16}{90}$$

$$= \frac{46}{90}$$

$$= \frac{23}{45}$$

The reader may easily check his computations for accuracy by noting that the sum of the three probabilities must equal one. That is, P(both students will be males) $+ P$(both females) $+ P$(one female and one male) $= 1$.

Exercises

6. Two bins contain handball gloves and balls, respectively. Bin A contains six fast and four slow handballs. Bin B contains three large, four medium, and two small pairs of gloves. One ball and one pair of gloves are selected at random from each of the two bins. Determine the probabilities of:
   a. selecting a fast ball and a small pair of gloves.
   b. selecting a slow ball or a large pair of gloves.
   c. selecting a fast ball and a small pair of gloves or a slow ball and a medium pair of gloves.
   d. not selecting either a fast ball or a small pair of gloves.
7. If the two teams competing in the World Series are evenly matched, what is the probability that the series will terminate at the end of the fourth game? The fifth game? The sixth game? The seventh game?
8. In a basketball game, Bill sets a pick allowing Ronnie to move to his favorite spot to attempt a shot. If the pick results in defensive men switching assignments, the probability that Ronnie will make a goal is 0.7. If the defensive men do not switch assignments, the probability that he will make a goal is 0.4. The probability that a switch will occur is 0.8. What is the probability that Ronnie will make a goal?
9. Cards identifying individual characteristics of 50 football players are randomly placed face down on a desk. The pertinent data given show:

Positions	CLASSIFICATION			
	Fr.	So.	Jr.	Sr.
Backs	1	4	4	6
Linemen	3	7	15	5
Ends	1	1	2	1

One card is randomly selected. What is the probability that:
   a. it is a freshman's card?
   b. it is a lineman's card?
   c. it is a junior back's card?
   d. it is a senior's card, given that a lineman's card was selected?
   e. it is either a senior's or a lineman's card?
   f. it is a back's card, given that a junior's card was selected?
10. On a given weekend, team A may win, lose, or tie. The probability of not winning is $\frac{10}{12}$, and the probability of not losing is $\frac{5}{6}$. Find the probability of a tie.
11. The probability that a certain baseball player will hit safely if he uses the correct bat is .350, and the probability of hitting safely with an incorrect bat is .250. In the bat rack are 20 bats, only 4 of which are correct for this batter. If he chooses a bat at random and takes his turn at bat, what is the probability that he will hit safely?
12. Three golfers are left with 10-foot putts on the green. The respective probabilities that they will sink the putts are $\frac{1}{2}$, $\frac{1}{3}$, and $\frac{1}{4}$. What is the probability that none of the putts will be successful?
13. On a given afternoon, the Alou brothers—Matty, Felipe, and Jesus—are playing in doubleheaders for their respective teams. The respective probabilities that they will hit safely at least once are .600, .500, and .400. What is the probability that at least two will get at least one hit on this afternoon?

5.3 COUNTING POSSIBLE OUTCOMES

PERMUTATIONS

Thus far we have defined the probability of an event A as the ratio of the number of outcomes (m) favorable to A divided by the total number of possible outcomes N. It is necessary, then, to count the numbers m and N. In the simplest cases, we can list all the possible outcomes and determine m and N by counting, but, in general, this would be an exhaustive process. In the more complicated experiments, rules to help us count are desirable. The present section considers some of these rules. Consider first an example.

Example 8 In how many ways can three sprinters, denoted by A, B, and C, finish a race?

SOLUTION The most obvious solution to this problem is to list the possible orders of finish and count them. Accordingly, we obtain

$$(ABC), (ACB), (BAC), (BCA), (CAB), (CBA)$$

giving six distinct orders of finish for the race.

There are many instances where we will need only the total number of possible outcomes. This suggests that we use some procedure for counting the possible outcomes without writing them down. Toward this end, suppose we represent each place of finish as follows:

1st   2nd   3rd

Now from the list of possible orders of finish it may be noted that any one of the three sprinters, A, B, or C, may finish first. Thus, the first place box may be filled in three ways.

1st   2nd   3rd

3

Once an individual has finished first in the race, only two sprinters remain to finish second.

1st   2nd   3rd

3   2

Finally, after two runners have finished first and second, only one runner remains to finish third. This gives

1st   2nd   3rd

3   2   1

By multiplying the numbers corresponding to the three orders of finish, we get the total number of possible finishes:

$$3 \times 2 \times 1 = 6$$

In this particular example, the order of finish is important. Thus, the arrangements (ABC) and (ACB) define two different orders of finish for the race, because runner B finished second in the former arrangement while runner C finished second in the latter. Such an ordering is referred to as a *permutation*. To *permutate* a collection of objects is *to arrange them in a specified order*.

In general, the number of permutations of a set of n different objects, taken all together, is

$$_nP_n = n! \tag{5.13}$$

where $n!$ is read "n factorial." The symbol $n!$ is defined as the product of all whole numbers from 1 to n, inclusive. That is,

$$n! = n(n-1)(n-2) \cdots (3)(2)(1) \tag{5.14}$$

where $\cdots$ represents all whole numbers between $(n-2)$ and 3 that should be included in the computations but have been left out for convenience.

Example 9 Suppose five sprinters run the 100-yard dash. How many possible ways may they finish?

SOLUTION Any casual attempt to write all the possible arrangements of five sprinters will soon demonstrate the difficulty involved. While writing each arrangement may be time consuming, determining the total number is not, thanks to Eq. (5.13). Since $n = 5$ we get

$$\begin{aligned} _5P_5 &= 5! \\ &= 5 \cdot 4 \cdot 3 \cdot 2 \cdot 1 \\ &= 120 \end{aligned}$$

Thus, there are 120 different ways the five sprinters may finish the race.

Example 10 Suppose we are interested only in the total number of ways five sprinters may finish first, second, and third in the 100-yard dash.

SOLUTION The number of specified orders of finish among five sprinters may be determined by the method given in Example 8. Thus, to assign a specified order of finish, the following places must be filled:

1st   2nd   3rd

The first place finish may be filled with one of five sprinters in five ways. Once a sprinter finishes first only four remain to finish second. Finally, after two sprinters finish first and second, only three remain to finish third. This gives

1st	2nd	3rd
5	4	3

or $5 \times 4 \times 3 = 60$ possible orders of finish.

A general formula that is useful for this type problem is: The number of permutations of n objects taken r at a time is

$$_nP_r = \frac{n!}{(n-r)!} \tag{5.15}$$

Example 11 How many different batting orders are possible for a baseball team if the team is to be selected from 12 players?

SOLUTION Nine players constitute a baseball team. Thus inserting $n = 12$ and $r = 9$ into Eq. (5.15) gives

$$\begin{aligned} _{12}P_9 &= \frac{12!}{(12-9)!} \\ &= \frac{12!}{3!} \\ &= 12 \cdot 11 \cdot 10 \cdot 9 \cdot 8 \cdot 7 \cdot 6 \cdot 5 \cdot 4 \\ &= 79{,}833{,}600 \end{aligned}$$

The permutation formula given above is applied to sets of objects or events that are different from each other. Quite frequently we may require counting procedures for the arrangement of objects some of which are identical. The corresponding formulae are significantly different from those already given. Consider again an example.

Example 12 Suppose a bin contains one green and two white tennis balls. How many ways may white and green balls be selected for use?

SOLUTION If the two white balls are stamped with numerals, the three balls are distinguishable and thus may be selected in

$$_3P_3 = 3! = 3 \cdot 2 \cdot 1$$
$$= 6 \text{ ways}$$

These may be written as

$$\begin{array}{cc} W_1W_2G & W_2W_1G \\ W_1GW_2 & W_2GW_1 \\ GW_1W_2 & GW_2W_1 \end{array}$$

But note that tennis balls are not normally numbered as shown in this example. Then, removing the subscripts on W_1 and W_2 gives the six arrangements

WWG   WWG

WGW   WGW

GWW   GWW

If we compare the orders of selection in any one row, we note that the two selections are exactly the same. Thus the one green and two white balls may be selected in only three distinguishable ways. Then, the six original arrangements must be reduced by the factor $\frac{1}{2}$ because of the nondistinguishable arrangements for the two white balls. That is,

$$_2P_2 = 2!$$
$$= 2$$

represents the proportion of the original arrangements that are nondistinguishable.

In general, *the number of permutations of N things, taken all together, when n_1 refers to the number of items of one kind, and n_2 the number of items of the other kind, is*

$$_NP_{n_1, n_2} = \frac{N!}{n_1! \, n_2!} \tag{5.16}$$

where $N = n_1 + n_2$; in other words where there are only two kinds of things.

This idea may be extended to any number of N things, taken all together, when there are n_1 items of one kind, n_2 items of another kind, and so forth up to n_k items of the same kind. This extension is not presented here for it is not needed to develop an understanding of the concepts to follow. The interested reader is referred to one of the references listed in the bibliography.

Example 13 A physical education instructor wishes to establish a circuit training program as part of his fitness class. He has three isometric and four isotonic exercises. How many arrangements are available if the instructor is interested only in the ordering of isometric and isotonic exercises and not in the individual exercises?

SOLUTION   Since individual exercises are not important we may consider the three isometric exercises as being alike and similarly the four isotonic can be considered alike. We may then use Eq. (5.16) with $N = 7$, $n_1 = 3$, and $n_2 = 4$ to get

$$_7P_{3,4} = \frac{7!}{3! \, 4!}$$

$$= \frac{7 \cdot 6 \cdot 5 \cdot 4!}{3 \cdot 2 \cdot 1 \cdot 4!}$$

$$= 35 \text{ arrangements}$$

COMBINATIONS

Let us now consider a related but somewhat different problem. Suppose we have a group of n things and want to know in how many ways we can select a subgroup of r without regard to arrangement. If we ignore the order of selection, there should be fewer possible ways objects may be selected. For example, two setbacks may be positioned in a pro-type offensive backfield in two different ways, AB or BA. These same two running backs, however, made up only one backfield, because AB and BA represent the same individuals. Order counts when plays are run from a set position. Thus, AB and BA are different. Order does not count when one is asked "Who makes up team X's backfield?"

To distinguish selection of objects when order counts from a selection of objects when order is not significant, we use, for the latter, the term *combination*. Computational formulae for determining combinations may be obtained from those of permutations.

Suppose three running backs are available for a pro-type backfield. How many backfields are possible? We know that the number of permutations of three things taken two at a time is

$$_3P_2 = 3 \cdot 2$$
$$= 6$$

We may write these as AB, BA, AC, CA, BC, and CB. However, we are interested only in the composition of the backfield, and not in where the players are positioned. Thus, backfield AB is made up of the same backs as BA, while AC is the same as CA, and BC is the same as CB. This gives only three different backfields. Since we are not concerned here with the order of selection of the two running backs, we can extract the groups of permutations that are alike by dividing $_3P_2$ by 2! which gives our number 3. This same procedure may be followed for any selection process where order does not count. In general,

The number of combinations of a set of n different objects, taken r at a time, is

$$\binom{n}{r} = \frac{n!}{r!(n-r)!} \tag{5.17}$$

Example 14   Three subjects are to be selected at random from a group of 30 individuals. How many possible combinations are there?

SOLUTION   In this case, the order of selection is of no importance. Thus, we use Eq. (5.17) with $n = 30$ and $r = 3$, to get

$$\binom{30}{3} = \frac{30!}{3!\,27!}$$
$$= \frac{30 \cdot 29 \cdot 28}{3 \cdot 2 \cdot 1}$$
$$= 4060$$

5.4 EMPIRICAL PROBABILITY

The classical definition of probability given by Eq. (5.1) has serious limitations. Quite frequently we will have difficulty outlining all possible outcomes. In addition, we can never be certain that each outcome is equally likely to occur. The definition does serve, however, as a model to follow in determining probabilities of events for experiments of interest. One may find the probability of an event as follows. Define in general the mathematical model for the experiment of interest stating at least the events to be considered. Then make many "independent" repetitions of the experiment under identical conditions and observe the relative frequency of the occurrence of the event, say, A. This relative frequency should be very close to the actual probability of A. Specifically, the relative frequency should approach the true probability as the number of repetitions increases. This probability may be referred to as the "empirical" probability of event A and is essentially an interpretation of the law of large numbers, which will be discussed later.

Example 15 We note from the classical definition of probability that if a coin is fair the probability of a head is $\frac{1}{2}$. Thus, if we toss the coin a number of times, we would expect the relative frequency for heads to be about $\frac{1}{2}$. In any one repetition of the experiment, the actual number of heads may differ from $\frac{1}{2}$, but in the long run, we would expect the combined relative frequencies to approach that value. An example to illustrate this property was reported by Huntsberger.* The results, plotted on a semilogarithmic scale to reduce the scale of the number of tosses, are presented in Figure 5.3.

Example 16 A mathematical model describing the association between heart disease and fitness levels in adult males is not available. We may empirically derive this model by randomly selecting, say, 1000 males from the population of males in the United States. Upon assessing their fitness level and examining for heart disease, we might obtain the data in Table 5.2.

TABLE 5.2

Hypothetical Data Showing Fitness Level and Heart Disease Association[a]

	HEART DISEASE		
Fitness Level	Present	Absent	Totals
High	.02	.13	.15
Medium	.08	.27	.35
Low	.10	.40	.50
Totals	.20	.80	1.00

[a] Tabled values are relative frequencies.

* D. V. Huntsberger, *Statistical Inference*, Boston: Allyn and Bacon, 1967, p. 70.

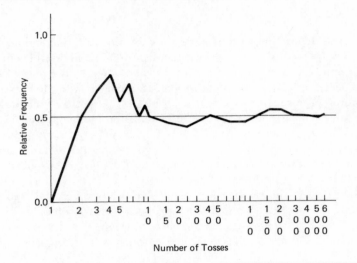

Number of Tosses

FIGURE 5.3

Relative frequency of heads

If we may assume that the empirical data in Table 5.2 represent the true mathematical model for the population, we may compute approximate probabilities for certain events of interest. For example, the empirical probability that an individual will have heart disease (D) given he is high fit (H) is

$$\text{Empirical } P(D \mid H) = \frac{RF(DH)}{RF(H)} = \frac{0.02}{0.15} = 0.133$$

That is, a high fit person's chances of having heart disease is 0.133, or 13.3 percent. On the other hand, the empirical probability that a low fit (L) person will have heart disease is suggested from Table 5.2 to be

$$\text{Empirical } P(D \mid L) = \frac{RF(DL)}{RF(L)} = \frac{0.10}{0.50} = 0.20$$

The reader may compute other empirical probabilities of interest.

5.5   IN RETROSPECT

Let us look in retrospect at the essence of this chapter. We have presented a number of rules of probability and have outlined examples to demonstrate their application. Taken on their own merit, these examples are for the most part simple, impractical, and only of academic interest. The reader should not, however, judge us too harshly because we have chosen to pause for a moment to flip coins and shuffle cards. The sequence of this treatise on statistics is based on the premise that probability concepts are fundamentally important to the understanding of statistical applications. Because of the nature of the subject, the sketch developed in an introductory text is completed only at the end of the book. Thus, the reader does not obtain a meaningful whole until the end. We recommend that the reader review the introductory remarks at the beginning of this chapter that outline the interrelationship among an experiment, a mathematical model, and probability. In addition, we suggest that the student construct a complete experiment or two for ready reference as we proceed through the text. For example, think of an experiment involving the average tar content of a make of cigarette, say, brand A. Obviously, it would be impossible to measure tar content of every cigarette made by brand A. This necessitates taking a sample, but we're interested in making some statement about a body of measurements that is larger than just the sample. That body is the population of brand A cigarettes. Suppose it has definitely been established that 30 milligrams of tar per cigarette will cause cancer. The statement we wish to make about the population of brand A cigarettes is either " each cigarette in the population possesses a tar content that is less than 30 milligrams " or " each cigarette possesses a tar content of 30 or more milligrams." In symbolic terms, let X represent the tar content of a random cigarette, then either $A: X < 30$ or $B: X \geqslant 30$. This problem involves more complicated techniques than those presented in this chapter. The reader should recognize, however, that by observing the tar content of a sample of cigarettes we are, in effect, applying the principle of empirical probability. The relative frequency of each of the two possible events (A and B) outlined above would serve as a basis for deciding which is more likely to occur. These observations in the form of probability statements would then serve to determine the reliability of the conclusion drawn.

As we continue the development of statistical concepts, we ask that you bear with us and recognize the fact that much of the information given is preliminary to some yet to be developed concept. In the final analysis, the parts should fit into the whole. Throughout we shall strive to present examples that will suggest the part each bit of information plays in the solution of statistical problems in physical education, recreation, and health.

Exercises

14. Referring to Exercise 4, compute each probability by using formulae for combinations.

15. Referring to Exercise 4, suppose two cards are drawn without replacement from one of the decks. Given the results of the two-card draw, you are asked to decide which of the two decks was used. Compute:
    a. the number of events favorable only to a bridge deck.
    b. the number of events favorable only to a pinochle deck.

    c. the total number of distinct two-card draws for each deck.

    d. the probability of selecting two cards that permit you to conclude without error that the deck selected was the bridge deck. What is the probability with pinochle deck?

    e. Which deck is suggested if two honor cards not of the same number and suit are selected?

    f. What risk is involved with the conclusion in (e)?

    g. What risk is involved in concluding the pinochle deck was selected?

16. On our nine-man baseball squad, we have four men who can play the infield (excluding pitcher and catcher). Assuming that the remaining team members can play any of the other five positions, how many different defensive lineups are possible?

17. A true-false test is to contain 20 questions with 8 answers that are false and 12 that are true. How many different arrangements of true and false answers are possible for this test?

18. A basketball coach has five different plays he may run from the high-low post offense. Generally, he prefers to run a sequence of three plays in an attempt to get a man open for a shot. If one of the three does not give a man an open shot, the ball is passed out to a guard and a new sequence of three plays is run. How many sequences are possible?

6

Numbers Determined by Experiments: Random Variables

In Chapter 5, we were interested in obtaining the probability of the occurrence of a single chance event. When an experiment is performed, however, we may want to know the probabilities of various outcomes or events associated with the experiment. Subsequently, we may wish to predict the outcomes of related experiments.

Recall that an experiment is the process of collecting a measurement or observation under a given set of conditions. Most experiments of interest yield a numerical value that varies from one conduction of the experiment to another. This is called a *random variable*.

The random selection of a single element or observation from a population may result in any of a number of possible outcomes, and we cannot know in advance of the sampling which element or value will be obtained. Therefore, the random selection of *n* elements from a population may be equated with the conduct of *n* independent trials of a random experiment. Thus, whenever we take a random sample we are performing a random experiment whose outcomes are the sample values. *In general, we define a random variable as one whose events or outcomes are the result of chance and vary from observation to observation or from experiment to experiment.*

In the following text, it is necessary to distinguish between patterns of behavior of numerical values arising from actual experiments and patterns of behavior of random variables governed by probability laws. Examples of the former were outlined in Chapter 2 in the form of frequency distributions. The latter comprises an array of values, together with their probabilities, that the random variable can assume. This is defined as a *probability distribution*.

In the context of Chapter 5, probability distributions may be equated with mathematical models. Thus, in analyzing data derived from an actual experiment, we may frequently hypothesize that the observations are *values* of a random variable which behave according to its associated probability distribution. An example will serve to clarify the concept.

Example 1 It is suspected that a particular die is loaded. How might we conduct an experiment to test this supposition?

Discussion The outcome of a toss of any die represents a chance occurrence and thus may be any number between 1 and 6, inclusive. We cannot know in advance of any toss of the die what the outcome will be, but if the die is fair we know that in the long run each side should appear an equal number of times. This knowledge provides us with a means of establishing a probability distribution (mathematical model) that might serve as a basis for comparing the outcomes that result from tossing the suspected die a reasonable number of times. That is, to each side of an unbiased die we attach a probability of $\frac{1}{6}$ that it will appear on any one roll. Thus we may construct the following probability distribution:

Outcome	1	2	3	4	5	6	
P(outcome)	$\frac{1}{6}$	$\frac{1}{6}$	$\frac{1}{6}$	$\frac{1}{6}$	$\frac{1}{6}$	$\frac{1}{6}$	(6.1)

Suppose we agree to toss the suspected die 36 times and record the number of times each side turns face up. Let the actual outcomes be represented by the frequency distribution in (6.2).

Outcome	1	2	3	4	5	6	
Actual frequency	3	7	9	4	8	7	(6.2)
Theoretical frequency	6	6	6	6	6	6	

Now, since our mathematical model for an unbiased die suggests that each side should appear about one-sixth of the time, or $\frac{1}{6} \times 36 = 6$ times for this experiment, the actual frequencies obtained in (6.2) do not agree with the theoretical frequencies. One might ask whether the actual frequencies are sufficiently different from the theoretical frequencies to justify the conclusion that the die is biased. All the mechanics needed to answer this question have not yet been presented, but the reader should get a general idea as to how the problem is approached.

By using probability distributions as mathematical models we can describe chance happenings to a *random variable* in a population of *objects* without observing the entire population. Once an experiment is defined (i.e., once the conditions are set), the probability distribution for a random variable of interest is fixed and does not vary. The probability distribution, therefore, provides a stable base for making decisions concerning the behavior of the random variable in a sample.

The actual outcomes recorded in (6.2) represent observations based on one set of tosses. No guarantee is given that the same set of frequencies will be obtained for a second set of 36 tosses. In fact, it would be a rare occurrence indeed. Thus, we cannot say, simply because the frequencies recorded in (6.2) are not all 6's, that the die is biased. However, let us recall our discussion of empirical probability in Chapter 5. If the die is unbiased, we will expect that in the long run the combined relative frequencies of the tosses will approach the corresponding probabilities in the probability distribution. If they do not, then evidence would be given that the die may be biased.

6.2 DISCRETE RANDOM VARIABLES AND THEIR PROBABILITY DISTRIBUTIONS

A discrete random variable is easily identified by examining the number and nature of the values that it may assume. In most practical problems, discrete random variables represent counting events such as chins successfully completed, cavities noted in sixth-grade students, points scored in a basketball game, and color of hair or eyes.

It may seem a bit awkward at first, but we will frequently wish to distinguish between a random variable and one of its values. The capital letter X will be used for the random variable and the subscript (i) on the letter X (i.e., X_i) will denote one of its values. For example, the random variable "cavities noted in sixth-grade students" replaces the symbol X. We have no way of knowing in advance how many cavities each student has, so we represent these unknown values by the symbol X_i. After a particular random sample is taken, X_i will be a number, but before the sample is drawn, X_i is a random event capable of assuming any value that the variable X can assume.

In general, the probability distribution for the random variable X may be represented as

$$
\begin{array}{c|c|c|c|c}
X_i & X_1 & X_2 & \cdots & X_k \\
\hline
p(X_i) & p_1 & p_2 & \cdots & p_k
\end{array}
\tag{6.3}
$$

For convenience, the X_i's are assumed to be arranged in increasing order from left to right, and since the events cannot overlap they constitute mutually exclusive events. Summing P's over all values of X_i will equal the sum of the probabilities of all events, and thus, $\sum p = 1$. We do not generally include any X_i whose probability is 0 in a probability distribution.

In order to judge quickly how a random variable is distributed, that is, how its probabilities change as values of the variable change, we can form a graphic representation of the probability distribution. The graph of the probability distribution (6.1) is shown in Figure 6.1. The vertical lines have

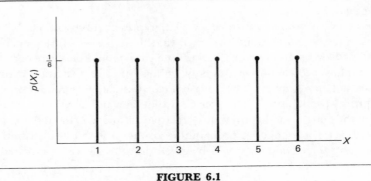

FIGURE 6.1

Probability distribution for the toss of a die

lengths proportional to the probabilities. The probability distribution in Figure 6.1 is called a *rectangular distribution* because all the probabilities associated with the events in the range 1 to 6 are equal.

Another illustration describes the distribution for a simple ping-pong ball toss game. Suppose three concentric rings constitute the target as described in Figure 6.2. The probability distribution associated with the ping-pong toss game is

X_i	0	1	2	3
$p(X_i)$	0.4	0.3	0.2	0.1

(6.4)

Its graph looks like the graph in Figure 6.3.

In general, the probability distribution of a discrete random variable X may be graphically represented as shown in Figure 6.4.

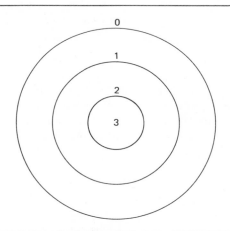

FIGURE 6.2

Ping-pong ball toss target

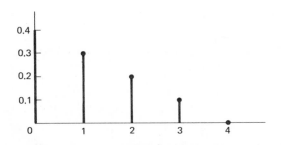

FIGURE 6.3

Probability distribution for ping-pong ball toss game

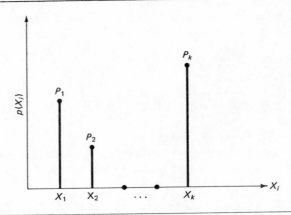

FIGURE 6.4

General probability distribution

Graphs of probability distributions also provide a convenient means of physically interpreting probabilities for specified intervals of random values. The sum of probabilities in any interval represents the probability that the value of the random variable X will be in that interval.

We give some examples.

Example 2   Consider the probability distribution (6.1) for the random variable "number appearing" on the toss of an unbiased die. The probability associated with the interval $1 < X_i < 4$ (1 is less than X_i and X_i is less than 4) asks for the probability that, on the roll of a die, either the number 2 or the number 3 will occur. Thus

$$P(1 < X_i < 4) = p(X_i = 2) + p(X_i = 3)$$

$$= \frac{1}{6} + \frac{1}{6} = \frac{2}{6} = \frac{1}{3}$$

Graphically, $P(1 < X_i < 4)$ is represented as the probabilities included in the shaded areas in Figure 6.5.

The probability

$$P(X_i < 4) = P(X_i = 1) + P(X_i = 2) + P(X_i = 3)$$

$$= \frac{1}{6} + \frac{1}{6} + \frac{1}{6} = \frac{3}{6} = \frac{1}{2}$$

Graphically, it may be represented as shown in Figure 6.6.

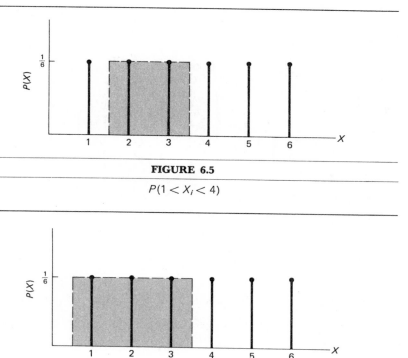

FIGURE 6.5

$$P(1 < X_i < 4)$$

FIGURE 6.6

$$P(X_i < 4)$$

The reader may note from Figure 6.6 that the shaded area accounts for about one-half of the total area occupied by the six events and their probabilities. It should also be noted that for discrete random variables we will begin our shaded area one-half unit below the lowest value in the interval and stop it one-half unit above the largest value.

Example 3   Consider the probability distribution for the tossing of a pair of dice. The probability for the sum of the two faces is

X_i	2	3	4	5	6	7	8	9	10	11	12
$P(X_i)$	$\frac{1}{36}$	$\frac{2}{36}$	$\frac{3}{36}$	$\frac{4}{36}$	$\frac{5}{36}$	$\frac{6}{36}$	$\frac{5}{36}$	$\frac{4}{36}$	$\frac{3}{36}$	$\frac{2}{36}$	$\frac{1}{36}$

$$(6.5)$$

Graphically, the probabilities $P(1 < X_i < 4)$, $P(5 < X_i < 10)$, and $P(X_i > 10)$ are represented in the respective shaded areas in Figure 6.7.

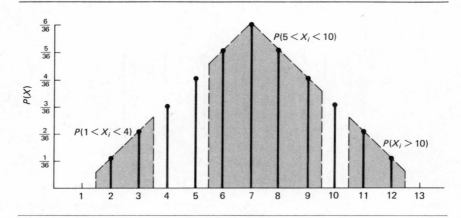

FIGURE 6.7

$P(1 < X_i < 4)$, $P(5 < X_i < 10)$, and $P(X_i > 10)$

It should be noted that the above probabilities may be represented as

$$P(1 < X_i < 4) = P(2 \leqslant X_i < 4)$$
$$= P(2 \leqslant X_i \leqslant 3)$$
$$= P(1 < X_i \leqslant 3)$$
$$P(5 < X_i < 10) = P(6 \leqslant X_i < 10)$$
$$= P(6 \leqslant X_i \leqslant 9)$$
$$= P(5 < X_i \leqslant 9)$$
$$P(X_i > 10) = P(X_i \geqslant 11)$$

Also, we note that in general

$$P(1 < X_i < 4) \neq P(1 \leqslant X_i < 4)$$

for the probability on the right-hand side of the inequality, $P(X_i = 1)$ is included in the interval but is not on the left-hand side.

In general, the probability for an interval is

$$P(a < X_i < b) = C\% \tag{6.6}$$

where a and b are two specific numbers, not necessarily among those in the set of X_i's, $a < b$, and C is some number between 0 and 100 inclusive.

A physical interpretation of (6.6) can be made which has implications for the general application of probability in repeated random experiments.

First, we note that the tossing of a die or coin as a random experiment may be likened to random sampling from a population of objects such as names placed in a hat, all individuals in a given city, or all students in a given class or university. This similarity may be visualized if we label each object in a large population of objects with a value that occurs in a probability distribution. All the values of the distribution will be used in labeling the objects. The number of objects to be labeled with each value will depend on the probability of that value. In other words, the number of objects with the same value *divided by* the total population will equal the probability of that value occurring in the distribution.

For example, the probability distribution for the random variable $X =$ "number appearing" on the toss of a die may be physically represented by filling a bin with white balls. Each ball is stamped with a value from 1 to 6. The percentage of balls stamped with a particular value is equal to that value's probability. The reader should easily relate selecting a ball at random with the tossing of an unbiased die. Note, for the die-tossing experiment, the probability distribution could not be physically represented with any number of balls other than six or a multiple of six.

In general, $P(a < X_i < b) = C\%$ implies that:

A. The probability that X_i falls between a and b is $C\%$, because

B. $C\%$ of the X_i's making up the probability distribution lie between a and b. Accordingly,

C. $C\%$ of the time, on the average, an object taken (observed) at random from the population will exhibit a value for X between a and b, and

D. With $C\%$ confidence, we can say "an object taken at random from the population will exhibit a value for X between a and b," or

E. We can say with $(100 - C)\%$ risk "an object taken at random from the population will exhibit a value for X between a and b."

The latter two interpretations suggest that the words "confidence" and "risk" may be substituted for the word "probability," with "risk" denoting the opposite of "confidence."

Example 4 Interpret the probability statement $P(5 < X_i < 10)$ for the random variable $X =$ "sum of dots" appearing on the toss of a pair of dice.

SOLUTION   The probability distribution of X is given by (6.5). Thus,

$$P(5 < X_i < 10) = P(X_i = 6) + P(X_i = 7) + P(X_i = 8) + P(X_i = 9)$$

$$= \frac{5}{36} + \frac{6}{36} + \frac{5}{36} + \frac{4}{36}$$

$$= \frac{20}{36} \quad \text{or} \quad 55.56\%$$

Now from (A)–(E), we can say:

A'. The probability that the "sum of dots," appearing on the toss of a pair of dice, is between five and ten is $^{20}\!/_{36}$ or 55.56%.

B'. 55.56% of *all* possible tosses of a pair of dice will have a "sum of dots" between five and ten.

C'. 55.56% of the time, on the average, the tossing of a pair of dice will exhibit a "sum of dots" between five and ten.

D'. With 55.56% confidence, we can say "the 'sum of dots' on the roll of a pair of dice will be between five and ten."

E'. With 44.44% risk, we can say "the 'sum of dots' on the roll of a pair of dice will be between five and ten."

Because of reference to the "all possible tosses" in (B'), this interpretation may confuse some readers. If you were to begin tossing a pair of dice now and continue the rest of your life, you would not begin to approach the population of possible outcomes or "all possible tosses." In this sense, we can say the population of values is infinite. Note, however, that (B) permits us to determine, in the form of a percentage, the number of "sum of dots" between five and ten that will occur in an infinite population of values.

A finite example may be given to intuitively demonstrate the truth of interpretations (B) and (B'). Let the probability distribution (6.5) be represented as tennis balls in a bin. In this context, each ball will be stamped with a value between 2 and 12, inclusive. The number of balls stamped with a particular value will be proportional to the probability associated with that value. Suppose 36 balls constitute the population for this example. Then the number of balls associated with each value is given by the population frequency distribution.

X_i	2	3	4	5	6	7	8	9	10	11	12
$f(X_i)$	1	2	3	4	5	6	5	4	3	2	1

$$(6.7)$$

Twenty of the 36 balls making up the population are stamped with values between five and ten. Since $20\!/_{36}$ is 55.56% we get the percentage that was indicated in (B').

Exercises

1. Suppose five green and three white tennis balls are in a bin. Construct a mathematical model for the number of green balls selected if four balls are taken, at random, one at a time and replaced before the next ball is selected. Calculate, graphically illustrate, and interpret the following probabilities:

   a. $p(0 < X_i < 3)$

   b. $p(0 \leqslant X_i \leqslant 2)$

   c. $p(1 < X_i < 4)$

   d. $p(1 < X_i < 3)$

   e. $p(X_i \geqslant 3)$

   f. $p(X_i \leqslant 3)$

2. Using the same number of green and white tennis balls in a bin as in Exercise 1, construct a mathematical model for the number of green balls selected out of four selections if each selection is made without replacement. Calculate, graphically illustrate, and interpret the probabilities requested in (a)–(f) of Exercise 1, using the new mathematical model.

3. Determine the probability distribution for the total score made on three tosses at the three concentric rings described in Figure 6.2 and probability distribution (6.4). Calculate, graphically illustrate, and interpret the following probabilities:
   a. $p(0 \leqslant X_i \leqslant 4)$
   b. $p(X_i \geqslant 3)$
   c. $p(X_i \geqslant 6)$
   d. $p(X_i < 2)$
   e. $p(6 \leqslant X_i \leqslant 10)$
   f. $p(X_i \leqslant 4)$

4. Toss a pair of dice simultaneously and record the number of points obtained. Perform this experiment 90 times and compare the resulting relative frequencies with those given by probability distribution (6.5).

5. If 70% of male high school freshmen can do between 66 and 82 inches in the standing broad jump, with what confidence can we say "An individual selected at random from this population will either jump less than 66 inches or more than 82 inches"?

6. A football coach wishes to select three running backs out of five candidates. All five candidates appear to have equal ability, but we assume that they can be ranked from 1 to 5. Let X equal the number of correct backs selected. Construct a probability distribution for X. What is the probability that the coach selects at least two of the three best backs to start a game? What risk is assumed if the coach states "I have selected at least two of the three best backs to start the game"? Why?

6.3   EXPECTATION AND VARIANCE

Probability distributions possess two characteristics that are important to the general theory of statistics. These characteristics are the *expected value* and the *variance* for the random variable X.

The expected value of the random variable X, denoted by $E(X)$, with probability distribution given by (6.3), is defined by

$$E(X) = X_1 p(X_1) + X_2 p(X_2) + \cdots + X_k p(X_k) \qquad (6.8)$$

or

$$E(X) = \sum_{i=1}^{k} X_i p(X_i) \qquad (6.9)$$

The expected value of X is also called the *mean* of X or the *population mean*. The reader should note the similarity between formulas (6.9) and (3.4). $E(X)$ will also be abbreviated by the greek letter μ. When more than one random variable is to be considered, subscripts will be added to μ to indicate the means associated with the appropriate random variable.

Example 5 Find the expected value for the single toss of an unbiased die.

SOLUTION Using Eq. (6.9), and referring to (6.1), we compute

$$E(X) = \mu$$

$$= \left(1 \cdot \frac{1}{6}\right) + \left(2 \cdot \frac{1}{6}\right) + \left(3 \cdot \frac{1}{6}\right) + \left(4 \cdot \frac{1}{6}\right) + \left(5 \cdot \frac{1}{6}\right) + \left(6 \cdot \frac{1}{6}\right)$$

$$= \frac{21}{6}$$

$$= 3.5$$

Example 6 Find the expected score for the toss of a single ping-pong ball at the target described by Figure 6.2.

SOLUTION Using Eq. (6.9), and referring to probability distribution (6.4), we compute

$$E(X) = \mu$$
$$= (0 \cdot 0.4) + (1 \cdot 0.3) + (2 \cdot 0.2) + (3 \cdot 0.1)$$
$$= 1.0$$

Notice that the statement "most likely" is not an appropriate interpretation of $E(X)$ in this example. The most likely score on any one toss is zero because it possesses the greatest probability of occurring. However, if we required a student to toss, say, 10 ping-pong balls and we took the average of his scores, we might say his expected score was 1.0. This score is expected for every individual required to attempt 10 tosses. Notice that not every individual may achieve an average score of 1.0. Some will be higher and some lower.

Thus, the expected value is not something we expect in the ordinary sense of the word. What the term implies is a value that will be close to the long-run average for random samples of the variable X. That is, if we take all individuals together, the expected value is the one single value that can be positioned closest to every score. It may not be an observed score because the expected value itself may not be possible. Consider for example the expected values obtained in Example 5.

A second useful measure that provides a quick means of summarizing the probability distribution is its *variance*. Probability distributions are characterized by the fact that some are rather compact while others exhibit a wide range of dispersion. If the random variable X assumes values far from the expected value with moderately large probabilities, then the variance will be large. If the probabilities are massed close to the expected values, the variance will be small. The reader should note the similarity between this interpretation of a variance and that given in Chapter 3.

The variance of the random variable X, denoted by $\text{Var}(X)$, with probability distribution given by (6.3), is defined by

$$\text{Var}(X) = \sum_{i=1}^{k} (X_i - \mu)^2 p(X_i) \tag{6.10}$$

Since $\text{Var}(X)$ is expressed as squares of the units of X, taking the square root of the variance will often make the concept of spread or variability more meaningful. This, of course, gives us our familiar measure the standard deviation, denoted by σ, namely

$$\sigma = \sqrt{\text{Var}(X)} \tag{6.11}$$

and, likewise,

$$\text{Var}(X) = \sigma^2 \tag{6.12}$$

Example 7 Compute the variance and standard deviation for the probability distribution that describes the experiment of tossing a die.

SOLUTION We first require the value of μ. Its value may be obtained by referring to Example 5. That is, $\mu = 3.5$. Then, using Eq. (6.10), we get

$$\text{Var}(X) = \left[(1 - 3.5)^2\left(\frac{1}{6}\right)\right] + \left[(2 - 3.5)^2\left(\frac{1}{6}\right)\right] + \left[(3 - 3.5)^2\left(\frac{1}{6}\right)\right]$$
$$+ \left[(4 - 3.5)^2\left(\frac{1}{6}\right)\right] + \left[(5 - 3.5)^2\left(\frac{1}{6}\right)\right] + \left[(6 - 3.5)^2\left(\frac{1}{6}\right)\right]$$
$$= 2.9167$$

The standard deviation, by Eq. (6.11), is obtained by taking the square root of the variance. This gives

$$\sigma = \sqrt{2.9167} = 1.7078$$

Example 8 What is the variance and standard deviation for the ping-pong ball toss game described by the probability distribution (6.4)?

SOLUTION From Example 6 we get $\mu = 1.0$. Then, using Eq. (6.10), we obtain

$$\text{Var}(X) = [(0 - 1)^2(0.4)] + [(1 - 1)^2(0.3)] + [(2 - 1)^2(0.2)]$$
$$+ [(3 - 1)^2(0.1)]$$
$$= 1.0$$

The standard deviation is

$$\sigma = \sqrt{1.0}$$
$$= 1$$

Exercises

7. Calculate the values of μ and σ for the distributions obtained in Exercises 1, 2, and 3. How does the mean and standard deviation of Exercise 3 compare with that determined for probability distribution (6.4)?

8. Calculate the values of $\bar{X}$ and s for the sample distribution obtained in Exercise 4. How do these values compare with μ and σ of probability distribution (6.5)?

9. Calculate the probabilities $p(\mu - \sigma \leqslant X_i \leqslant \mu + \sigma)$ for each probability distribution given in Exercises 1, 2, and 3. Interpret these probabilities.

10. The probability distribution describing the total number of bases made per time at bat by a major league baseball player is:

X_i	0	1	2	3	4
$p(X_i)$	0.7	0.12	0.08	0.03	0.07

For the player's next time at bat, determine:
a. the expected number of total bases.
b. the variance and standard deviation for the total number of bases.
c. the probability that he will make at least two total bases (i.e., he will hit at least a double).
d. With what confidence can the player make the statement "I will hit at least a double"?
e. What risk is assumed when the player makes the statement in (d)? With what confidence can he make the statement "Today I will get at least two hits"? Assume he goes to bat four times.

11. Refer to Exercise 3 in Chapter 5.
a. What is the expected true value of three golf balls selected at random without replacement?
b. Can the golfer expect more or less for his money if the balls are sold at $3.00 for three balls?

12. In a single elimination match play golf tournament the following events take place:

A defeats B, on the average, three out of eight times
A defeats C five out of six times, and D seven out of ten times
C defeats D two out of five times.

A plays B, C plays D in the first round with the winners vying for first place while losers vie for third place. If first place is worth $1000, second $500, and third $200, determine the following:
a. the expected winnings for A.
b. the risk that A will lose money if the entry fee is $250.
c. the expected net gain or loss for A.

6.4   REPEATED INDEPENDENT TRIALS WITH TWO OUTCOMES: THE BINOMIAL DISTRIBUTION

Previous sections of this chapter have dealt with probability distributions for some simple discrete random variables. The emphasis was on the general properties of probability distributions as mathematical models that are useful for the study of simple random experiments.

We will now discuss a special type of distribution, which is more complex than the previous ones, and which, accordingly, will permit us to study more complex random experiments. The *binomial distribution* serves as a mathematical model for the study of variations that may occur from repeated independent trials of a random experiment that permits only two outcomes per trial. The binomial distribution merits attention because it serves as a model for the study of a great many real-life experiments and because it has important properties that appear in other probability models, particularly the normal distribution to be discussed later. A few examples will serve to introduce the nature of the binomial distribution.

Free Throw Shooting   A highly skilled basketball player shoots 10 free throws. For repeated sets of 10 shots, the number of baskets made varies. On any given set, he may be successful from 0 to 10 times. What is the probability associated with each of the possible number of baskets?

Coin-tossing Experiment   A balanced coin is tossed three times. What is the probability associated with each of the possible number of heads?

Drug Effectiveness Experiment   A new serum is tested for effectiveness in preventing the common cold. Ten people are injected with the serum and observed for a period of one year. If the probability of surviving the year without a cold, when a serum is not used, is $\frac{1}{3}$, how many of the ten must survive without a cold before we may conclude that the serum is effective?

Quiz Result Experiment   John received a perfect score on a five-question true-false quiz and immediately proclaimed his responses were made by flipping a coin. Is his statement reasonable?

Attitude Toward Physical Activity Experiment   Consider a sample survey conducted at a large university to determine the proportion of individuals expressing a favorable attitude toward physical activity. If 50 individuals are selected at random and interviewed, how many must express a favorable attitude before we can conclude that this attitude represents the feelings of the majority of the students at this university?

Each experiment above is described as a binomial experiment because it possesses the properties that

1. there must be a fixed number of trials;
2. each trial must result in a "success" or a "failure," that is, it must have two mutually exclusive outcomes;
3. all trials must have identical probabilities of success; and
4. the trials must be independent of each other.

Very few real-life situations will satisfy perfectly the properties stated above; however, many situations will come close to having these properties, and thus the binomial distribution can be used as a mathematical model for their study.

The general characteristics of the binomial distribution may now be derived by considering the following example.

Example 9 A bin contains three red and two green tennis balls. What is the probability of selecting exactly one red ball out of three random draws? (One ball is drawn at a time, replaced, and the balls are mixed before the next selection.)

SOLUTION   On any given draw we note that

$$p(\text{red}) = \frac{3}{5}$$

$$p(\text{green}) = \frac{2}{5}$$

The elementary events favorable to the event $X =$ "exactly one red ball" are (red and green and green), (green and red and green), and (green and green and red). From Chapter 5, we note by extension of the law of independence, that

$$p(R \text{ and } G \text{ and } G) = p(R) \cdot p(G) \cdot p(G) = \left(\frac{3}{5}\right) \cdot \left(\frac{2}{5}\right) \cdot \left(\frac{2}{5}\right)$$

$$= \left(\frac{3}{5}\right)^1 \cdot \left(\frac{2}{5}\right)^2$$

$$p(G \text{ and } R \text{ and } G) = p(G) \cdot p(R) \cdot p(G) = \left(\frac{2}{5}\right) \cdot \left(\frac{3}{5}\right) \cdot \left(\frac{2}{5}\right)$$

$$= \left(\frac{3}{5}\right)^1 \cdot \left(\frac{2}{5}\right)^2$$

$$p(G \text{ and } G \text{ and } R) = p(G) \cdot p(G) \cdot p(R) = \left(\frac{2}{5}\right) \cdot \left(\frac{2}{5}\right) \cdot \left(\frac{3}{5}\right)$$

$$= \left(\frac{3}{5}\right)^1 \cdot \left(\frac{2}{5}\right)^2$$

Thus, for any possible order of one red and two green balls, the probability is the same. The probability that $X =$ "exactly one red ball," then, is

$$p(X = \text{exactly one red ball}) = 3 \cdot \left(\frac{3}{5}\right)^1 \cdot \left(\frac{2}{5}\right)^2 \qquad (6.13)$$

The number of elementary events favorable to the event $X =$ "exactly one red ball" is the permutation of one red and two green balls. Thus, we can rewrite (6.13) as

$$p(X = \text{exactly one red ball}) = {}_3P_{1,2} \cdot \left(\frac{3}{5}\right)^1 \cdot \left(\frac{2}{5}\right)^2 \tag{6.14}$$

or

$$p(X = \text{exactly one red ball}) = \binom{3}{1} \cdot \left(\frac{3}{5}\right)^1 \cdot \left(\frac{2}{5}\right)^2 \tag{6.15}$$

because

$${}_nP_{n_1,n_2} = \binom{n}{n_1} \text{ with } n_1 + n_2 = n$$

The reader should easily apply the same logic to obtain the probabilities of drawing, say, zero, two, or three red balls under the conditions described.

Following the procedure above, we now derive the general formula for a binomial experiment. The language of trials, successes, and failures will be used in this discussion instead of selections, red balls, and green balls. Suppose we conduct a random experiment such that, for any given trial, the outcome can result in either a success or a failure. Let $P(\text{success}) = p$ and $P(\text{failure}) = (1-p)$ for any given trial of the experiment. If the experiment is conducted n times, what is the probability of obtaining exactly x successes and $(n-x)$ failures?

The number of elementary events favorable to exactly x successes and $(n-x)$ failures is given by the permutation formula of two kinds of objects (Chapter 5). That is, the number of ways of getting exactly x successes is

$${}_nP_{x,n-x} = \frac{n!}{x!\,(n-x)!}$$
$$= \binom{n}{x} \tag{6.16}$$

a typical elementary event favorable to the event "exactly x successes" is

$$\underbrace{S, S, \ldots, S}_{x} \quad \underbrace{F, F, \ldots, F}_{(n-x)}$$

If we assume the outcomes for the n trials are independent, then the probability of the typical elementary event occurring is

$$\underbrace{p \cdot p \cdots p}_{x} \cdot \underbrace{(1-p) \cdot (1-p) \cdots (1-p)}_{n-x} = p^x(1-p)^{n-x}$$

Since there are $\binom{n}{x}$ elementary events favorable to the event "exactly x successes," and each has the same probability of occurring, we get by the law of mutually exclusive events

$$p(X) = \binom{n}{x}p^x(1-p)^{n-x}$$
$$= \binom{n}{x}p^x q^{n-x} \tag{6.17}$$

where $q = 1 - p$.

Equation (6.17) is the general term of the binomial distribution. Given the value p, Eq. (6.17) can be used to determine the probability that the discrete random variable equals X for n trials of a random experiment when the conditions for a binomial experiment are met.

Example 10: *Free Throw Shooting Experiment* Suppose the outstanding basketball player referred to at the beginning of this section has a probability of 0.8 of making a basket on a single shot. What is the probability that he will make eight shots out of ten attempts?

SOLUTION   Using Eq. (6.17), with $p = 0.8$, $q = 0.2$, and $n = 10$, we get

$$p(X = 8) = \binom{10}{8}(0.8)^8(0.2)^2$$
$$= 0.302$$

It is interesting to note that some people interpret $p = 0.8$ to mean that the player is certain to make eight shots out of ten attempts. The solution of 0.302 is far from certainty. This confusion arises because with $p = 0.8$ the expected (or mean) number of free throws made out of one set of ten is eight. Thus, the confusion is between a mean and a probability.

Let us determine the general formula for the expected number of successes in n trials of a binomial experiment. We recall from (6.9) that

$$E(X) = \sum_{i=1}^{n} x_i p(x_i)$$

In this formula, each $p(x_i)$ becomes the binomial probability

$$P(X_i) = \frac{n!}{(x_i)! \, (n - x_i)!} p^{x_i} q^{n - x_i} \tag{6.18}$$

and the values X_i become the values 0, 1, 2, ..., n. Thus,

$$E(X) = \sum_{x=0}^{n} x \cdot p(X)$$
$$= \sum_{x=0}^{n} x \cdot \frac{n!}{x! \, (n - x)!} p^x q^{n - x}$$

A small amount of algebraic simplification reduces this equation to

$$E(X) = np \tag{6.19}$$

We can use Eq. (6.19) to determine the expected number of free throws made in ten attempts by the player cited in Example 10.

$$E(X) = 10(0.8)$$
$$= 8$$

Example 11: *Drug Effectiveness Experiment* The expected number of people to survive the year without a cold, when a serum is not used, is found by using Eq. (6.19) with $n = 10$ and $p = \frac{1}{3}$,

$$E(X) = 10 \cdot \frac{1}{3}$$

$$= 3.33 \text{ people}$$

This expected value provides us with a reference point for determining the number of individuals, injected with the serum, that must survive without a cold before we will conclude that the serum is effective. Intuitively, we suggest that the number must be greater than 3.33 people because individuals injected with the serum must exhibit survival characteristics that are better than those expected for individuals with no injection. How much greater the number of survivors must be will be answered later.

The reader should note that the expected value 3.33 is the parameter μ of the population distribution describing the chance occurrence of the common cold among ten random individuals not injected with any serum. Since the value μ, along with σ, designates a particular binomial distribution, we might require that results of our experiment with the new serum provide evidence of a larger expected value than 3.33.

The variance of the number of successes, x, in n trials of a binomial experiment is given here without proof.

$$\text{Var}(X) = \sigma^2 = npq \tag{6.20}$$

and

$$\sigma = \sqrt{npq} \tag{6.21}$$

Example 12 If the basketball player attempts ten free throws, his expected number of successes is eight. The standard deviation is

$$\sigma = \sqrt{(10)(0.8)(0.2)}$$
$$= 1.264$$

This means that if he attempts several sets of ten free throws per set, the standard deviation of 1.264, in a sense, indicates how the number of successes for individual sets might vary from the expected value of eight.

Example 13 If the drug effectiveness experiment is repeated several times, using ten subjects per repetition, the expected number of survivals if the serum is not effective is 3.33. The standard deviation is

$$\sigma = \sqrt{(10)\left(\frac{1}{3}\right)\left(\frac{2}{3}\right)}$$

$$= 1.49$$

Thus, while ordinarily we expect somewhere near 3.33 people out of 10 to survive the year without a cold when no serum is used, we would not be too surprised if as many as about 4.82 (i.e., $\mu + \sigma$) people or as few as only 1.84 (i.e., $\mu - \sigma$) people survived without a cold. We say this because we realize that variations from the expected do occur. The reader should note that the mean and standard deviation provide us with a better means of characterizing this variation.

A Decision Problem The binomial distribution will help us to describe how probability theory is utilized in decision making. Let us consider our drug effectiveness experiment.

A little reflection on our part suggests that a test for the effectiveness of the serum must be based on an experiment consisting of a small sample of individuals. A small sample is desired because of the expense involved in producing a serum that may not be effective, because of the control problems involved with observing a large group of subjects, and because of the danger of possible undesirable side effects associated with the serum. Thus, we select ten individuals, at random, from a population of interest to conduct our experiment.

Let us compare the survival results for the ten individuals with respect to the mathematical model suggested by the results expected when a serum is not used. This model, in the form of a probability distribution, may be derived by using the binomial distribution. We do this because the experiment satisfies very closely the properties describing a binomial experiment. We specified a fixed number of ten subjects (trials). Either a subject will contact a cold or he will not; that is, there are two possible outcomes. The subjects were not selected with replacement, but the probability of drawing an individual surviving without a cold when the serum is not used, remains approximately constant from trial to trial as long as the population of subjects is relatively large in comparison with the sample.

With the probability distribution describing the survival characteristics of individuals not injected with the serum, we can determine if the experiment provides sufficient evidence to suggest that the serum is effective. Intuitively, we feel that if the serum is not effective, the subjects will exhibit survival characteristics similar to those expected when no serum is used. Conversely, we suggest that if the serum is effective, a greater proportion of individuals must survive without a cold than would be expected for a group that had no injection.

Thus, by using (6.17), we can find the probability distribution for the values 0, 1, 2, ..., 10 when no serum is used. This information is presented in Table 6.1. Table 6.1 is represented graphically by Figure 6.8 (note that the heights of the probabilities for the numbers 8, 9, and 10 are too small to be reproducible in the text).

TABLE 6.1

Probability Distribution for Drug Effectiveness Experiment

Number Survived Without a Cold	$P(x)$
0	1024/59,049 = 0.01734
1	5120/59,049 = 0.08670
2	11,520/59,049 = 0.19509
3	15,360/59,049 = 0.26012
4	13,440/59,049 = 0.22760
5	8064/59,049 = 0.13656
6	3360/59,049 = 0.05690
7	960/59,049 = 0.01625
8	180/59,049 = 0.00304
9	20/59,049 = 0.00033
10	1/59,049 = 0.00002

The probability that seven or more individuals will survive the year without a cold when a serum is not used is 0.01963. That is

$$p(7 \leqslant x \leqslant 10) = 0.01963$$
$$= 1.96\%$$

From the interpretation rules for the probability of an interval, we can say that with a sample of 10 individuals selected at random from the population of individuals not injected with a serum, only 1.96% of the time, on the average, will between seven and ten individuals survive without a cold. Then, in our sample of ten subjects injected with the serum, a survival proportion of seven or greater would be suggestive that the serum is effective.

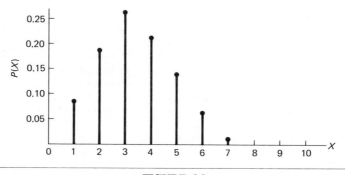

FIGURE 6.8

Graph of probability distribution for drug effectiveness experiment

Our *confidence* in concluding that the serum is effective if the number of survivors is seven or greater is given by

$$p(0 \leqslant x \leqslant 6) = 0.98037$$
$$= 98.04\%$$

The risk of being wrong when we conclude that the serum is effective for this decision rule is

$$p(7 \leqslant x \leqslant 10) = 0.01963$$
$$= 1.96\%$$

The reader should note that our risk (or the risk that the serum is not effective) is exactly the probability that seven or more individuals will survive even though no serum is used. Thus, we can never be sure on the basis of experiments of this type that the serum is effective. We have shown that seven or more individuals injected with the serum surviving without a cold is not consistent with the results expected for a sample of individuals receiving no serum. This somewhat negative approach is the basis for the decision-making process used in statistics. The approach will be expounded on in Chapter 9.

Exercises

13. The probability that a beginning golfer gets a good shot if he uses the correct club is one-third, and the probability of a good shot with an incorrect club is one-fourth. In his bag are five different clubs, only one of which is correct for any given shot. If he takes 60 shots during an afternoon of play and each time selects his club at random, how many good shots can he anticipate?

14. A sporting goods distributor is selling unmarked boxes of tennis shoes at $10.00 per box. If it is known that two-thirds of the boxes contain Converse All Stars valued at $14.00 and one-third contain rejects valued at $7.00, determine:
    a. the expected value of one box selected at random.
    b. the expected value of 10 boxes selected at random (assume no replacement but a very large population).
    c. the probability distribution for the number of Converse All Stars selected at random out of 10 boxes selected.

    Suppose you suspect that less than two-thirds of the boxes contain Converse All Stars. To prove his claim, the distributor has suggested you select 10 boxes at random and count the number of Converse All Stars.

    d. What number(s) will you accept as being consistent with the distributor's claim? What risk is associated with the number(s) you specified?
    e. What assumptions were made to complete (a)–(d)?

15. A major league baseball player has a batting average of .350. Assuming five times at bat, determine:
    a. the probability distribution for the number of hits made.
    b. the expected number of hits.
    c. the variance and standard deviation for the number of hits made.
    d. the probability that he will get less than two hits.
    e. the risk the opposing team's manager assumes when he states "We'll prevent him from getting more than one hit today."

   f. the confidence the player may assume when he states "They can't prevent me from getting more than one hit."

16. Calculate the probability distribution for a five-question true-false quiz assuming the respondent answers all five questions by flipping a coin. Under this assumption, determine (a) and (b) below.
   a. the expected number of questions correctly answered.
   b. the variance for this distribution.
   c. What risk is associated with the statement "Anyone correctly answering more than three questions could not have done so strictly by flipping a coin"?
   d. With what confidence can one make the statement in (c)?

17. In a dental study on preadolescent children, it is assumed that the probability is three-fifths that a child's teeth will have at least one cavity. Determine (a) and (b) below.
   a. the probability that five students must be examined before the first cavity is found
   b. the probability that 5 students out of 12 will have at least 1 cavity
   c. Suppose a tooth paste company claims its tooth paste will reduce the proportion of children with at least one cavity. How many children using this company's tooth paste must exhibit no cavities before you will accept their claim?
   d. What confidence and risk do you assign to the rule specified in (c)?
   e. What is the probability that the number of students out of ten having at least one cavity is between two and seven?

18. During deer season only one hunter in five kills a deer. If each hunter may kill only one deer, determine:
   a. the probability that less than four of eight hunters will kill a deer
   b. the expected number of deer killed by eight hunters

7

The Normal Probability Distribution

7.1 BASIC CONCEPTS

The probability distributions that we have discussed permit us to describe the behavior of random variables that have a *finite* or *countable* number of possible outcomes. These variables, which we call *discrete random variables*, have the distinct feature that when $p(X_i) = 0$, for some value X_i of the random variable X, we conclude that the value X_i is impossible. We now turn our attention to a type of random variable possessing the peculiar characteristic that when $p(X_i)$ is zero the value X_i may actually occur. This type of random variable is called a *continuous random variable*.

We recall from Chapter 2, the word *continuous* means "proceeding without interruption." This definition provides the key to the identification of continuous random variables. The fact that these variables are continuous without interruption means that any value X_i within a specified interval is possible. In physical measurement problems, for example, it is convenient to think of the measures as continuous. Length, weight, and time are typical of measurements that can take any value in an interval. The fact that in practice we choose to round off these measurements to the nearest fraction of an inch, ounce, or second does not take away the fact that they, theoretically, represent continuous measures. We round off continuous measurements to some convenient interval scale because we recognize that no one can measure, for example, the length of an object, and be sure the measurement is correct. That is, measurements made to the thousandth of an inch can be described as *precise* but they are not *exact*. The same can be said for measurements of time and weight or measurements taken of any continuous random variable.

AN INTUITIVE FRAMEWORK FOR
THE STUDY OF CONTINUOUS RANDOM VARIABLES

Suppose we throw darts at a rectangular dart board that is 10 in. long and 5 in. high, as diagramed in Figure 7.1. Let us score each throw as the horizontal distance from line zero and rethrow any dart that misses the dart board. What is the probability of hitting the board exactly 3 in. to the right of line 0? By "exactly," we mean 3.00... in. with zeros carried out forever. This is the same as saying "What is the probability of hitting any one of the geometric points lying within the geometric line* exactly 3 in. to the right of line 0?" Clearly, there is no chance at all, making the probability zero. The same holds true for any line X_i within the interior of the dart board. Since we rule out darts missing the board, the probability that a dart strikes the board is one. That is, some line will be hit. But, if we attempt to add probabilities for all the lines within the dart board, we add nothing but zeros.

---

* A *point*, as defined in geometry, has no length, breadth, or thickness; that is, it has no size. Therefore, a geometric point cannot be seen and could not be identified as being hit by the dart. A *geometric line* can be thought of as being composed of many geometric points placed side by side in a straight line. Thus, a geometric line cannot be seen because it has no width or thickness. That is, a geometric line has only one dimension—length.

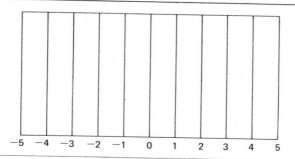

FIGURE 7.1

Rectangular dart board

That is,

$$\sum_{\substack{\text{all} \\ \text{lines}}} p(\text{exactly line } X_i \text{ is hit}) = 0$$

The reason for the zero probabilities is that we cannot identify the geometric points and lines necessary for "exact" measurements. We do recognize, however, that we can identify intervals of geometric lines even though we cannot single out individual lines within that interval. Thus, assigning probabilities to intervals suggests a possible solution to our problem.

We note the similarities between determining probabilities and computing areas. The area of a rectangle is equal to the length of its base times its height. But, since the area of every interior line segment perpendicular to its base is zero, we cannot get the area of the rectangle by adding areas of interior line segments. Similarly, we cannot get the probability of striking a specified interval (identified by a rectangle) by adding the probabilities associated with each line segment within the interval. It is in this sense that we might say that the probability that a dart strikes within a specified interval is proportional to its area.

Let us apply this thought to our dart board game. If our players are assumed to be unskilled, we might argue that the probabilities of hitting any two intervals of equal area on the board are equal. Since each interval identified in Figure 7.1 is of unit length, the area of any given interval is equal to its height (i.e., area = base × height = 1 × height = height). If the height of the board is 5 in., then the area of each interval is 1 in. × 5 in. = 5 in.² (square inches), and the total area of the board is 10 × 5 in.² = 50 in.². We might then say that the probability of hitting a specified interval is:

$$p(\text{hitting interval } i) = \frac{5 \text{ in.}^2}{50 \text{ in.}^2}$$

$$= \frac{1}{10} \qquad (i = -1, -2, \ldots, 1, 2, \ldots, 5)$$

Example 1   A player tosses one dart that strikes the dart board. What is the probability that the dart hits within -2 and $+2$ in. of line 0?

SOLUTION   The area between the numbers -2 and $+2$ in. is four-tenths of the total area. We conclude, then, that the probability is four-tenths. Graphically, the probability is shown as the shaded area in Figure 7.2.

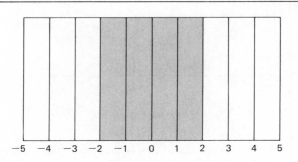

FIGURE 7.2

Area between -2 and $+2$ in.

For continuous measures, we cannot distinguish between $p(-2 \leqslant X \leqslant +2)$ and $p(-2 < X < +2)$, because the difference between these two quantities is zero. Technically, the difference is $p(X = -2)$ and $p(X = +2)$, but we note that the area for each of these is zero.

Example 2   Given that a second dart has been thrown, what is the probability that it hits 1 in. to the right of line 0?

SOLUTION   Technically, the probability is zero. However, a practical solution may be obtained by letting all lines between $+\frac{1}{2}$ and $+1\frac{1}{2}$ in. from line 0 represent 1 in. Then the area for the interval $+\frac{1}{2}$ to $+1\frac{1}{2}$ is one-tenth of the total area and we might say that the probability is one-tenth. Graphically, the probability is given in Figure 7.3.

We might note that this example serves to illustrate how elementary events for physical measurement problems may be determined.

It should be made clear, however, that these events are not elementary events in the classical sense given in Chapter 5. Instead they are elementary events that are of practical value to the experimenter. Thus, when we are measuring height, we assign all measurements between $66\frac{1}{2}$ and $67\frac{1}{2}$ in. the value 67, and we follow a similar procedure for all heights recorded. Then, for practical purposes, 67 is called an elementary event for the random

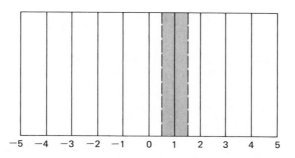

FIGURE 7.3

The elementary event, $X_i = 1$

variable height, although we recognize that 67 only represents the midpoint of the interval identifying the possible heights from $66\frac{1}{2}$ to $67\frac{1}{2}$.

The key to specifying elementary events for continuous random variables is to determine the smallest interval of values that is of practical interest to the experimenter. In our height measurement example, we chose to assign the same value to all measurements within an interval of 1 in. We could just as well have chosen a smaller interval, say, of $\frac{1}{2}$ in. In this case, our measurement of 67 in. would represent all values between $66\frac{3}{4}$ and $67\frac{1}{4}$ in.

The nature of the problem, the amount of variability present, the variable to be measured, and the accuracy desired are just a few of the criteria that one might use to determine the interval of practical value for a given experiment. If an experiment involves measuring 50-yd dash times, the interval can very well be $\frac{1}{10}$ sec. On the other hand, measures of reaction time require accuracies to at least $\frac{1}{100}$ sec because most simple reaction time scores will lie between $\frac{1}{10}$ and $\frac{1}{20}$ sec.

7.2 CONTINUOUS RANDOM VARIABLES AND THEIR PROBABILITY DISTRIBUTION

The concept of area as probability, developed in the previous section, will be used as a means of describing probability distributions of any continuous random variable. Let us select a sample of 100 adult males from the population of males in the United States. Suppose we measure height to the nearest inch and construct a histogram for the resulting measures, as given in Figure 7.4. If we assume that each of the 100 individuals is represented by 1 in.^{2}, then the area of each bar within the histogram is equal to the frequency for each height interval recorded. Thus, the area for a given interval indicates

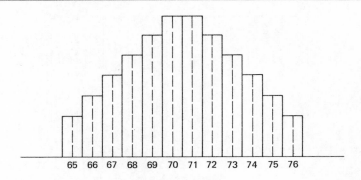

FIGURE 7.4

Histogram for height of 100 males

the frequency of occurrence for that particular interval of heights. For example, if 10 males had recorded heights between 69½ and 70½ in., the rectangle identified as 70 in. would have an area of 10 in. × 1 in. = 10 in.²

Suppose we connect the midpoint of each rectangle in the histogram with a smooth continuous line, as indicated in Figure 7.5. We note that the rectangles enclosed by the curve very closely approximate the area under the smooth curve. The rectangles do not exactly indicate the area because one part of each rectangle overlaps above the curve and another part of each rectangle fails to enclose part of the area immediately under the curve.

If we increase our sample to 1000 males and decrease our interval of values to, say, ¼ in., we obtain a histogram like the one given in Figure 7.6. In this figure, as opposed to Figure 7.5, the area of rectangles under the curve better approximates the area under the curve. This is because a lesser area

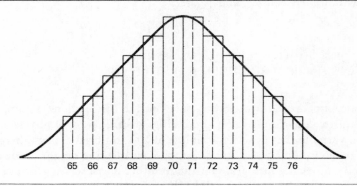

FIGURE 7.5

Superimposed histogram and frequency polygon for height of 100 males

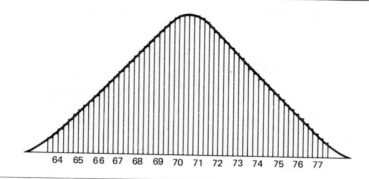

FIGURE 7.6

Histogram for height of 1000 males

of each rectangle protrudes above and falls below the curve than was the case for the rectangles identifying the histogram in Figure 7.5.

If we were to continue to increase the sample size and decrease the interval width, the resulting rectangles would approach the smooth curve as a limit. Our approximation of the area under the curve would become better and better as we proceeded. In view of this concept, it should be easy to see how we can define the probability of an event for a continuous random variable as the area under a curve.

7.3 THE NORMAL CURVE AND THE NORMAL PROBABILITY DISTRIBUTION

Probabilities calculated as areas under the curve for the dart game example were easy to determine since the areas in question were rectangles. Probabilities as areas under the curve for the measure of height were a little more difficult to calculate since a uniform distribution of intervals failed to result. An approximation method was suggested, but we note that its use might be prohibited in many practical situations. For example, with this method we cannot know the exact nature of the distribution without measuring every member of the population. Since this will seldom be possible, we must find some alternate approach.

The necessary approach is made possible by the use of a special curve, called the *normal probability curve* or simply the *normal curve*. The normal curve describes the random behavior of a special kind of random variable, called the *normal random variable*. Before we describe the method of deriving probabilities for events of certain continuous random variables, let us look at the properties of the normal curve.

The normal curve is represented graphically in Figure 7.7. The curve looks like the curves that we diagramed to describe the behavior of random samples

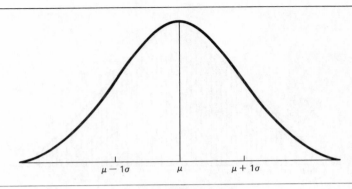

FIGURE 7.7

The normal curve

of adult male's heights. This was done deliberately because height is one of the many continuous random variables that closely follows the normal curve.

The curve is bell-shaped and has a single peak or mode at $X = \mu$. It is symmetric about $X = \mu$, which means that the part of the curve to the left of $X = \mu$ is a mirror image of the curve to the right of $X = \mu$. The curve is concave downward between $X = \mu - 1\sigma$ and $X = \mu + 1\sigma$, and concave upward for values of X outside that interval. As the curve moves away from $X = \mu$ in either direction, it falls closer and closer to the base line but never touches it no matter how far the curve is extended. The total area under the curve and above the base line is equal to 1.

The convenient mathematical properties of the normal curve make much of the theory of statistics readily available to the researcher for practical applications. For example, many naturally occurring continuous random variables follow very closely the normal curve. Other random variables can be easily transformed to approximate the normal random variable. Also, the normal curve describes fairly well the behavior of the random variable derived from calculating sample means no matter what the shape of the original variable's probability curve. This property will be discussed in greater detail later. In short, the normal probability curve serves as a mathematical model for many experiments involving continuous random variables.

7.4   COMPUTATIONS OF PROBABILITIES USING THE NORMAL CURVE

The mathematical expression for the normal curve is

$$f(X) = \frac{1}{\sqrt{2\pi}\,\sigma}\,e^{-(1/2\sigma^2)(X-\mu)^2} \tag{7.1}$$

This expression describes any normal random variable X as long as we specify its mean (μ) and standard deviation (σ). The remaining terms in the equation are constants; π is approximately 3.14159 and e, the base of the natural logarithms, is approximately 2.71828.

Regardless of the value of μ or σ, the properties outlined in Section 7.3 hold. However, the positioning of the curve on the base line is dependent on the value of μ and the general spread of the curve is dependent on the value of σ. Figure 7.8 describes the normal curve for three normal random variables having the same σ but different μ's.

When σ is constant, a change of μ causes the normal curve to shift to the right or left. The shape remains constant with the same peak and spread.

Figure 7.9 describes the normal curve for three normal random variables having the same μ but different σ's. All three curves have the same central position at $X = \mu$. But the smallest σ_1 describes a normal curve with a tall

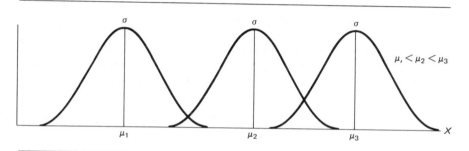

FIGURE 7.8

Normal curves with different means

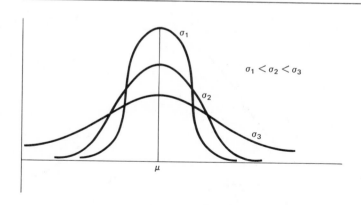

FIGURE 7.9

Normal curves with same mean, different standard deviations

peak at μ and little spread, while the largest σ_3 describes a normal curve with a short peak at μ and considerably more spread. It should be noted that, regardless of the value of μ or σ, each curve has a total area of 1. Thus, if the curve elevates above the base line, then it must decrease rapidly as the value of X gets further and further from μ.

We emphasize that μ and σ are constant values not subject to change for a specified population at a specified time. They may, however, change from population to population or within the same population over time. As descriptive characteristics of a normal probability curve, they are referred to as *parameters*. If we provide a value for each of the parameters μ and σ, we specify a single normal probability curve for the random variable X. We can then find the probabilities associated with specific values of X. Probabilities are *not* associated with the parameters μ and σ, since μ and σ are constant values. It is important that we make the distinction between a random variable and a parameter.

Probabilities associated with the normal curve have been calculated by using Eq. (7.1). These probabilities are tabulated in Appendix B as Table I, "The Normal Distribution." Since Eq. (7.1) is dependent on the numerical values of μ and σ, it can be used to generate an infinite number of normal curves, with each curve somehow related to the single table of areas described above. For this purpose, a convenient transformation is available. The transformation is

$$Z = \frac{X - \mu}{\sigma} \tag{7.2}$$

where Z is the *standard normal random variable* and also represents the values used to determine areas in Table I, Appendix B. The standard normal random variable has zero mean and unit standard deviation; that is, $\mu_Z = 0$ and $\sigma_Z = 1$. The standard normal random variable follows the *standard normal*

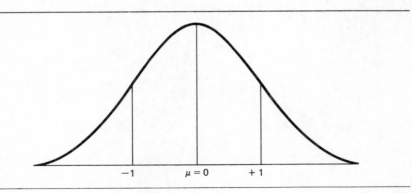

FIGURE 7.10

Standard normal curve

curve (Figure 7.10). It is the basic normal curve employed in statistics since all other normal curves can be transformed to it by means of Eq. (7.2). A few examples will serve to illustrate how Table I is used to find probabilities.

Example 3 Find the probability that a standard normal random variable takes a value between 0 and 1.

SOLUTION $P(0 < Z < 1) = A(1)$. $A(1)$ is the area under the standard normal curve from $Z = 0$ to $Z = 1$, as shown in Figure 7.11. Table I,

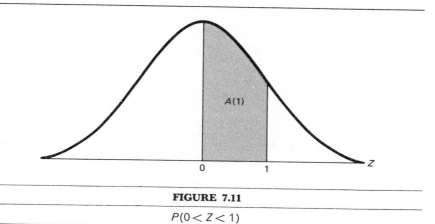

FIGURE 7.11

$P(0 < Z < 1)$

Appendix B describes areas under the standard normal curve from $Z = 0$ to $Z = C$ (where C is a constant). Thus, $A(1)$ is the tabulated value, 0.3413, corresponding to $Z = 1$. Then, $P(0 < Z < 1) = A(1) = 0.3413$.

Example 4 Find the probability that a single random value of Z will be between -1.0 and 2.42.

SOLUTION The shaded area in Figure 7.12 is equal to the desired probability.

Since the normal curve is symmetric about $Z = 0$, the area $A(-1)$ is the same as $A(1)$. Thus

$$P(-1 < Z < 2.42) = A(-1) + A(2.42)$$
$$= A(1) + A(2.42)$$
$$= 0.3413 + .4922$$
$$= 0.8335$$

Note that the area for $Z = 2.42$ was found by referring to the row corresponding to $Z = 2.4$ and the column labeled $Z = 0.02$.

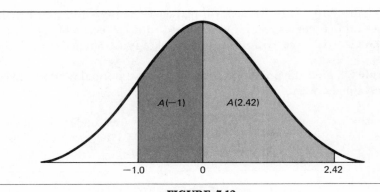

FIGURE 7.12

$$P(-1.0 < Z < 2.42)$$

Example 5   What is the probability that a standard normal random variable takes a value between 0.5 and 3.4?

SOLUTION   The required probability is the area between 0.5 and 3.4, as shown in Figure 7.13. The probability is the area from 0 to 3.4 minus the area from 0 to 0.5. That is,

$$
\begin{aligned}
P(0.5 < Z < 3.4) &= A(3.4) - A(0.5) \\
&= 0.4988 - 0.1915 \\
&= 0.3073
\end{aligned}
$$

Example 6   Let $X =$ "standing broad jump" be a normal random variable with $\mu = 80$ in. and $\sigma = 5$ in. Find the probability of selecting one individual from the population described as possessing a score between 75 and 88 in.

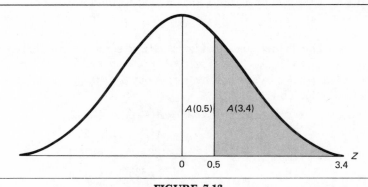

FIGURE 7.13

$$P(0.5 < Z < 3.4)$$

SOLUTION   We make use of Eq. (7.2) to transform into Z-units. This gives:

$$X = 75 \quad \text{corresponds to} \quad Z = \frac{75 - 80}{5} = -1.0$$

$$X = 88 \quad \text{corresponds to} \quad Z = \frac{88 - 80}{5} = 1.6$$

Then,

$$
\begin{aligned}
P(75 < X < 88) &= P(-1.0 < Z < 1.6) \\
&= A(-1.0) + A(1.6) \\
&= A(1.0) + A(1.6) \\
&= 0.3413 + 0.4452 \\
&= 0.7865
\end{aligned}
$$

The graphic transformation is given in Figure 7.14. The reader should note that the area under the standard normal curve within the interval $(-1.0 < Z < 1.6)$ may be used to determine the area under the original normal curve because the two areas are equal. Thus, while the form of the

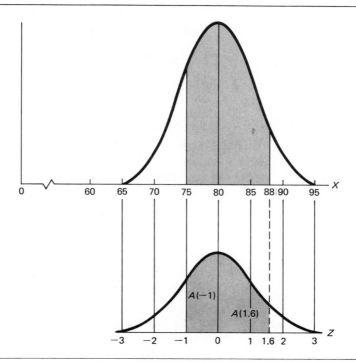

FIGURE 7.14

Area correspondence between X and Z

curves may change somewhat, the transformed curve will always retain the shape of the normal curve.

Example 7   Find the 30th percentile for the standing broad jump variable having $\mu = 80$ and $\sigma = 5$.

SOLUTION   The 30th percentile is that number P_{30} that divides the distribution of scores into the lower 30% and the upper 70%. That is,

$$P(X_i \leqslant P_{30}) = 0.30$$

Assuming that scores for the standing broad jump are normally distributed, we may find P_{30} by transferring from X to Z using the equation

$$Z_{0.30} = \frac{P_{30} - 80}{5}$$

where $Z_{0.30}$ is the Z-value that divides the standard normal curve into the lower 30% and upper 70%. Then,

$$P(X_i \leqslant P_{30}) = P(Z_i \leqslant Z_{0.30}) = 0.30$$

Graphically, the probabilities are shown in Figure 7.15. To find $Z_{0.30}$, we have to rewrite the probability statement as follows

$$P(Z_i \leqslant Z_{0.30}) = 0.5 - P(Z_{0.30} < Z_i < 0)$$

or

$$P(Z_{0.30} < Z_i < 0) = 0.5 - P(Z_i < Z_{0.30})$$
$$= 0.5 - 0.3$$
$$= 0.2$$

Thus, from Table I, Appendix B, we find that $A(-0.52) \approx 0.20$. This gives us

$$Z_{0.30} = -0.52.$$

Then,

$$-0.52 = \frac{P_{30} - 80}{5}$$

and

$$P_{30} \approx 77.4$$

Example 8   As a convenient summary, we note that if Z is the standard normal random variable and $Z = 1.68$, then

$$A(1.68) = P(0 < Z < 1.68) = 0.4535$$
$$P(Z > 1.68) = 0.0465$$
$$P(Z < 1.68) = 0.9535$$
$$P(-1.68 < Z < 1.68) = 0.9070$$

Figure 7.16 gives the graphic display for $A(1.68) = P(0 < Z < 1.68) = 0.4535$.

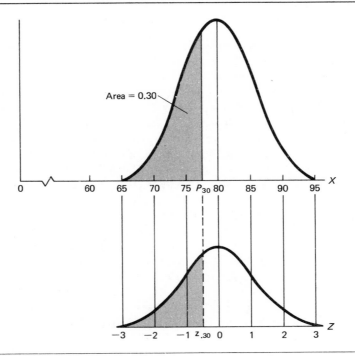

FIGURE 7.15

$$P(X_i < P_{30}) = 0.30$$

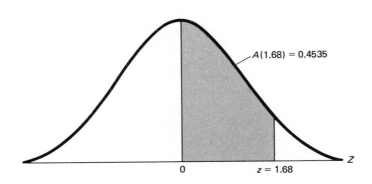

FIGURE 7.16

$$P(0 < Z < 1.68) = 0.4535$$

7.5 SAMPLING DISTRIBUTIONS

One of the most important ideas that the user of statistics must understand is that even though the data we work with in numerical form arise from a single random sample, that sample is but one of many different samples that might have been selected. Thus, *any* numerical result arrived at on the basis of a random sample of values must also be referred to as a random variable. This implies that the sample mean, $\bar{X}$, and the sample standard deviations, for example, are random variables because each is computed using outcomes X_i ($i = 1, 2, \ldots, n$) of a random sample, and these outcomes vary from sample to sample as was demonstrated in Chapter 4. Just like any random variable, a probability is associated with each of the possible sample means, $\bar{X}_i$, or the standard deviation, s_i. That is, just as there is some probability that the height of an American male selected at random from the population lies between 69 and 73 in., so there is some probability that the mean height of a random sample of, say, 50 American men lies between 69 and 73 in. Obviously, the two probabilities do not have the same numerical value. Thus, a probability distribution exists for each of the random variables $\bar{X}$ and s.

Let us develop the important concepts for sampling distributions using a familiar example. Recall the probability distribution for $X = $ "number appearing" on the toss of a single die is

$$
\begin{array}{c|cccccc}
X_i & 1 & 2 & 3 & 4 & 5 & 6 \\
\hline
P(X_i) & \frac{1}{6} & \frac{1}{6} & \frac{1}{6} & \frac{1}{6} & \frac{1}{6} & \frac{1}{6}
\end{array}
\tag{7.3}
$$

We note that this distribution might be represented physically by a very large number of white tennis balls, numbered 1–6 in a bin. Thus, tossing a die might be likened to selecting a white ball at random from the bin. Suppose we toss the die twice and compute the mean, $\bar{X}$, of the two throws. This experiment is the direct counterpart of selecting two tennis balls from the bin or the hypothetical example presented in Chapter 4. That is, this experiment represents a sample size of $n = 2$. Let us denote the outcome on the first throw of the die as X_1 and the outcome of the second throw as X_2. There are $6^2 = 36$ possible samples for (X_1, X_2). Since each of the outcomes for the first toss has the same probability of occurring (i.e., one-sixth) and since this probability also applies for the second toss, the probability associated with each sample (X_1, X_2) is $\frac{1}{36}$. We compute the mean, $\bar{X}$, using the formula

$$
\bar{X} = \frac{X_1 + X_2}{2}
$$

Thus, $\bar{X}$ may take the values: 1, 1.5, 2, 2.5, 3, 3.5, 4, 4.5, 5, 5.5, or 6. The probability associated with each sample mean value is computed by counting the number of samples yielding that particular mean. For example, the sample mean, $\bar{X} = 3.0$, may occur if samples $(1, 5)$, $(2, 4)$, $(3, 3)$, $(4, 2)$, or $(5, 1)$ are selected. Thus, the probability that a sample mean of $\bar{X} = 3.0$ will occur is the sum of the probabilities associated with these individual samples, or $\frac{1}{36} + \frac{1}{36} + \frac{1}{36} + \frac{1}{36} + \frac{1}{36} = \frac{5}{36}$. The same procedure is followed to arrive at the probability for each of the other sample means. The probability distribution for the random variable $\bar{X}$, based on a sample size of $n = 2$, is then

$\bar{X}_i$	1	1.5	2	2.5	3	3.5	4	4.5	5	5.5	6	
$P(\bar{X}_i)$	$\frac{1}{36}$	$\frac{2}{36}$	$\frac{3}{36}$	$\frac{4}{36}$	$\frac{5}{36}$	$\frac{6}{36}$	$\frac{5}{36}$	$\frac{4}{36}$	$\frac{3}{36}$	$\frac{2}{36}$	$\frac{1}{36}$	(7.4)

The reader may note that this distribution is the same as that recorded for the sum of the throws of a pair of dice. This is logical since the mean is based on the sum of X_1 and X_2; that is, the mean is a function of the random variable X.

The basic point to remember is that Eq. (7.4) represents the mathematical model describing the random behavior of the variable $\bar{X}$ based on random samples of size $n = 2$. Since the concept of a random sample plays a central role in the derivation of the probability distributions described, these distributions are commonly referred to as *sampling distributions*. Thus, Eq. (7.3) represents the sampling distribution for random variable X when a single element from the population is randomly observed (selected), while (7.4) represents the sampling distribution for random variable $\bar{X}$ when two elements from the same population are randomly observed (selected) and an average taken.

We recall that the mean of the random variable X identified by (7.3) is $\mu_X = 3.5$. The mean of the sampling distribution (7.4) for $\bar{X}$ is found by using Eq. (6.9). This mean is denoted by $\mu_{\bar{X}}$ and is also found to be 3.5. That is, the two random variables X and $\bar{X}$ have the same population means. In general, it is possible to show that the mean of $\bar{X}$ for samples of any size is the same as the mean of the sampling distribution for X; i.e., $\mu_{\bar{X}} = \mu_X$.

Using Eq. (6.11), we find the standard deviation for X to be $\sigma_X = 1.7078$. However, from (6.11), we find the standard deviation for $\bar{X}$ to be $\sigma_{\bar{X}} = 1.2076$. As you might expect an average has less variability than a single random value. This is because extreme values of $\bar{X}$ are not as likely to occur as extreme values for X. [Compare, for example, the probabilities $P(X = 6)$ and $P(\bar{X} = 6)$.] The reason for this variability concept is that for the die-tossing experiment only one 6 is required to obtain the value $X = 6$, while two are required to obtain the average $\bar{X} = 6$.

Another interesting relationship involving σ_X and $\sigma_{\bar{X}}$ may be derived from the above example. If we divide σ_X by $\sqrt{2}$ we obtain

$$\frac{1.7089}{\sqrt{2}} = 1.2083.$$

But this is precisely the value of $\sigma_{\bar{X}}$. Since $n = 2$ for this example, we derived $\sigma_{\bar{X}}$ from σ_X by dividing σ_X by $\sqrt{2}$. For samples of size n, we may state the general rule that $\sigma_{\bar{X}}$ may be computed from σ_X by dividing σ_X by $\sqrt{n}$.

$$\sigma_{\bar{X}} = \frac{\sigma_X}{\sqrt{n}} \tag{7.5}$$

The reader will note that this discussion is similar to the discussion in Chapter 4.

The preceding discussion did not mention the geometric shape of the probability distribution for the sample mean, $\bar{X}$. We emphasize that knowing the mean and variance for a probability distribution tells us *nothing* about the shape of the distribution. Specifically, the same mean, μ, and standard deviation, σ, may result from a variety of probability distributions. But the graphs of these distributions may exhibit little resemblance to each other. Consider, for example, the distributions

x	-3	-2	-1	0	3
$P(x)$	$\frac{1}{8}$	$\frac{1}{8}$	$\frac{1}{8}$	$\frac{3}{8}$	$\frac{1}{4}$

x	-2	2
$P(x)$	$\frac{1}{2}$	$\frac{1}{2}$

Each distribution has a mean $\mu = 0$ and standard deviation $\sigma = 2$. But the probability that $X > 0$ is one-fourth for the first distribution and one-half for the second. Thus, even if we know the values of μ and σ, we still have no information concerning the probability of a given event. This implies that for a discrete random variable the exact probabilities must be known and for a continuous random variable the probability curve must be known.

Exercises

1. For the standard normal variate Z, evaluate and sketch the following probabilities under the normal curve.

   a. $p(Z < -0.6)$
   b. $p(Z > 1.8)$
   c. $p(-0.6 < Z < 1.8)$
   d. sum of $a + b + c$
   e. $p(Z > 1.4)$
   f. $p(Z < -1.4)$
   g. $p(Z < 1.4)$
   h. $p(Z > -1.4)$
   i. $p(|Z| < 1.4)$
   j. $p(1.6 < Z < 2.3)$
   k. $p(-1.10 < Z < 1.3)$
   l. $p(-2.50 < Z < 1.25)$
   m. $p(-1.25 < Z < -1.10)$
   n. $p(0 < Z < b) = 0.40$
   o. $p(Z > b) = 0.60$
   p. $p(Z < b) = 0.60$
   q. $p(b < Z < 0) = 0.40$
   r. $p(-b < Z < b) = 0.80$

2. Calculate and sketch the cumulative probability function for the standard normal variate Z.

3. For the standard normal variate Z, determine the shortest interval containing 80% of the area under the normal curve. Justify your answer.

4. The number of cigarettes smoked daily by individuals in a given population is approximately normally distributed with a mean of 18 cigarettes and a standard deviation of 10.
   a. What percentage of the people smoke more than a pack a day?
   b. What percentage smoke more than two packs per day?
   c. What percentage of this population do not smoke?
   d. Would you question the accuracy of your answers to (a), (b), or (c)? If so, which ones?

5. Suppose it has definitely been determined that 3.0 mg of nicotine per cigarette will cause cancer in long-term smokers. If brand X's nicotine content is normally distributed with a mean of 2.5 mg and a standard deviation of 0.4, what proportion of these cigarettes are potentially carcinogenic?

6. Larry Brown, of the Washington Redskins, averages 5.4 yd per carry with a standard deviation of 2 yd. If his number of yards gained is normally distributed, determine (a) and (b) below:
   a. the probability that he will make a first down on the first play from scrimmage.
   b. the interval of values that is likely to include 70% of his carries. Interpret this probability interval. Is it possible to calculate a second interval containing 70% of his carries, but yielding different upper and lower limits? If so, what criterion should be used to select the best 70% interval?
   c. What is the probability that he will make a first down on a play from scrimmage if 4 yd are needed for the first down?
   d. What is the risk that he won't make the first down under the conditions described in (c)?

7. A typical system for assigning handicaps to individuals in golf is derived from the formula

$$n_i = 0.8(\mu_i - \text{Par for course})$$

Suppose Charles G. and Charles D. have average golf scores of 80 and 84, respectively, with a standard deviation of $\sigma = 4$ for each. Calculate each golfer's handicap if par $= 72$. If adjustments are made for handicaps and a normal distribution is assumed for each golfer's scores, determine (a) and (b) below:
   a. the probability that Charles G. will defeat Charles D. at medal play if Charles D. shoots his average score.
   b. the probability that Charles D. will defeat Charles G. at medal play if Charles G. shoots his average score.
   c. Why are the probabilities in (a) and (b) not equal?
   d. What handicap system will completely equalize competition?

8. A state university is constructing a new basketball arena. The attendance to each game in the old arena was normally distributed with a mean of 5000 and a standard deviation of 500. What should be the capacity of the new arena if similar attendance is expected and University officials desire that no more than 1% of the games during a season be sold out?

9. Suppose the systolic blood pressure (SBP) in hypertensive individuals is normally distributed with a mean of 160 mm and a standard deviation of 10 mm. Determine:
   a. $p(130 < \text{SBP} < 160)$
   b. $p(\text{SBP} > 180)$
   c. $p(\text{SBP} < 130)$
   d. $p(\text{SBP} < b) = 0.95$
   e. $p(\text{SBP} > b) = 0.05$
   f. $p(a < \text{SBP} < b) = 0.95$ where $b > a$ and $b - a$ is a minimum.

7.6   THE CENTRAL LIMIT THEOREM

We recall that many random variables of practical interest are similar to the normal random variable in their behavior. For these variables, we are justified in the use of the normal curve to arrive at probabilities of interest. Fortunately, under certain conditions, the normal curve can be used with a broad class of nonnormal random variables. The basis for this statement is one of the most interesting and important mathematical theories of statistics. It is stated here in a simplified form:

The *central limit theorem*: If random samples of n observations are drawn from a population with mean μ and standard deviation σ, the sample mean $\bar{X}$ will have a distribution with mean μ and standard deviation $\sigma/\sqrt{n}$ that approaches the normal distribution as n increases.

Proof of the theorem is beyond the scope of this discussion. For convenience, however, some illustrations may be given in place of a rigid proof.

Suppose we consider the random experiment defined as observing the results of tossing a single unbiased die. The probability distribution describing this random experiment is given by (7.3). We note that each of the values of X have a one-sixth probability of occurring. A graph of these probabilities is perfectly horizontal. It is not difficult to see that the distribution is far removed from that of the normal curve. Now, suppose we consider the sampling distributions for the mean $\bar{X}$ based on all possible samples of size $n = 1, 2, 3, 4$, and 5. The graphs of the probability distribution for each of these sample sizes are presented in Figure 7.17.

The truth of the central limit theorem is visual. Clearly, as the size of n increases, the distribution for $\bar{X}$ becomes increasingly bell-shaped, even though the original distribution for X is horizontal. For sample sizes as small as $n = 5$, the distribution of $\bar{X}$ is very close to the normal curve. These results suggest that probabilities for the random variable $\bar{X}$ may be approximated by using areas under the normal curve. For example, the probability $p(\bar{X} \geq 5)$, when $n = 5$, is 0.0324 when computed from the exact distribution and 0.0333 when computed by means of the normal approximation. The latter method provides an error of only 0.0009. This error is small despite the fact that the approximation is usually better for values nearer the mean than for those further from μ.

Sampling distributions for $\bar{X}$ tend to approach the model of the normal curve more slowly when the original distribution for X is asymmetrical rather than symmetrical. The approach to normal, nevertheless, still occurs as the sample size increases. Suppose we conduct an experiment by tossing a ping-pong ball at the target of concentric rings shown in Figure 6.2.

Let us assume that experience has demonstrated that (7.6) gives the probability distribution for the score X on a single toss.

X_i	0	1	2	3	
$P(X_i)$	0.4	0.3	0.2	0.1	(7.6)

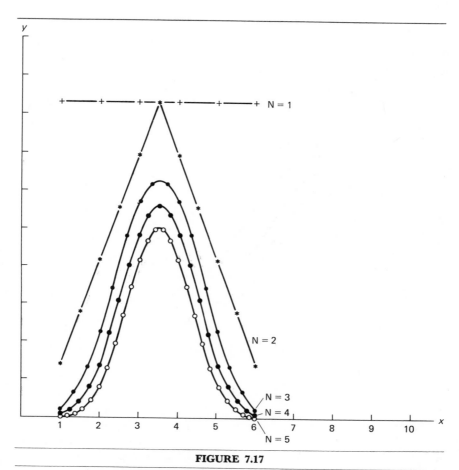

FIGURE 7.17

Probability distributions for mean die tosses based on samples
of $n = 1, 2, 3, 4,$ and 5

This type of experiment is typical of physical performance tasks wherein the degree of difficulty of the task is not uniform across all possible scores of X. That is, it is more difficult to hit the center ring valued at three points than it is to hit the outer ring valued at one point. Naturally, this is reflected in the probabilities given. Thus, (7.6) describes an asymmetrical distribution for a random variable X which by no means resembles the normal curve.

Using the procedure we used with the die-tossing experiment, we may derive the sampling distributions for the random variable $\bar{X}$ when samples of size $n = 1, 2, 3, 4,$ and 5 are taken from (7.6). A graphic display of the resulting distributions is presented in Figure 7.18. The curve labeled $n = 1$ is, of course, a graph of the original distribution and is obviously asymmetrical. The curves describing the sampling distributions of X based on sample sizes of $n = 2$ to $n = 5$ are seen to rapidly approach the shape of the normal

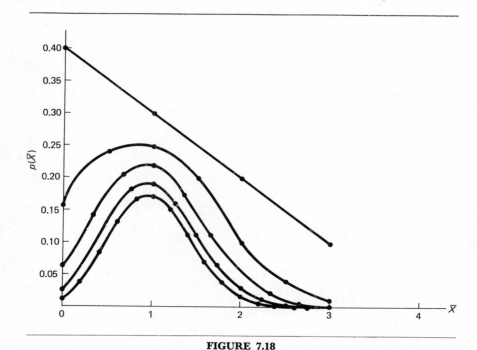

FIGURE 7.18

Probability distribution for mean ping-pong tosses based on samples
of $n = 1, 2, 3, 4,$ and 5

curve. It can also be seen that the curve for each sampling distribution up to and including $n = 5$ remains somewhat asymmetrical. Probability examples based on the exact and normal distributions will serve to demonstrate that the approximation to the normal curve is still quite good even for sample sizes as small as $n = 5$. That is, calculating the probability of, say, $p(X \leqslant 0.2)$ using the exact distribution yields 0.04864 while the normal approximation gives 0.05880, or an error of 0.01016. Thus, even though the approximation is quite good, the latter example yields a greater error than was obtained in the die-tossing experiment (i.e., a greater error than was obtained with a symmetrical distribution).

The value of the central limit theorem cannot be overemphasized. It enables us to use the normal distribution to compute approximate probabilities for mean scores even though we don't know the exact distribution yielding the sample values of X. In fact, exact distributions are often hard to realize. It is fortunate that such approximations are available. The usefulness of the theorem is that initially we need only the assumptions of random sampling and the existence of a mean and standard deviation. With this information, we can apply the central limit theorem and conclude that a wide class of distributions—whether continuous, discrete, skewed, symmetric, unimodal, or multimodal—will yield sample means with distributions approaching the normal curve. Remarkable results indeed!

We see that since n is constant for a given sample, the central limit theorem can be restated to apply to the sum of the independent sample measurements $(X_1 + X_2 + \cdots + X_n)$ or $\sum_{i=1}^{n} X_i$. In this context, the theorem states that the sum of a number of independent random variables is approximately normally distributed. This realization helps explain why a large number of variables possess, approximately, a normal distribution. For example, intelligence is a variable that is approximately normally distributed. One might argue that intelligence consists of the sum of a number of independent random variables. The measure of adult height, too, closely follows the normal curve. One justification for this is that height is a variable that is subject to a wide variety of hereditary, environmental, endocrinological, nutritional, and developmental factors.* Thus, height may be thought of as a sum of all these independent factors.

One must exercise caution in extending the preceding argument to include any random variable of interest. There have been enough measures of intelligence and height for their frequency distributions to be graphically constructed. The results closely resemble the normal distribution. Proof, however, has not been presented that each of these measures is normally distributed *because* it represents sums of independent random variables.

While adult height follows approximately the normal distribution, adult weight does not. Yet, it might be argued that the small factors influencing height also have an effect on weight. Additionally, we know that body weight is a function of calories consumed vs. calories used. It is easier for the former to produce positive effects on weight than for the latter to work negatively. The result is a positively skewed distribution.

The key to the use of the central limit theorem to support the argument that a variable, complex in nature and resulting from summing, is approximately normally distributed, lies in the requirement that the many small effects making up the sum operate independently of each other. This, of course, is difficult to justify in practice. For example, it can be argued that pushups consist of the sum of a number of factors. But, since we do not have readily available empirical evidence to indicate that all of these factors are independent, we are prevented from arguing that pushups are approximately normally distributed. Thus, while we may employ the theorem in arguing that the mean number of pushups (or any physical performance variable) derived from a random sample of adults is approximately normally distributed, we cannot readily extend this argument to the original variable.

In certain circumstances, the central limit theorem can be explicitly employed so that a set of data will more closely follow the normal curve. An assessment of *independent* physical performance scores can be averaged to give

---

* Richard D. Remington and Anthony M. Schork, *Statistics with Applications to the Biological and Health Sciences*, Prentice-Hall, Inc., Englewood Cliffs, New Jersey, 1970, p. 418.

assurance that the resulting measure will be *nearer* to the normal distribution than were the individual scores. For example, we can gain such assurance by basing an average standing broad jump score on, say, three trials rather than any one of the individual jumps. A sum of tennis skill test items or a battery of motor ability items will provide us with the same assurance. Of course, the utility of this technique is rather limited unless the number of assessments is large and the departure from normalcy is only slight.

One final comment is warranted concerning the central limit theorem. The approach to normal depends completely on the size of the random sample n. Unfortunately, there is no clear cut rule for choosing a value of n that will assure good approximations to the normal curve. The size of n that will allow us to assume reasonable normality depends on (1) the original probability distribution, (2) the use we will make of the approximation, and (3) a definition of the word "reasonable." If the original distribution is not too far removed from depicting the normal curve, or if we are willing to take rough approximations for derived probabilities, our sample size need not be large. On the other hand, if the original distribution is badly skewed and/or we demand good probability approximations, the sample size must be large.

A popular rule of thumb for the sample size is $n \geqslant 30$. The design of a particular research project must be realized before reasonably accurate observations regarding sample size, n, are in order. We note, simply, that there are times when n may be less than 30 and times when it must be a great deal more. Statisticians provide varying responses to the question of sample size. Often financial considerations will dictate the number used. More information about sample size will be presented in Chapters 8 and 9.

7.7 NORMAL APPROXIMATION TO THE BINOMIAL DISTRIBUTION

Suppose in the free throw shooting experiment (Example 6.10) we wished to determine the probability that the player would make, say, 45 shots out of 50 attempts or more practically the probability that he would make 45 or more shots out of 50. Using (6.17) for $X = 45$, $n = 50$, and $p = 0.8$, we get

$$p(X = 45) = \binom{50}{45}(0.8)^{45}(0.2)^5$$

and for $X \geqslant 45$ we get

$$p(X \geqslant 45) = \sum_{X=45}^{50} \binom{50}{X}(0.8)^X(0.2)^{50-X}$$

Immediately we recognize that the former probability involves laborious computations while the latter requires the additional burden of computing a complicated sum. The reader should now understand, at least in one sense, why we leaned toward the simplest examples when we previously discussed the binomial distribution. Fortunately, for examples like the above, the central limit theorem can be used to show that, when n is "large," a good approximation to the binomial distribution may be obtained by using the normal distribution. Before investigating the nature of this approximation in general, let us reconsider the drug effectiveness experiment discussed in Chapter 6. One probability of interest in the drug effectiveness experiment was that seven or more individuals out of ten will survive the year without a cold when a serum is not used. This probability, using the binomial distribution, was computed to be

$$P(7 \leqslant X \leqslant 10) = 0.01963$$

Graphically, the probability is the area of that part of the probability distribution in Figure 7.19 that lies to the right of 6.5 (to include the probability that $X = 7$).

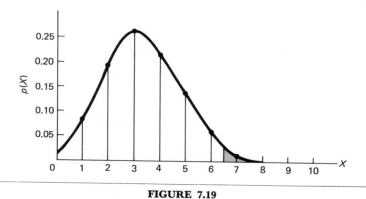

FIGURE 7.19

Binomial distribution of untreated survivors of common cold

The normal curve approximation for the binomial distribution is the one with the same mean and standard deviation as the specific binomial distribution of interest. Accordingly, with $n = 10$, and $p = \frac{1}{3}$, the mean and standard deviation were computed previously, by means of Eqs. (6.19) and (6.21), to be

$$\mu = 3.3333$$

and

$$\sigma = 1.4907$$

To approximate the probability $P(7 \leqslant X \leqslant 10)$ by the normal curve, it is necessary to find the area under that part of the fitted normal curve that lies to the right of 6.5. Since the fitted curve has $\mu = 3.3333$ and $\sigma = 1.4907$, it follows that

$$Z = \frac{X - \mu}{\sigma} = \frac{6.5 - 3.3333}{1.4907} = 2.12$$

From Table I, Appendix B, the area to the right of $Z = 2.13$ is 0.01700. When this value is compared with the correct value of 0.01963, the error is only 0.0026.

A similar approximation may be made for a shorter interval—for example, the probability that exactly six individuals will survive the year without a cold. From Table 6.1, the correct answer is

$$P(X = 6) = 0.05690$$

To approximate this probability using the normal curve it is necessary to specify an interval that represents $X = 6$. Let us follow the idea (suggested in Example 2) of defining the interval containing a specific value as being an interval that contains all values from one-half unit below to one-half unit above the value of interest. This gives

$$P(X = 6) = P(5.5 \leqslant X \leqslant 6.5)$$

where the probability on the right-hand side is computed using the normal curve with $\mu = 3.3333$ and $\sigma = 1.4907$. Then

$$Z_2 = \frac{6.5 - 3.3333}{1.4907} = 2.12 \quad \text{and} \quad A(2.12) = 0.4830$$

$$Z_1 = \frac{5.5 - 3.3333}{1.4907} = 1.45 \quad \text{and} \quad A(1.45) = 0.4265$$

Upon subtracting $A(1.45)$ from $A(2.12)$, we get the required approximation as

$$P(5.5 \leqslant X \leqslant 6.5) = 0.0565$$

which is in error by only 0.0004.

These two examples suggest that even when the sample size is small, we can use the normal curve to get a good approximation of the probabilities associated with the binomial distribution. Let us now establish the general conditions permitting the normal approximation to the binomial.

If X represents the number of successes in n independent trials of an event, with a probability p of occurring in a single trial, then X is approximately normal with mean $\mu = np$ and standard deviation $\sigma = \sqrt{npq}$ if the condition $np > 5$ when $p \leqslant \frac{1}{2}$ or $nq > 5$ when $p > \frac{1}{2}$ is met.

Justification of the approximation method results from the central limit theorem. If p is close to zero or one, a skewed binomial distribution is produced preventing a close normal approximation even when n is large. Thus, if $np < 5$ when $p \leqslant \frac{1}{2}$, or if $nq < 5$ when $p > \frac{1}{2}$, the normal approximation should ordinarily not be used.

Example 9   Determine the probability $P(X \geqslant 45)$ for the basketball shooting experiment when $n = 50$, and $p = 0.8$.

SOLUTION   Since $nq = n(1 - p) = 50(0.2) = 10$ is greater than 5, we may use the normal approximation. Accordingly,

$$\mu = np = 50(0.8) = 40$$

$$\sigma = \sqrt{npq} = \sqrt{50(0.8)(0.2)} = 2.8284$$

and

$$Z = \frac{45 - 0.5 - 40}{2.8284} = \frac{4.5}{2.8284} = 1.59$$

giving

$$P(X \geqslant 45) = P(Z \geqslant 1.59) = 0.0559$$

When we apply the normal approximation technique, the adjustment (of 0.5) is required because a transition is made from the discrete (binomial) variable to the continuous (normal) variable.

Exercises

10. A golf ball manufacturer knows that, on the average, 2% of his products are defective. What is the probability that 100 golf balls selected at random will contain exactly five defectives?

11. By use of the normal curve, find how many free throws are required in order that the probability of getting at least seven goals will have the value one-half if $p = 0.4$.

12. The university intramural director distributes, on the average, 500 towels per day to 700 regular intramural participants. How many towels should he stock each day so that he can expect, on the average, to run short of towels only about one day per month (25 days)? What binomial distribution assumption might be violated here?

13. In a discrimination reaction time test, the probability of a correct response on a single trial, due to chance alone, is one-fourth. Given 25 trials, what is the probability of 10 or more correct responses due to chance alone? Twenty or more? Determine $p(\mu - \sigma \leqslant X \leqslant \mu + \sigma)$ for 25 trials. Interpret each of the three probabilities requested.

14. A true–false examination contains 100 questions. If a student flips a coin to answer the questions, determine:
    a. $p(\mu - \sigma < X < \mu + \sigma)$.
    b. the probability that the student receives at least a passing grade of 60.
    c. the range of score you feel is inconsistent with the student's contention that he answered each question by flipping a coin.

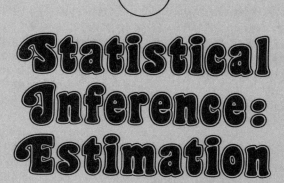

Statistical
Inference:
Estimation

8.1 INTRODUCTION

Until now our study has been confined to the problem of developing concepts that describe probability and probability distributions. We generally provided the essential information needed to describe a given population and then proceeded to ask questions concerning probabilities of specific events. In this chapter, we reverse our viewpoint and ask questions relative to the characteristics of a population of interest.

When we perform experiments we recognize that many random variables will be of interest; but little may be known about the parameters describing their probability distributions. Often, knowledge of these parameters is essential for intelligent decision making. For example, our decision to smoke brand A cigarettes depends, in part, on the magnitude of the population mean μ describing the average tar content of each cigarette (see Section 5.5).

There are other examples of how knowing parameters can affect decision making. Other instances are the individual who may be admitted into a particular university curriculum only if his predicted grade point average, based on aptitude tests, is greater than the minimum accepted, or the individual, on a particular weight-reducing program, who may wish to know the total amount of weight he can expect to lose. Also note that to aid the physical education department in planning an elective physical activity program, the department may wish to know how students perceive the benefits of physical activity.

Without knowing the constant values or parameters of a population, we can use statistical inference to provide information about these parameters. This technique, which is referred to as *statistical estimation*, may be classified into two types, *point estimation* and *interval estimation*. A point estimation procedure uses information from a random sample to arrive at a single numerical value or point on the interval scale which estimates the population parameter of interest. The interval estimation procedure specifies two numerical values or points that define an interval of values that are believed to contain the population parameter of interest.

8.2 POINT ESTIMATION

The basic problem of point estimation is to determine how the values of a random sample are to be used to estimate the unknown parameter of interest. For example, the average tar content of each brand A cigarette may be estimated using the sample mean $(\bar{X})$, the median (mdn), or some other sample measure of central tendency. Whatever the method of estimate, we recognize that it is not likely to equal the population parameter exactly. The extent to which the estimate is in error will depend on the random sample selected and the estimation procedure used. It is reasonable, then, to require that the estimate be close to the actual value *on the average* as repeated random samples of the same size are taken. This implies that the mean of the sampling distribution describing the estimator should be equal to the parameter being estimated. That is, if the parameter being estimated is denoted by θ (the Greek letter theta) and the estimator by $\hat{\theta}$ (where the "hat" indicates that we are estimating the parameter immediately beneath), then

$$E(\hat{\theta}) = \theta \tag{8.1}$$

This is the property of *unbiasedness*, which is referred to in Chapter 4, and which merely states that the random variable $\hat{\theta}$ possesses a sampling distribution whose mean is the parameter θ being estimated. From Sections 7.5 and 4.3, we recall that the mean μ_X of the sampling distribution describing the random variable $\bar{X}_i$ is equal to the population mean μ_X. Thus, the sample mean $\bar{X}$ is an unbiased estimator of the population mean μ and may be used as an estimate of that parameter. In general, the sampling distributions for an unbiased estimator and a biased estimator may be shown as in Figure 8.1(a) and (b).

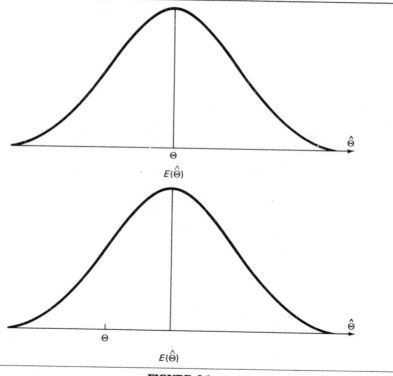

FIGURE 8.1

(a) Sampling distribution for unbiased estimator. (b) Sampling distribution for biased estimator

Since the sample mean $\bar{X}$ is an unbiased estimate of the population mean μ, it is logical to ask if the same property holds for s^2 as an estimate of the population variance σ^2. From Chapter 4 we recall that s^2 may be computed by the formula

$$s^2 = \frac{1}{n} \sum_{i=1}^{n} (X_i - \bar{X})^2$$

Then, the expected value of s^2, with n in the denominator, can be shown to be

$$E(s^2) = E\left[\frac{1}{n} \sum_{i=1}^{n} (X_i - \bar{X})^2\right] = \frac{n-1}{n} \sigma^2$$

This shows that computing s^2 by dividing the sum of squared deviations by n is not an unbiased estimator of σ^2. That is, the average of the sampling distribution for the random variable s^2 obtained from repeated samples of size n will not equal σ^2, but will be consistently too small by the factor $(n-1)/n$. The sample variance, s^2, can be made an unbiased estimate of σ^2 by dividing the sum of squares of deviations by $(n-1)$ rather than by n, as was pointed out in Chapter 4. That is,

$$s^2 = \frac{1}{n-1} \sum_{i=1}^{n} (X - \bar{X})^2 \tag{8.2}$$

is an unbiased estimate of σ^2 and justifies our use of Eq. (8.2) to compute s^2, as introduced in Chapter 3.

Returning to our discussion of unbiased estimators of the parameter μ defining a normal population, we note that the sample median (mdn) is also an unbiased estimate of μ. Thus, the property of unbiasedness alone does not allow us to select the best estimator of μ. A second property is required to help us select the one best estimate. Intuitively, we would like our estimators to vary as little as possible with repeated sampling. This property implies that the variance of the sampling distribution for the random variable $\hat{\theta}$ should be as small as possible. If we are given two unbiased estimators, $\hat{\theta}_a$ and $\hat{\theta}_b$, we would prefer to use the one with the smaller variance. The essence of this property is seen in Figure 8.2.

We recall from Chapter 7 that the variance identifying the sampling distribution of $\bar{X}$ is σ^2/n. By way of contrast, the variance identifying the sampling distributions of the median can be shown to be approximately $1.57\sigma^2/n$. Then the sampling distribution of the median, for a given sample size n, shows more variability than the sample mean. This implies that the sample median as an estimator of the population mean, μ, can be expected on the average to differ from μ by a larger amount than is expected for the sample mean, $\bar{X}$. This concept also implies that when $\bar{X}$ is used to estimate μ, a smaller sample can be used (without loss of efficiency) than when the median is used to estimate μ.

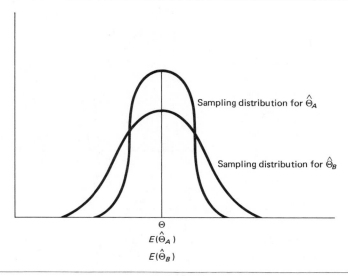

FIGURE 8.2

Two unbiased estimators of θ with different efficiencies

8.3 INTERVAL ESTIMATION

The criteria of unbiasedness and minimum variance presented in Section 8.2 for point estimates of population parameters have one characteristic in common. They each recognize that a single estimate of a population parameter obtained from a random sample is likely to be in error when estimating the parameter. Since there is zero probability that a continuous random number will equal exactly a specified number, it seems logical to ask what interval of sample values is likely to contain the population parameter being estimated. Only when this question is answered can we provide some measure of assurance that the true parameter is being closely estimated.

In any interval estimation procedure, we wish the one interval of values used to be as small as possible and possess the highest probability that the parameter being estimated is contained within the interval's limits. Since the normal curve will frequently serve as the probability distribution of the estimator of interest, *symmetrical limits* with their midpoint at μ (the center of the normal curve) will provide interval estimates that satisfy the above criteria. That is, if the interval I has its midpoint at the mean of the standard normal random variable, as shown in Figure 8.3, then, for a normally distributed variable, this symmetric interval has the two properties stated here without proof: (1) Among all possible intervals of the same length, the symmetric interval has the greatest probability of containing within its

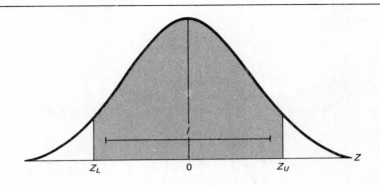

FIGURE 8.3

The symmetric interval

limits the value of a random object chosen from the population, and (2) among all possible intervals having the same probability, the symmetric interval has the shortest length. If we incorporate the idea of confidence, as defined in Chapter 6, with the concept of symmetric intervals, we may define a confidence interval as the interval estimate given by the equation

$$P(Z_L \leqslant Z \leqslant Z_U) = C\% \tag{8.3}$$

where Z is the standard normal random variable, Z_L and Z_U are the lower and upper limits of the symmetric interval, and $C\%$ represents the confidence, before the sample is drawn, that the interval between Z_L and Z_U will contain Z. Since Eq. (8.3) represents symmetrical limits we note that $Z_L = -Z_U$. Upon making this substitution in Eq. (8.3), we get

$$P(-Z_U \leqslant Z \leqslant Z_U) = C\% \tag{8.4}$$

Exercises

1. Determine probabilities for the following symmetric intervals:
   a. $P[-2 \leqslant Z \leqslant 2]$
   b. $P[-1.96 \leqslant Z \leqslant 1.96]$
   c. $P[-1.645 \leqslant Z \leqslant 1.645]$
   d. $P[-2.57 \leqslant Z \leqslant 2.57]$
   e. $P[-1.0 \leqslant Z \leqslant 1.0]$
   f. $P[-0.5 \leqslant Z \leqslant 0.5]$
   g. $P[-3 \leqslant Z \leqslant 3]$
2. Referring to symmetric intervals computed in Exercise 1 in answering the following questions.
   a. What is the relationship between the length of each symmetric interval and its corresponding probability?
   b. For each symmetric interval, select three different intervals of the same length and determine their probability. How do these latter probabilities compare with the original symmetric intervals' probability? Give reasons for your answer.

c. For each symmetric interval, determine three alternate intervals possessing the same probability. How do the lengths of these latter intervals compare with the original symmetric interval? Give reasons for your answer.
3. Determine symmetric intervals for the following degrees of confidence.
   a. 92%
   b. 68.26%
   c. 99%
   d. 80%
   e. 95%
   f. 99.9%
   g. 50%
4. Given: The steady-state heart rate for adult women exercising at 600 kpm on a bicycle ergometer is normally distributed with a mean of 160 and a standard deviation of 9.0.

   Find: The probability that the mean heart rate of a random sample of size 25 will not be less than 154 nor greater than 167.

8.4 CONFIDENCE INTERVAL FOR THE MEAN OF A NORMAL DISTRIBUTION WITH KNOWN VARIANCE

The confidence interval for the parameter μ describing the normal distribution of the random variable X, with σ^2 known, may be derived using Eq. (8.4). We know that the sample mean, $\bar{X}$, is an unbiased estimate of μ. If the random variable X is normally distributed, the random variable $\bar{X}$ is also normally distributed. Then, the normal random variable $\bar{X}$ is related to the standard normal random variable Z by the equation

$$Z = \frac{\bar{X} - \mu_{\bar{X}}}{\sigma_{\bar{X}}} \tag{8.5}$$

Now substituting the right-hand side of Eq. (8.5) in Eq. (8.4) for Z, we obtain

$$P\left[-Z_U \leqslant \frac{\bar{X} - \mu_{\bar{X}}}{\sigma_{\bar{X}}} \leqslant Z_U\right] = C\% \tag{8.6}$$

Using the properties of inequalities, we may multiply each term by $\sigma_{\bar{X}}$ to obtain

$$P[-Z_U\,\sigma_{\bar{X}} \leqslant \bar{X} - \mu_{\bar{X}} \leqslant Z_U\,\sigma_{\bar{X}}] = C\% \tag{8.7}$$

In addition, we may subtract $\bar{X}$ from the three parts of our chain inequality to get

$$P[-\bar{X} - Z_U\,\sigma_{\bar{X}} \leqslant -\mu_{\bar{X}} \leqslant -\bar{X} + Z_U\,\sigma_{\bar{X}}] = C\% \tag{8.8}$$

We may eliminate the negative sign on $\mu_{\bar{X}}$ by multiplying the terms in the three-part inequality chain by the factor -1. This gives:

$$P[\bar{X} + Z_U\,\sigma_{\bar{X}} \geqslant \mu_{\bar{X}} \geqslant \bar{X} - Z_U\,\sigma_{\bar{X}}] = C\% \tag{8.9}$$

Note that the multiplication process reversed the sense of the inequalities. Let us rewrite Eq. (8.9) in a more convenient form.

$$P[\bar{X} - Z_U\,\sigma_{\bar{X}} \leqslant \mu_{\bar{X}} \leqslant \bar{X} + Z_U\,\sigma_{\bar{X}}] = C\% \tag{8.10}$$

Equation (8.10) provides an expression of probability that, before a sample of size n is selected, the interval between the limits $(\bar{X} - Z_U\,\sigma_{\bar{X}})$ and $(\bar{X} + Z_U\,\sigma_{\bar{X}})$ will contain the mean $\mu_{\bar{X}}$ identifying the sampling distribution for $\bar{X}$.

Now since the mean of the sampling distribution of $\bar{X}$ is equal to the mean of the distribution of X and $\sigma_{\bar{X}} = \sigma/\sqrt{n}$, we may rewrite Eq. (8.10) to give the confidence interval for the parameter μ as:

$$P\left[\bar{X} - Z_U\,\frac{\sigma}{\sqrt{n}} \leqslant \mu \leqslant \bar{X} + Z_U\,\frac{\sigma}{\sqrt{n}}\right] = C\% \tag{8.11}$$

Example 1   Suppose a sample of 25 cigarettes was randomly selected from the population of brand A cigarettes and each cigarette's tar content was assessed. Compute a 95% confidence interval for the average tar content of brand A cigarettes if $\bar{X} = 28$ and it is known from previous work that the population variance is $\sigma^2 = 25$.

SOLUTION   A 95% confidence interval for the standard normal random variable is given in Figure 8.4. Z_U is the value given in Table I, Appendix B, corresponding to the area under the curve from $Z = 0$ to $Z = Z_U$, which is $A(Z_U) = 0.475$. Then, $Z_U = 1.96$, and Eq. (8.11) is found, by substituting for Z_U, $\bar{X}$, σ, and n, to be

$$P\left[28 - (1.96)\,\frac{5}{\sqrt{25}} \leqslant \mu \leqslant 28 + (1.96)\,\frac{5}{\sqrt{25}}\right] = 95\%$$

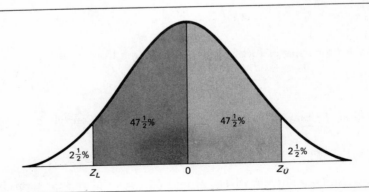

FIGURE 8.4

Ninety-five percent confidence limits on Z

or

$$P[26.04 \leqslant \mu \leqslant 29.96] = 95\% \qquad (8.12)$$

Thus, we can say with 95% confidence that the true average tar content of brand A cigarettes is between 26.04 and 29.96.

Note that we do not say the probability is 95% that μ is between the two limits. We may use the word "probability" *prior* to taking the sample but not after. Since this concept can be confusing, it deserves an explanation. Notice that the only random variable in Eq. (8.11) is $\bar{X}$. The quantities μ, σ, n, C, and Z_U are *constants* when C is specified. Thus, prior to the selection of a sample, Eq. (8.11) describes a *random interval's* position, which is dependent on the random variable $\bar{X}$. But, after a random sample is selected, $\bar{X}$, itself, becomes a *fixed* or constant value. That is, it is constant for that sample. The reason for this, of course, is that $\bar{X}$ varies only from sample to sample but is fixed for a given sample. Thus, after a sample has been taken, all values in Eq. (8.11) are constant, meaning that the interval (8.12) involves no random variables at all. Then, either μ is between 26.04 and 29.96 or it is not; there is no probability that can be attached to the statement that μ is between these limits.

The discussion above was not presented to add confusion to the concept of confidence intervals but to add interpretation to these intervals. We note that $\bar{X}$ is dependent on the particular random sample of size n selected. Thus, from sample to sample, $\bar{X}$ will vary. This, in turn, implies that the interval's position will also vary and cause the interval to slide up and down the interval scale. Note that once $C\%$ is specified, the length of different confidence intervals is the same, but since the intervals' positions are random, depending on the random samples selected, some intervals will contain the parameter μ and some will not. The question is "How many will contain μ?" The answer for the problem in Example 8.1 is 95% and, in general, the answer is $C\%$. Thus, when we say we are 95% confident that the mean tar content of brand A cigarettes is between 26.04 and 29.96 we are expressing confidence that this interval is one of 95 out of 100 intervals that contain the parameter μ. Figure 8.5 provides a graphic illustration of the random variability of confidence intervals thought to contain the parameter μ.

The preceding discussion suggests that some confidence intervals may not contain the parameter being estimated. It is logical to ask why we can't increase our confidence to 100%, thereby making sure that every confidence interval contains the estimated parameter. The answer is that this confidence interval (for there is only one) would not be of practical value. In Example 8.1, a 100% confidence interval for the mean tar content would yield limits of zero and ∞. These limits imply that the mean tar content could be any value, and this gives us no more information than we started with.

Suppose we ask "What is the mean grade point average (GPA) of undergraduate students at the University of Maryland?" Obviously, we could

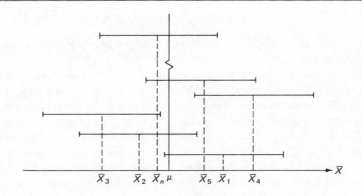

FIGURE 8.5

Confidence intervals covering μ

state with 100% confidence that the mean lies somewhere between zero and four (assuming GPA is computed on a four-point basis). Note that we didn't have to sample individual GPA's to make this statement, but neither did we provide any useful information concerning the mean GPA. By assuming a small risk that we will incorrectly estimate the true mean GPA, we can greatly reduce the limits of the interval that we believe will contain the constant value desired. This reduced range of scores increases the usefulness of the estimate for decision making. For example, if a random sample of 100 students yields a mean GPA of 2.4, and if we know from previous years that $\sigma = 0.7$, then we can say with 95% confidence that the population mean GPA is between 2.2628 and 2.5372.

The discussion above suggests that the degree of confidence influences the length of the confidence interval believed to contain the population parameter being estimated. We might logically ask what other factors influence the length of the confidence interval and what effect does their influence have on the nature of the interval estimate. In general, we note that three factors influence the confidence interval's length.

1. Confidence level
2. Magnitude of σ^2
3. Sample size n

A decrease in the confidence level will produce narrower confidence intervals. For example, in the tar content experiment, the 95% confidence interval is 3.92 mg long, while the 90% confidence interval based on the same sample is only 3.3 mg long. The latter, obviously, reduces the range of possible values believed to contain the population mean. That is, $\bar{X} = 28$ is expected to be in error as an estimate of μ by ± 1.96 mg for the former but only ± 1.65 mg for the latter. The cost of reducing the interval's length, however, is an increase in the risk that the population mean may not be contained within the specified interval. Conversely, we note that a 99% confidence interval increases the interval's length to 3.98 mg, thereby reducing the risk that the interval will miss μ. The confidence level one should select depends on the cost to be incurred should the interval fail to contain the estimated parameter. In particular, what are the consequences to be incurred if the parameter is incorrectly estimated? This concept is discussed at greater length in Chapter 9.

The smaller the variance σ^2, the narrower the length of the confidence interval. We note, however, that σ^2 is a constant and for a given population cannot be changed. It may be possible to classify the population according to some meaningful factor, such as sex, race, or grade level, and reduce σ^2 by using subgroups from the classified population. For example, suppose we divide the population of university students into four groups according to number of credit hours earned (i.e., freshman, sophomore, etc.). Very likely, for each group of students, this classification would produce a smaller σ^2, and would permit us to express a shorter confidence interval for the mean GPA. This approach, however, requires random sampling within each classification of students, thereby increasing the total number of sample values to be selected. It may be too costly in time or money to obtain the necessary samples. Sampling from only one classification of students, such as the freshman group, would limit inferences to only the freshman group.*
Finally, it may be noted that greater precision in measurement sometimes can be employed, leading to a reduced σ^2 by eliminating errors of measurement which are included in σ^2.

Since the standard error of estimate for μ is $\sigma/\sqrt{n}$, this quantity may be reduced by increasing the sample size n, yielding a narrower confidence interval. Suppose, for example, that 100 brand A cigarettes were selected in Example 8.1. The standard error in this case would be

$$\sigma_{\bar{X}} = \frac{5}{\sqrt{100}} = 0.5$$

and the confidence interval for the mean tar content would be (assuming $\bar{X} = 28$ in the larger sample)

$$P[27.02 \leqslant \mu \leqslant 28.98] = 95\%$$

Thus, the confidence interval's length has been cut in half. The size of the sample, however, may be dictated by economic or other factors. In addition,

---

* It should be noted that if 100 samples were to be taken from the total population vs. 25 from each group the stratified sampling would in general be superior for the same total number of samples (100).

notice that it was necessary to increase the size of the original sample four times just to reduce the interval's length by one-half.

It is possible to reverse the above approach and determine the sample size needed to yield an interval length of predetermined size. That is, since the factor $\sigma/\sqrt{n}$ is contained in the confidence interval for the parameter μ we may approximate μ as closely as we wish simply by taking a large enough sample. The basis for this fact can be easily seen from Eq. (8.11). We note that the accuracy of estimation is determined by the factor:

$$Z_U \frac{\sigma}{\sqrt{n}} \tag{8.13}$$

The value of Z_U is determined by the confidence desired. Once confidence is specified, the magnitude of (8.13) for a given problem is a function only of the sample size n. Since $\sqrt{n}$ is in the denominator of (8.13), increasing n will decrease the quotient and vice versa. Thus, to determine the sample size needed to provide a specified accuracy (a) on the estimate of μ, for a given level of confidence, we set (8.13) equal to the accuracy desired as follows:

$$a = \frac{Z_U \sigma}{\sqrt{n}} \tag{8.14}$$

Example 2   Suppose we wish to estimate the mean tar content of brand A cigarettes to within 1 mg. How large a sample of brand A cigarettes must be selected to provide the desired accuracy with 95% confidence?

SOLUTION   Using Eq. (8.14), we set $a = 1$, $\sigma = 5$, and $Z = 1.96$. This gives us:

$$1 = 1.96 \frac{5}{\sqrt{n}}$$

$$\sqrt{n} = 1.96 \frac{5}{1}$$

$$\sqrt{n} = 9.80$$

$$n = 96.04 \text{ or } 97 \text{ cigarettes}$$

Then, using a sample size of 97, we would be reasonably certain (95%) that an estimate of mean tar content for brand A cigarettes could be made within 1 mg of the brand's true mean value. An alternative statement is if repeated random samples of size $n = 97$ are selected from the population of brand A cigarettes, 95 out of 100 samples will yield a sample mean $\bar{X}$ that is within 1 mg of the true population mean μ.

8.5   CONFIDENCE INTERVAL FOR THE MEAN OF A NONNORMAL POPULATION, σ KNOWN

In general, we may have prior information from which the value of σ may be determined, but we may feel that the distribution of scores is not normally distributed. We may still be interested in deriving an interval estimate of the population mean μ. The central limit theorem indicates that the distribution of $\bar{X}$ will be approximately normal with mean μ and $\sigma^2/\sqrt{n}$ for samples taken from a nonnormal population, provided that n, the sample size, is sufficiently large. Since the sample mean, $\bar{X}$, is still an unbiased estimate of the population mean μ, when σ is known and a sufficiently large sample is taken, Eq. (8.11) holds equally well as a general formula for determining confidence intervals for the mean μ of a nonnormal population.

Example 3   Suppose 25 male university students complete the Harvard Step Test. The average heart rate determined for the recovery period 1 to $1\frac{1}{2}$ min after exercise was 150 beats/min. If we know from previous experience that $\sigma^2 = 25$, compute a 66% confidence interval for the population's average recovery heart rate.

SOLUTION   We make use of the central limit theorem to justify the use of Eq. (8.11). Then, $Z = 0.95$, by interpolation in Table I, Appendix B, and $\sigma_{\bar{X}} = 1$, giving

$$P[150 - (0.95)(1) \leqslant \mu \leqslant 150 + (0.95)(1)] = 66\%$$

or

$$P[149.05 \leqslant \mu \leqslant 150.95] = 66\%$$

Exercises

5. An Exergenie, set at 120 lb, should resist a force of 120 lb when a subject attempts to pull the rope through a full range of motion. However, the resistance varies from one exertion to another. The instructor periodically attaches a strain gauge to the rope to determine the resistance offered by the Exergenie. How many measurements should be taken to estimate the true resistance within 4 lb, with 98% confidence, if it is known from past experience that the standard deviation is 10 lb?

6. The director of the physical education service program needed an estimate of the average neck size of male students enrolled in physical activity courses. A random sample of 100 students was selected and neck size assessments yielded $\bar{X} = 15$ in. If the population standard deviation was known to be 2 in. and the director wished to estimate the population mean with 90% confidence, what is the interval estimate? What assumptions were necessary to compute the interval estimate?

7. A physical education instructor needs an estimate of the mean showering and dressing time of students enrolled in his classes. In order to make such an estimate, he randomly selects 50 students and secretly records the time required. The mean time was 6 min with a standard deviation of 2 min. Use a 95% level of confidence to estimate the overall mean.

8. A kinesiology professor has noted from past experience that the standard deviation of each student's test scores for 16 weekly exams is 0.6 point out of 10. He is considering selecting only a few exam scores from the 16 to arrive at an overall grade. If he wishes to estimate each student's 16-test average within ½ point at a confidence level of 95.4%, how many exams must he select at random from each student? How many with 99% confidence? Suppose that a student will protest this method of exam score assessment only if his true average is higher than the upper limit of the confidence interval recorded. How many protests can the professor anticipate for each confidence level stated above?

9. Have each member of the class shoot 20 sets of 10 free throws and record the number made. Compute the binomial coefficient p for each student based on the total number of goals made out of 200. Estimate the true shooting percentage with 95% confidence. Employing the number made out of each set of 10 free throws, determine the number of sets exhibiting a shooting percentage within the confidence limits computed?

10. From past experience the standard deviation of 50-yd dash scores of 10th-grade males in a school system is 0.6 sec.
    a. The sample mean of 25 randomly selected 10th-grade males will be how accurate as an estimate of the mean of all 10th-grade males?
    b. How will this accuracy be affected if the sample size is made four times greater?

11. One hundred male students enrolled in physical activity courses at a large university ran, on the average, 1.46 miles in 12 min. The standard deviation of their performances was 0.15 mile. How accurate is 1.46 as an estimate of the average distance run in 12 min by the male students at this university?

8.6　CONFIDENCE INTERVAL FOR THE DIFFERENCE BETWEEN THE MEANS OF TWO POPULATIONS

Estimating the difference between the means μ_1 and μ_2 of two populations may be as important a procedure as estimating a population mean. For example, the difference between male and female subjects may be sought for various physical and/or motor performance measures; the effectiveness of two different drugs in relieving arthritic pain may be compared; and a new method of instruction may be compared with an old one.

These examples imply that two populations exist. The first is characterized by the parameters μ_1 and $\sigma_1{}^2$, and the second by the parameters μ_2 and $\sigma_2{}^2$. To estimate μ_1 and μ_2, we may use $\bar{X}_1$ and $\bar{X}_2$, respectively, calculated from a random sample of n_1 measurements drawn from population 1 and n_2 measurements drawn from population 2. We assume that the samples have been drawn independently of each other.

We wish to determine confidence intervals for the difference $\mu_1 - \mu_2$. A point estimate of this difference may be provided by subtracting the sample means, $\bar{X}_1 - \bar{X}_2$. It may be shown that this difference is an unbiased estimate of the population means difference since

$$E(\bar{X}_1 - \bar{X}_2) = \mu_1 - \mu_2 \tag{8.15}$$

In addition, if the population variances $\sigma_1{}^2$ and $\sigma_2{}^2$ are known, we can show that the variance of the sampling distribution for $\bar{X}_1 - \bar{X}_2$ is

$$\sigma^2_{\bar{X}_1 - X_2} = \frac{\sigma_1{}^2}{n_1} + \frac{\sigma_2{}^2}{n_2} \tag{8.16}$$

If the random variables X_1 and X_2 are normally distributed or if the sample sizes are sufficiently large, we may state that the difference between the random variables $\bar{X}_1$ and $\bar{X}_2$ is normally distributed and may be related to the standard normal random variable by the equation

$$Z = \frac{\bar{X}_1 - \bar{X}_2 - (\mu_1 - \mu_2)}{\sqrt{(\sigma_1{}^2/n_1) + (\sigma_2{}^2/n_2)}} \tag{8.17}$$

Thus, if we employ the steps we would follow to derive confidence intervals for the mean of a single population, we will obtain the confidence interval for the difference between two population means.

$$P\left[(\bar{X}_1 - \bar{X}_2) - Z_U \sqrt{\frac{\sigma_1{}^2}{n_1} + \frac{\sigma_2{}^2}{n_2}} \leqslant \mu_1 - \mu_2 \leqslant (\bar{X}_1 - \bar{X}_2) + Z_U \sqrt{\frac{\sigma_1{}^2}{n_1} + \frac{\sigma_2{}^2}{n_2}} \right]$$
$$= C\% \tag{8.18}$$

Equation (8.18) should not be difficult to remember once the similarity between Eqs. (8.18) and (8.11) is recognized. For example, we may derive Eq. (8.18) from Eq. (8.11) if we replace $\bar{X}$ in (8.11) with $(\bar{X}_1 - \bar{X}_2)$ and if we replace $\sigma/\sqrt{n}$ with $\sqrt{(\sigma_1{}^2/n_1) + (\sigma_2{}^2/n_2)}$. Our earlier remarks about confidence intervals for μ also hold here and will continue to hold throughout the remainder of this chapter.

Example 4 The following data represent submaximal exercise heart rates of male and female university students. Heart rates were assessed during steady-state work at 600 kpm/min. Calculate a 95% confidence interval for the difference between the means of the two populations.

Males	Females
$\bar{X}_1 = 140$	$\bar{X}_2 = 150$
$\sigma_1{}^2 = 144$	$\sigma_2{}^2 = 81$
$n_1 = 24$	$n_2 = 27$

SOLUTION The sample mean difference is

$$\bar{X}_1 - \bar{X}_2 = 140 - 150 = -10$$

The variance of each sample mean is

$$\frac{\sigma_1{}^2}{n_1} = \frac{144}{24} = 6, \qquad \frac{\sigma_2{}^2}{n_2} = \frac{81}{27} = 3$$

Then

$$\sqrt{\frac{\sigma_1{}^2}{n_1} + \frac{\sigma_2{}^2}{n_2}} = \sqrt{6 + 3} = \sqrt{9} = 3$$

and $Z_U = 1.96$, giving

$$P[-10 - (1.96)(3) \leqslant \mu_1 - \mu_2 \leqslant -10 + (1.96)(3)] = 95\%$$

or

$$P[-15.88 \leqslant \mu_1 - \mu_2 \leqslant -4.12] = 95\%$$

Because the negative interval limits may prove confusing to some, we can restate the equation above in words. That is, we can say with 95% confidence that when the exercise workload is 600 kpm/min. the mean submaximal exercise heart rate for males is 15.88 to 4.12 beats/min *lower* than the mean value for females.

The reader may note that the ordering of population means in Eq. (8.18) is arbitrary. Thus, we may easily reverse the mean difference to read $\mu_2 - \mu_1$ provided we also reverse the order of the sample means. The effect on the resulting confidence interval is to eliminate the negative numbers. By making these adjustments, we can state the mean submaximal heart rate difference is

$$P[4.12 \leqslant \mu_2 - \mu_1 \leqslant 15.88] = 95\%$$

We may interpret the confidence interval as follows: With a 95% confidence we can say that the mean submaximal exercise heart rate for females is 4.12 to 15.88 beats per minute *higher* than the mean rate for males when recorded at an exercise load of 600 kpm/min.

It is important to point out that the distribution of the random variables X_1 and X_2, individual heart rates for males and females, respectively, was not assumed to follow the normal curve. Yet the basis for the confidence interval computed is the normal curve. We may justify using the normal curve by again invoking the central limit theorem. That is, if the sample size is sufficiently large, the distribution of the sample mean is approximately normally distributed. In this case, the sample mean is the mean difference $\bar{X}_1 - \bar{X}_2$. Furthermore, the sample size employed to compute this difference is $n_1 + n_2 = 51$, the combined sample size from the two independent populations.

Exercises

12. Given: The mean number of situps performed by college freshman women is 26 with a standard deviation of 5. For college senior women, the mean is 30 and the standard deviation is 6. The number of situps is normally distributed for each population.

Find: The probability that if a random group of 9 freshman women and a random group of 16 senior women are drawn, the freshman sample's mean will exceed the mean of the seniors.

13. The maximal heart rates of young and middle-age men were compared. A random sample of 40 young (Y) and 50 middle-age (M) men gave heart rates of $\bar{X}_Y = 200$ and $\bar{X}_M = 180$. It was known previously that $\sigma_1 = 10$ and $\sigma_2 = 8$. Compute an 85% confidence interval for the difference in mean maximal heart rates. Interpret the significance of your results.

14. A physical education teacher has two tennis classes, one scheduled during the morning (M) and one during the afternoon (A). He wishes to estimate the mean difference in performance between the two classes so he administers a tennis skill test at the end of the semester. The results are $\bar{X}_M = 68$ and $\bar{X}_A = 60$ with $n_M = 35$ and $n_A = 30$. He knows from previous classes that the variability of tennis skill is consistent from class to class and thus he assumes that $\sigma_M = \sigma_A = 10$. Compute a 92% confidence interval for the mean difference in tennis skill for the two sessions. Interpret your results.

8.7   THE *t*-DISTRIBUTION

We required, without justification at the time, that the variance(s) σ^2 or σ_1^2 and σ_2^2 be known to derive confidence intervals for μ and $\mu_1 - \mu_2$. We conveniently satisfied this requirement by assuming that the variances were known from previous work. Many times the population variances will be known and thus the previous confidence interval formats can be used. Admittedly, many times the variances will not be known. What then can be done to compute desired confidence intervals? A complete answer to this question cannot be given but some useful guidelines may be offered.

Since σ^2 is unknown, it seems logical that an estimate may be derived from the sample values. Section 8.1 suggests that the sample variance s^2 possesses some good properties and may serve as an acceptable estimator of the parameter σ^2. It would therefore appear that a solution to the problem had been found and we could proceed, as before, by simply replacing σ^2 with s^2 where needed. This is, in fact, the case *when the sample size is large*. This method of solving the problem is subject to one serious objection when the sample size is small. That is, for small sample sizes, the sample variance s^2 will not be an accurate estimate of σ^2 and we cannot equate the quantity

$$\frac{\bar{X} - \mu}{s/\sqrt{n}} \tag{8.19}$$

to the standard normal random variable Z for fear of introducing serious error. The effect of the substitution of s for σ is to prohibit us from employing Z-values from Table I to compute confidence intervals.

If (8.19) is not a normally distributed random variable, what is the nature of its distribution? We note that (8.19) is a random variable since its value depends on the two random variables $\bar{X}$ and s. When the random variable $\bar{X}$ is normally distributed or the sample size is large, the quantity (8.19) follows

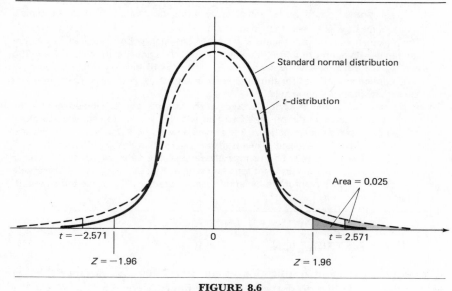

FIGURE 8.6

The t- and standard normal distributions

a distribution known as the *student's t-distribution*. The quantity (8.19) may be equated to student's t as follows:

$$t = \frac{\bar{X} - \mu}{s/\sqrt{n}} \qquad (8.20)$$

The distribution identifying the random variable t and the standard normal random variable Z is given in Figure 8.6. It may be noted from Figure 8.6 that the t-distribution resembles the standard normal distribution. It is, in fact, a symmetrical distribution with mean equal to zero. The exact shape of the t-distribution, however, depends on the sample size used to compute the variance s_X^2 or $s_{\bar{X}_1 - \bar{X}_2}^2$. A different t-distribution exists for every sample size that might be used. To identify a given t-distribution, we introduce the parameter v as a subscript on the quantity t, which gives us t_v. The subscript v is commonly referred to as the *degrees of freedom* of t. When confidence intervals on μ are desired, v will be equal to $n - 1$, where n is the sample size. When confidence intervals on $\mu_1 - \mu_2$ are desired, v will be equal to $n_1 + n_2 - 2$, where n_1 and n_2 are the sample sizes selected from populations 1 and 2, respectively.

In general, degrees of freedom are associated with the divisor used to compute the variance estimate of interest. For example, $n - 1$ is the divisor for the variance estimate $\hat{\sigma}^2$ giving $v = n - 1$ whereas $n_1 + n_2 - 2$ is the divisor for $\hat{\sigma}^2_{\bar{X}_1 - \bar{X}_2}$ giving $v = n_1 + n_2 - 2$. The t-distribution will approximately follow the standard normal distribution when the degrees of freedom are large. However, the t-distribution possesses more area in the tails of the distribution and is more peaked than the standard normal distribution when the degrees of freedom are small. Thus, t-values corresponding to areas under the curve at the extremes of the distribution will be quite different from Z-values corresponding to the same areas when the degrees of freedom are small. For example, the area under the normal curve for $Z \geqslant 1.96$ is 0.025 while the same area under the t-distribution is found for $t \geqslant 2.54$ when the degrees of freedom (d.f.) for t is 5. These values are graphically portrayed in Figure 8.6. Additionally, we may note that the t-values corresponding to the same area (0.025) as above are $t = 2.228$ for d.f. $= 10$, $t = 2.042$ for d.f. $= 30$, and $t = 1.96$ for d.f. $= \infty$. The latter value is the value of Z, and simply denotes that we know the value of σ because we used every observation of the population to compute s. In addition, these values support our earlier statement that the t-distribution approximates the standard normal distribution for sufficiently large samples.

Table II, Appendix B gives percentage points of the t-distribution. The tabled values correspond to points on the t-axis such that the probability of a smaller t is equal to the area specified at the head of each column. But we note that different t-values correspond to the same area depending on the value of v. To denote a specific t-value, we will employ the notation $t_{p, v}$, which identifies the t-value corresponding to the $100p$ percentile and degrees of freedom v. That is, $t_{p, v}$ is the value on the t-axis such that

$$P(t \leqslant t_{p, v}) = p \qquad (8.21)$$

Since the distribution is symmetric about the mean zero, only t-values for $p > 0.5$ are recorded in Table II, Appendix B. Values of t corresponding to $p < 0.5$ may be found from the table by attaching negative signs to the corresponding t-value for $p > 0.5$. For example, $t_{0.20, v} = -t_{0.80, v}$, $t_{0.025, v} = -t_{0.975, v}$, and, more generally,

$$t_{p, v} = -t_{1-p, v} \qquad (8.22)$$

8.8 CONFIDENCE INTERVALS FOR THE MEAN μ WHEN σ^2 IS UNKNOWN

Confidence intervals for the mean μ of a normal population for any sample size or a nonnormal population when the sample size is sufficiently large and σ^2 is unknown, may be obtained using

$$P[\bar{X} - t_{1-\alpha/2, (n-1)}(s/\sqrt{n}) \leqslant \mu \leqslant \bar{X} + t_{1-\alpha/2, (n-1)}(s/\sqrt{n})] = C\% \qquad (8.23)$$

where $\alpha = 1 - C$ or the risk that the interval (8.23) *will not* contain the population mean μ.

Example 5 Find a 95% confidence interval for the mean hemoglobin level for white males over the age of 11 years if a sample of 20 males yielded the following data.

Subject	Hemoglobin	Subject	Hemoglobin
1	14.40	11	14.55
2	14.55	12	15.00
3	13.90	13	13.98
4	14.75	14	15.25
5	12.95	15	13.90
6	14.91	16	14.55
7	14.00	17	15.03
8	14.20	18	13.85
9	14.46	19	13.75
10	16.25	20	15.63

SOLUTION   The necessary computations are determined as follows:

$$\sum X = 289.86 \qquad \sum X^2 = 4211.3404$$
$$\bar{X} = 14.49 \qquad s_X^2 = 11.6024$$
$$s_X = 3.4062 \qquad s_{\bar{X}} = 0.7617$$

Now, since $\alpha = 1 - 0.95 = 0.05$ and $v = 20 - 1 = 19$, we determine the appropriate t-value from Table II of the Appendix B by finding the value corresponding to $v = 19$ and $p = 0.975$. This gives $t = 2.093$. Then, using Eq. (8.23) we get

$$P[14.49 - (2.093)(0.7617) \leqslant \mu \leqslant 14.49 + (2.093)(0.7617)] = 0.95$$

or

$$P[12.90 \leqslant \mu \leqslant 16.09] = 0.95$$

Example 6 Suppose the population variance was unknown for the tar content of brand A cigarettes assessed in Example 8.1. Assume also that the sample variance for the 25 cigarettes included in the experiment was $s^2 = 36$. Compute 95 and 99% confidence intervals for the mean tar content μ.

SOLUTION   Using Eq. (8.23), we set $\alpha = 0.05$ to obtain the 95% limits. Since $v = n - 1$, we get $t_{0.975, 24} = 2.064$ from Table II, Appendix B. Recalling that $\bar{X} = 28$, we get 95% confidence limits on μ of

$$P[28 - (2.064)(6/5) \leqslant \mu \leqslant 28 + (2.064)(6/5)] = 95\%$$

or

$$P[25.52 \leqslant \mu \leqslant 30.48] = 95\%$$

We set $\alpha = 0.01$ to obtain 99% confidence limits. This gives $t_{0.995, 24} = 2.797$ and

$$P[28 - (2.797)(\tfrac{6}{5}) \leqslant \mu \leqslant 28 + (2.797)(\tfrac{6}{5})] = 99\%$$

or

$$P[24.64 \leqslant \mu \leqslant 31.36] = 99\%$$

The 95% confidence interval using t is longer than the corresponding interval obtained in Example 8.1 using Z. This increase in length comes from two sources: the replacement of σ by s and the replacement of Z by $t_{1-\alpha/2, (n-1)}$. We note from Table II, Appendix B, that replacing Z by t will always increase the length of the interval, but we can never know in advance how replacing σ by s will affect the interval since s is a random variable. Thus, an increase in the interval's length is logical since we could not maintain the same degree of confidence in an estimate when two sources of error existed instead of one.

8.9   CONFIDENCE INTERVALS FOR THE DIFFERENCE BETWEEN THE POPULATION MEANS μ_1 AND μ_2, $\sigma_1{}^2$ AND $\sigma_2{}^2$ UNKNOWN

Two cases must be considered here. First we may assume that the variances $\sigma_1{}^2$ and $\sigma_2{}^2$ are equal (i.e., $\sigma_1{}^2 = \sigma_2{}^2 = \sigma$). Under this assumption the random samples of size n_1 and n_2, taken independently, may be combined to estimate the single population variance σ. Thus, an unbiased estimate of σ is provided by the equation

$$s_p{}^2 = \frac{(n_1 - 1)s_1{}^2 + (n_2 - 1)s_2{}^2}{n_1 + n_2 - 2} \tag{8.24}$$

where the subscript p indicates that the two samples have been combined or "pooled." Using Eq. (8.24), we may compute confidence intervals for the difference between means, $\mu_1 - \mu_2$, as follows:

$$P\left[(\bar{X}_1 - \bar{X}_2) - t_{1-\alpha/2, (n_1 + n_2 - 2)} s_p \sqrt{\frac{1}{n_1} + \frac{1}{n_2}} \right.$$

$$\leqslant \mu_1 - \mu_2$$

$$\left. \leqslant (\bar{X}_1 - \bar{X}_2) + t_{1-\alpha/2, (n_1 + n_2 - 2)} s_p \sqrt{\frac{1}{n_1} + \frac{1}{n_2}} \right]$$

$$= (1 - \alpha)\% \tag{8.25}$$

where it should be noted that

$$s_{\bar{X}_1 - \bar{X}_2}^2 = s_p{}^2 \left(\frac{1}{n_1} + \frac{1}{n_2} \right) \tag{8.26}$$

Example 7   The resting systolic blood pressures of a group of smokers and nonsmokers are given as follows:

	Smokers	Nonsmokers
	$\bar{X}_1 = 134$	$\bar{X}_2 = 122$
	$s_1^2 = 45$	$s_2^2 = 36$
	$n_1 = 25$	$n_2 = 31$

Assume that $\sigma_1^2 = \sigma_2^2$ and that the random sample $(X_{11}, X_{12}, \ldots, X_{1n_1}, X_{21}, X_{22}, \ldots, X_{2n_2})$ are all independent observations. Compute 99% confidence intervals for the mean difference $\mu_1 - \mu_2$.

SOLUTION   We compute first the value of s_p^2 using Eq. (8.24). This gives

$$s_p^2 = \frac{(24 \cdot 45) + (30 \cdot 36)}{54} = 40$$

Then, using Eq. (8.26), we get

$$s_{\bar{X}_1 - \bar{X}_2} = \sqrt{40\left(\frac{1}{25} + \frac{1}{31}\right)} = 1.7$$

Next we determine the value of t by using $\alpha/2 = 0.005$ and $v = 55$ (nearest tabled value to $v = 25 + 31 - 2 = 54$).* This gives $t_{0.995, 55} = 2.669$. Substituting the values for $\bar{X}_1$, $\bar{X}_2$, $s_{\bar{X}_1 - \bar{X}_2}$, and t in Eq. (8.25), we get

$$P[12 - (2.669)(1.7) \leqslant \mu_1 - \mu_2 \leqslant 12 + (2.669)(1.7)] = 99\%$$

or

$$P(7.46 \leqslant \mu_1 - \mu_2 \leqslant 16.54) = 99\%$$

An interpretation of the confidence interval indicates that we may say with 99% confidence that the average systolic blood pressure of smokers is 7.46 to 16.54 mm Hg higher than the average value for nonsmokers.

The second confidence interval considered in this section is the case when $\sigma_1^2 \neq \sigma_2^2$. When the two variances cannot be assumed equal, the pooling concept employed in the previous confidence interval may not be used because the statistic $(\bar{X}_1 - \bar{X}_2)/s_{\bar{X}_1 - \bar{X}_2}$ does not lead to a t-distribution. The problem of computing confidence intervals for the difference $\mu_1 - \mu_2$ has been debated extensively and several approaches have been suggested. We will not pursue these approaches here but will offer one approach that seems justified for the present level of discussion.

---

* When a tabled value for a specific v does not exist one may refer to the nearest tabled value or interpolate between tabled values to more closely estimate the t-value corresponding to the degrees of freedom of interest.

If our sample sizes are large, we may assume that s_1^2 and s_2^2 are good estimates of σ_1^2 and σ_2^2, respectively. We may then use Eq. (8.18) with s_1^2 substituted for σ_1^2 and s_2^2 substituted for σ_2^2. The size of n_1 and n_2 determines the accuracy with which s_1^2 and s_2^2 estimate σ_1^2 and σ_2^2. The degree of accuracy depends on the individual researcher and his particular problem. We suggest, however, that n_1 and n_2 should each be in the neighborhood of 50 when s_1^2 and s_2^2 are substituted for σ_1^2 and σ_2^2 in Eq. (8.18).

Exercises

15. A random sample of 17 students enrolled in physical fitness classes at a large university were tested in the physical fitness laboratory. Their average maximal oxygen intake was 3.64 liters per minute with a standard deviation of 0.52. Estimate, using a 95% level of confidence, the average maximal oxygen intake for all students in the fitness program. Interpret the confidence interval computed.

16. A football coach wishes to estimate the average yards gained for a particular play run against a set defensive alignment. Records indicate the following yards gained for the last 10 times this play was run under the defensive alignment of interest:

$$3, \ 2, \ -2, \ 6, \ 8, \ 1, \ 4, \ 10, \ -1, \ 5$$

Establish a 90% confidence interval for the average gain, in yards, expected for this particular play. What assumptions are necessary to compute this confidence interval?

17. A sample of 20 brand A cigarettes was tested for nicotine content and gave $\bar{X} = 6$ mg and $s = 1$ mg. Use the t-distribution to find 99% confidence limits for μ.

18. The mean residual lung volume of college-age males (CAM) was compared with that of middle-age males (MAM). Random samples of 24 young men and 14 middle-aged men gave the following results:

$$\bar{X}_{CAM} = 1.526 \qquad s_{CAM} = 0.165$$
$$\bar{X}_{MAM} = 1.764 \qquad s_{MAM} = 0.211$$

Compute a 95% confidence interval for the mean difference in residual volume assuming homogeneous variances. Interpret your results.

19. The following 18-hole golf scores were recorded for Charles and Clyde:

Charles: 80, 77, 74, 78, 72, 80, 82, 81, 75, 74
79, 76, 77, 80, 74, 73, 73, 79, 76, 75

Clyde: 85, 74, 80, 76, 77, 79, 82, 81, 80, 78
76, 79, 80, 81, 80, 79, 83, 77, 76, 78

Compute a 95% confidence interval for the mean difference in golf scores. What is the largest margin that Charles can anticipate defeating Clyde by in Medal Play? The least margin? What assumption(s) is (are) necessary to complete the analysis of this exercise?

COMPUTER APPLICATION

20. Employ the fitness data keypunched in Chapter 2 to compute a 95% confidence interval for the mean difference between males and females for each of the variables given. Repeat for seniors and freshmen.

The following program may be utilized to complete Exercise 20.

FORTRAN IV PROGRAM

Confidence Interval for Difference Between Means for Independent Groups

Col. 7
↓

```
      DIMENSIØN FMT (80)
      READ (5,100) M, N
      READ (5,101) TC
      READ (5,102) FMT
      SUMX = 0.0
      SUMXSØ = 0.0
      DØ 50 J = 1, M
      READ (5,FMT) X
      SUMX = SUMX + X
   50 SUMXSØ = SUMXSØ + X**2
      L = M + N
      SUMY = 0.0
      SUMYSØ = 0.0
      DØ 60 J = M+1, L
      READ (5,FMT) X
      SUMY = SUMY + X
   60 SUMYSØ = SUMYSØ + X**2
      A = M
      B = N
      C = L
      XBAR = SUMX/A
      VARX = (SUMXSØ - (A*XBAR**2))/(A-1)
      SDX = SØRT(VARX) ·
      YBAR = SUMY/B
      VARY = (SUMYSØ - (B*YBAR**2))/(B-1)
      SDY = SØRT(VARY)
      VARSP = ((A-1)*VARX + (B-1)*VARY)/(C-2)
      SEDSØ = VARSP*(1/A + 1/B)
      SEDIFF = SØRT(SEDSØ)
      DIFBAR = XBAR - YBAR
      CUL = DIFBAR + TC*SEDIFF
      CLL = DIFBAR - TC*SEDIFF
      WRITE (6,103) XBAR, VARX, SDX
      WRITE (6,104) YBAR, VARY, SDY
      WRITE (6,105) DIFBAR, SEDIFF
      WRITE (6,106) CUL
      WRITE (6,107) CLL
  100 FØRMAT (2I2)
  101 FØRMAT (F3.2)
  102 FØRMAT (80A1)
  103 FØRMAT (' ','MEANX =',F10.3,'VARX =',F10.3,'SDX =',F10.3)
  104 FØRMAT (' ','MEANY =',F10.3,'VARY =',F10.3,'SDY =',F10.3)
  105 FØRMAT (' ','MEAN DIFF =',F10.3,'STD ERR ØF DIF =',F10.3)
  106 FØRMAT (' ','UPPER LIMIT =',F10.3)
  107 FØRMAT (' ','LØWER LIMIT =',F10.3)
      STØP
      END
```

Order of cards:

1. System cards
2. Program deck
3. Sample sizes card
     Cols. 1,2: Sample size for first group
           3,4: Sample size for second group
4. Critical *t*-value card (keypunched according to format statement 101)

5. Data format card
6. Data cards for first group
7. Data cards for second group
8. Job termination card

8.10 CONFIDENCE INTERVALS FOR PAIRED COMPARISONS

The previous confidence intervals for the difference between means $\mu_1 - \mu_2$ were based on samples drawn independently from the two populations. Often a particular experiment will dictate the drawing of two samples that are not independent. For example, we may wish to compare each individual's performance before and after an experimental treatment; to aid in controlling extraneous factors we may wish to assign twins to each of two experimental conditions. Further, we may wish to equate smokers and nonsmokers according to resting heart rate before comparing their resting blood pressure. All of these examples are popularly referred to as *paired comparisons*. The pair occurs because either one individual is assessed twice on the same variable and therefore is a member, so to speak, of both populations, or one individual in one population is matched or paired with a member of the second population because they possess similar characteristics. Thus, by pairing, it is meant that the observations for the two populations are associated as follows:

$$X_{11} \text{ is related to } X_{21}$$
$$X_{12} \text{ is related to } X_{22}$$
$$\vdots$$
$$X_{1n} \text{ is related to } X_{2n}$$

where X is the random variable of interest, and the first subscript on X denotes the population sampled, and the second denotes the particular individual or object in the sample. For example, X_{12} represents the value of the random variable X observed for the second individual or object taken from population 1 and X_{22} represents the value of the random variable X observed for the individual or object in population 2 matched with the individual or object 2 in population 1. Notice that the idea of independence of sampling is not suggested by this interpretation. That is, the selection of X_{12} for observation automatically requires the selection and observation of X_{22}.

To compute confidence intervals on the mean difference $\mu_1 - \mu_2$ for paired comparisons, it is necessary to compute the individual differences d_i for each matched pair. For example, $d_1 = X_{11} - X_{21}$, $d_2 = X_{12} - X_{22}$, etc. We may then note that

$$\mu_d = \mu_1 - \mu_2 \tag{8.27}$$

and

$$\bar{d} = \bar{X}_1 - \bar{X}_2 \tag{8.28}$$

is an unbiased estimate of μ_d.

Similarly, if σ_d^2 is unknown, we may use s_d^2 as an estimate of σ_d^2 where

$$s_d^2 = \frac{\sum (d_i - \bar{d})^2}{n-1} = \frac{\sum d_i^2 - n\bar{d}^2}{n-1} \qquad (8.29)$$

and compute the required confidence interval using

$$P[\bar{d} - t_{1-\alpha/2,\,(n-1)}\, s_d/\sqrt{n} \leqslant \mu_d \leqslant \bar{d} + t_{1-\alpha/2,\,(n-1)}\, s_d/\sqrt{n}] = (1-\alpha)\% \qquad (8.30)$$

In Eqs. (8.29) and (8.30), n is taken as the number of "pairs" contained in the two samples.

Example 8 Two methods of developing isometric wrist flexor strength were compared with two groups of college male subjects. Subjects were matched according to initial wrist flexor strength and one subject from each matched "pair" was assigned at random to one of the strength development programs. The following posttest data were recorded on 10 matched pairs:

Pair	X_1	X_2
1	88	85
2	85	80
3	90	84
4	88	82
5	80	75
6	82	77
7	79	73
8	77	70
9	80	72
10	75	70

Calculate a 95% confidence interval for μ_d.

SOLUTION Using the data above, we get

$$\bar{d} = 5.6 \qquad s_d^2 = 18.222$$
$$s_d = 4.268 \qquad s_{\bar{d}} = 1.35$$

The tabular value for $t_{0.975,\,9}$ is 2.262. Making these substitutions in Eq. (8.30) gives

$$P(2.55 \leqslant \mu_d \leqslant 8.65) = 95\%$$

Exercises

21. An experimental study was undertaken to determine the effect of pre-elimentary activity on the thickness of articular cartilage. The articular cartilage of the right elbow joint of 26 subjects, selected at random, was X-rayed from the lateral view before and immediately following 10 minutes of activity. The average change in thickness was 0.15 mm with a standard deviation of 0.02 mm. Estimate, using a

99% level of confidence, the average change in thickness that all athletes can anticipate. Discuss the significance of your estimate.

22. Twenty sixth-grade students in each of two health classes were matched according to intelligence test scores. One class learned health by the problem-solving (PS) approach, while the second class was taught by the lecture (L) method. The following results, based on a standard health knowledge test, were obtained:

Pair:	1	2	3	4	5	6	7	8	9	10
Problem solving	95	94	90	89	86	84	86	80	82	81
Lecture	90	86	88	79	80	75	78	80	72	76

Pair:	11	12	13	14	15	16	17	18	19	20
Problem solving	77	75	74	72	70	65	62	65	64	66
Lecture	70	78	77	65	68	70	55	68	60	50

Compute a 95% confidence interval for the mean difference in the two teaching methods. What assumptions are necessary to compute this interval? Interpret your results.

23. Reanalyze the data of Exercise 22; do not assume matched pairs. How much wider is the confidence interval? Explain.

24. From five sets of identical twins (pairs A, B, C, D, and E), one child was selected at random from each pair to participate in an "active games" program in addition to regular kindergarten activities. The other child from each pair participated only in the regular kindergarten program. At the end of the school year, the following first-grade readiness scores were obtained:

Pair	Active Games	Control
A	100	90
B	125	120
C	142	135
D	130	120
E	150	138

Estimate the mean difference in readiness scores using a 95% confidence interval. Analyze the data as though the experiment had been conducted in an unpaired manner. Does it appear that using identical twins increased the amount of information available in the experiment?

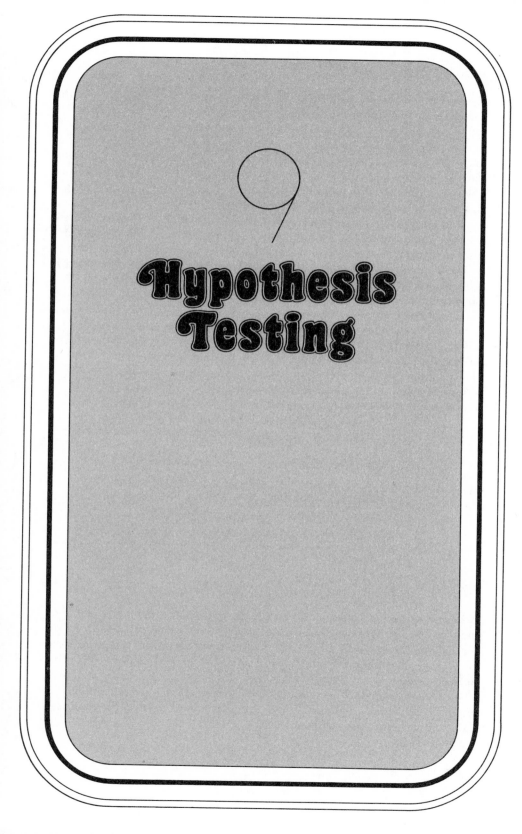

9

Hypothesis Testing

9.1 INTRODUCTION

One of the first steps in inferential statistics, as stated in Chapter 1, is the establishment of a hypothesis. More specifically, in inferential statistics, we establish a hypothesis concerning a population parameter, collect data from a random sample, determine the appropriate statistics from this sample, and on the basis of these statistics either accept or reject the population parameter hypothesis. It is important to understand that hypotheses are always concerned with population parameters rather than with sample statistics. As a result, there is a chance, or risk, that we will be wrong in making a generalized decision about a parameter from the incomplete information furnished by a sample statistic. Thus, probability statements are associated with the acceptance or rejection of hypotheses.

There are two possibilities for making an error in decision. If we reject a hypothesis when, in fact, it is true, we make a *type I* error in decision. The probability of making a type I error is denoted by α (alpha). The other decisional error which we may make is the acceptance of a hypothesis which is, in fact, false. This error is called *type II* error, and the probability of making it is denoted by β (beta). No error occurs whenever we reject a false hypothesis or accept a true hypothesis. There is no special name given to the acceptance of a true hypothesis, which has probability $(1 - \alpha)$. However, the probability of rejecting a false hypothesis $(1 - \beta)$ is referred to as *power*. If we denote a hypothesis by H_0, the decision possibilities may be summarized by Table 9.1.

TABLE 9.1

Decision Possibilities When Testing a Hypothesis H_0

Our Decision	ACTUAL SITUATION IN THE POPULATION	
	H_0 is True	H_0 is False
Accept	No error $(1 - \alpha)$	Type II (β)
Reject	Type I error (α)	No error $(1 - \beta)$ *power*

9.2 HYPOTHESIS TESTING OF μ: σ KNOWN

An example should be helpful in furthering your conceptualization of hypothesis testing. Suppose it has been established that cancer can be caused by the regular smoking of one pack of cigarettes per day if the cigarettes have an average tar content equaling or exceeding 30 mg per cigarette. We wish to determine whether a particular brand, say brand A, is safe to smoke. The stated hypothesis might be: The average level of nicotine content in brand A cigarettes is equal to 30 mg per cigarette. We would usually write a shorter version of this hypothesis:

$$H_0: \quad \mu = 30 \text{ mg}$$

where μ represents the mean tar content of the population consisting of all brand A cigarettes. In general, we state a hypothesis about a mean as $H_0: \mu = \mu_0$, where μ represents the population mean and μ_0 represents the hypothesized value. Such a hypothesis about a population parameter is called a *statistical hypothesis* or sometimes a *null hypothesis*. We want to provide evidence that this hypothesis should either be accepted or rejected.

If the null hypothesis is rejected, at least one alternative hypothesis must be available to take its place. As it now stands in our example, there are two alternatives to $H_0: \mu = 30$, either $\mu < 30$ or $\mu > 30$. Let's assume we are interested in only the first alternative, $\mu < 30$. If that is the case, then we will not reject our hypothesis if μ is equal to or greater than 30 ($\mu \geqslant 30$) but will reject it only if evidence exists that $\mu < 30$. Thus, we state our hypothesis and its alternative (denoted by H_A) as:

$$H_0: \quad \mu \geqslant 30 \text{ mg}$$
$$H_A: \quad \mu < 30 \text{ mg} \tag{9.1}$$

This more appropriately represents our intent since if H_0 is accepted, we will conclude that the cigarettes are unsafe; and if we reject H_0, we will conclude that the cigarettes are safe.

Obviously, we could never test all brand A cigarettes for tar content. Thus, it is necessary to base our decision on a sample of brand A cigarettes. Assume that we have a random sample of 64 brand A cigarettes, and we test the tar content of each cigarette with the use of a smoking machine and determine the sample mean $\bar{X}$. We wish to decide, on the basis of this sample mean, whether brand A is safe to smoke. There are two chances of being wrong in our decision to smoke brand A or not. If we reject our hypothesis and decide to smoke brand A when in reality the average tar level is equal to or greater than 30 mg, then we make a type I error. Likewise, if we conclude on the basis of our experiment that brand A cigarettes are dangerous when in actuality the average nicotine content is less than 30 mg, then we commit a type II error. The possibilities, and their respective probabilities, when testing our hypothesis are listed in Table 9.2.

TABLE 9.2

Decision Possibilities in Testing the Hypothesis $H_0: \mu \geqslant 30$ mg

Our Decision	ACTUAL SITUATIONS IN THE POPULATION	
	H_0 True: Brand A is Unsafe: $\mu \geqslant 30$	H_0 False: Brand A is Safe: $\mu < 30$
Accept H_0: Brand A is lethal: $\mu \geqslant 30$	No error	Type II error (β)
Reject H_0: Brand A is safe: $\mu < 30$	Type I error (α)	No error ($1 - \beta$)

The sampling distribution of sample means is used as the basis for testing a hypothesis about μ, the population mean. In our present example, assume from previous work that we know the population standard deviation for tar content is $\sigma = 8$. Thus, the standard deviation of the sampling distribution of means is

$$\sigma_X = \frac{\sigma}{\sqrt{n}}$$

$$= \frac{8}{\sqrt{64}}$$

$$= \frac{8}{8}$$

$$= 1$$

If we use $\mu = 30$ as our population mean, we will derive a sampling distribution of means that will look like the one in Figure 9.1.

Suppose that the sample mean we obtain is $\bar{X} = 28$. Is this value so extreme that we should reject the hypothesis that this sample comes from the population with $\mu \geqslant 30$ and $\sigma = 8$ or is $\bar{X} = 28$ sufficiently close to 30 for us to conclude that our sample does come from a population with $\mu \geqslant 30$? The answer to this question depends on how much risk we are willing to take. From Figure 9.1, we see that the sample mean, $\bar{X} = 28$, lies two standard deviations below the population mean (or $Z = 2$) in the sampling distribution of means. Assuming that this distribution is normally distributed, we find from the normal probability table that we can expect approximately 2% of samples drawn from this population to have means that are two or more standard deviations away from the population mean. Therefore, if we should conclude that our sample with $\bar{X} = 28$ could not have come from the population with $\mu = 30$, there is a 2% chance of being in error. If we reflect on what was just said, we see that we are talking about a type I error, namely

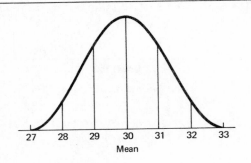

FIGURE 9.1

Sampling distribution of $\bar{X}$'s when $\mu = 30$ and $\sigma\bar{X} = 1$

rejecting our hypothesis when it is actually true. In this case, there would be a 2% chance of making such an error or, stated otherwise, $\alpha = 0.02$. In practice, the more appropriate procedure is to determine, before data are collected, the level of type I error we can risk and determine those values of $\bar{X}$ that will cause us to reject the hypothesis. *The values of $\bar{X}$ that cause us to reject a hypothesis are called rejection or critical values. The area under the normal curve corresponding to those values constitutes a rejection or critical region.* Both rejection and critical are common terms used to describe this region. Hereafter, we will refer only to a critical region or value. If we consider a type I error as relatively harmless, then we choose a relatively large α, such as $\alpha = 0.10$ or even $\alpha = 0.20$. If a type I error is serious, as in the present example, then we would want to reduce the chances of making such an error and we would set our α-level very low, $\alpha = 0.01$ or $\alpha = 0.001$ for instance. Traditionally, α is set at 0.01 or 0.05. However, there is nothing sacred about such α-levels. The level of α is set for the practical reasons just outlined.

The α-level is also called the *level of significance*. Assuming for the present example that we let our level of significance be small, say $\alpha = 0.01$, we find from the normal probability table that a sample mean must fall more than 2.326 standard deviations below the mean ($Z_{0.01} = -2.326$) in order to be in the lower 0.01 portion of a normal distribution. Therefore, in our example, we need to have a sample mean of less than 27.674 (or $\bar{X} < 27.674$) before we conclude that the sample did *not* come from a population with $\mu \geqslant 30$. Looking at our sampling distribution of means again (Figure 9.2), we see that the shaded portion indicates the region ($\bar{X} < 27.674$) that will cause rejection of the hypothesis H_0: $\mu \geqslant 30$. This is the *critical region*. In general, for this type of situation, the critical region is

$$\bar{X} < \mu_0 + \frac{Z_\alpha \sigma}{\sqrt{n}} \tag{9.2}$$

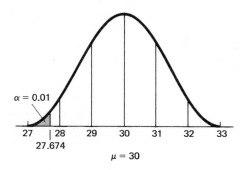

$\alpha = 0.01$

$\mu = 30$

FIGURE 9.2

Sampling distribution of $\bar{X}$'s showing the critical region ($\bar{X} < 27.674$)

where Z_α indicates the distance of a chosen α from the mean, in standard deviations, and μ_0 is the hypothesized value of μ. The term Z_α is referred to as the *critical value* for Z since, quite often, we find Z_α and then reject H_0 if $Z < Z_\alpha$ where

$$Z = \frac{\bar{X} - \mu_0}{\sigma/\sqrt{n}} \tag{9.3}$$

Since $\bar{X} = 28$ is not in the critical region for our example, we are unable to reject the hypothesis, $H_0: \mu \geqslant 30$, and would therefore conclude that, on the basis of our experiment, it is not advisable to smoke brand A cigarettes.

Although we do not reject our hypothesis $\mu \geqslant 30$, there is a chance that in actuality it should have been rejected. If this were the case, we would be making a type II error. It is impossible, however, to determine the probability of making such an error (β) unless we know the actual population mean value. In our example, if the population from which we take our sample has a mean of say 26 instead of the 30 we hypothesized, then the true sampling distribution is shifted to the left by four standard deviations. This new sampling distribution and our original distribution have been placed for illustrative purposes on the same graph in Figure 9.3.

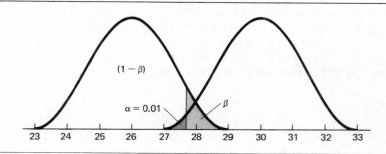

FIGURE 9.3

Sampling distributions showing alpha and beta

The shaded portion represents $\alpha = 0.01$, while the lined portion represents β, the probability of accepting the hypothesis $\mu = 30$, if in fact, $\mu = 26$. We can see there would be a different area (value) for β if the true sampling distribution was positioned differently than shown. Therefore, it is an impossibility to determine or directly control the value of β since we never know the actual value of μ.

Certain factors that can be controlled indirectly affect the magnitude of β. In Figure 9.4, the amount of β is shown in our example for two different values of α, namely $\alpha = 0.05$ and $\alpha = 0.01$. We can see quite clearly from Figure 9.4 that *with a larger α, we have a smaller β or vice versa.*

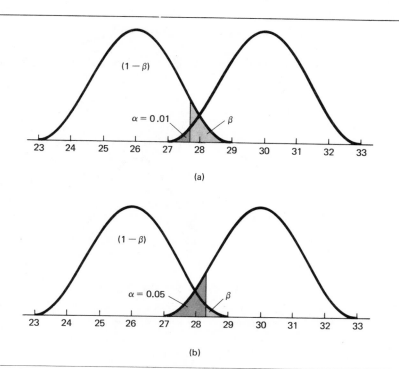

(a)

(b)

FIGURE 9.4

Graphical representation showing the effects of the size of alpha on beta

Another factor that affects β is the sample size. The larger the sample size, the smaller the size of β. Figure 9.5 illustrates this for our example. The different sampling distributions of $\bar{X}$'s are represented for sample sizes of 16 and 64, with hypothesized $\mu = 30$ and actual $\mu = 26$. We can see that since the standard error is smaller for the larger sample, the resultant β for a particular population mean is considerably smaller. Therefore, *the power of a hypothesis test is increased by increasing the size of the sample.*

Obviously, we would like to be able to keep α and β at a minimum. Although it is generally quite easy to control α, since we usually select the level of type I error we are willing to risk, there is *no* such convenient method for directly controlling the level of β. We have seen three factors that affect β: (1) the value of the actual population mean; (2) the level of significance chosen, α; and (3) the size of the sample. Since the actual population mean value will *not* be known (if we know the population value, there would be no need to test the hypothesis), only the latter two factors exist for controlling type II error (β). However, we have seen that to decrease the size of β we must increase the risk of a type I error (α). Therefore, if we want to reasonably control α and β concurrently, our only alternative is to increase the sample

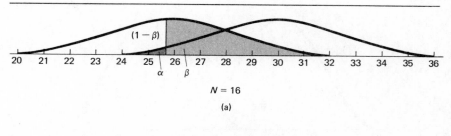

$N = 16$

(a)

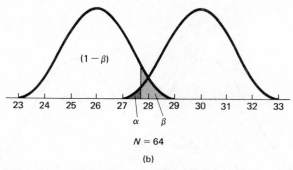

$N = 64$

(b)

FIGURE 9.5

Graphical representation showing the effects of sample size on β

size. It must be realized, however, that we do not want to dilute the quality of an experiment in order to have a larger sample size. We should select as large a sample as is feasible in terms of time, quality of data collection, and economics. But the test of hypothesis must have reasonable power. More information concerning this problem is given in a later section of this chapter.

Since it is generally difficult to control the size of a type II error, the way in which we state our hypothesis becomes very important. In the cigarette smoking example, we chose the hypothesis and its alternative:

$$H_0: \quad \mu \geqslant 30 \text{ mg}$$
$$H_A: \quad \mu < 30 \text{ mg}$$

The direction of the alternative hypothesis was not chosen without thought. With our hypothesis stated as it is, if we commit a type I error, α (rejecting a true hypothesis), we will conclude that brand A cigarettes are safe when, in fact, they are not. A type II error, on the other hand, would result in our declaring the cigarettes unsafe when, in fact, they are safe. We certainly want to have direct control over the first type of error since such an error in decision might result in death. Thus, we stated our hypothesis so that this serious and possibly life-and-death situation would be a type I error whose probability could be directly controlled. Our type II error would be less harmful, since if it were made, the result would be loss of smoking a non-carcinogenic cigarette.

Had we stated our null hypothesis and its alternative as:

$$H_0: \quad \mu \leqslant 30 \text{ mg}$$
$$H_A: \quad \mu > 30 \text{ mg}$$

a type I error would result in concluding the cigarettes are dangerous to health when in fact they are safe. However, a type II error would result in the decision to smoke carcinogenic cigarettes. Therefore, the original statement of the hypothesis ($H_0: \mu \geqslant 30$) and its alternative ($H_A: \mu < 30$) are preferred. It is extremely important in all such situations to carefully weigh the manner in which a hypothesis is stated.

There are many situations in which we are interested in both alternatives to a hypothesis of equality. Suppose, for example, that we are interested in knowing if the 16-year-old girls at Roosevelt High differ significantly from the AAHPER National norm group in the performance of the 50-yd dash. Given that the population mean and standard deviation of the 50-yd dash for 16-year-old girls is $\mu = 8.3$ sec, $\sigma = 0.6$ sec, our hypothesis would be:

$$H_0: \quad \mu = 8.3$$
$$H_A: \quad \mu > 8.3 \quad \text{or} \quad \mu < 8.3$$

Both alternatives, $\mu > 8.3$ and $\mu < 8.3$, are stated, since it would be of interest if the girls were either superior or inferior to the national norm group. These two alternatives may be combined to give one statement:

$$H_A: \quad \mu \neq 8.3$$

Assume that we select a random sample of 36 girls and an $\alpha = 0.05$. Then

$$\sigma_{\bar{X}} = \frac{0.6}{\sqrt{36}}$$

$$= \frac{0.6}{6}$$

$$= 0.1$$

The sampling distribution of the mean with critical regions is presented in Figure 9.6. We can see that the critical region is split between the two *tails* of the distribution with $\alpha/2$ or 0.025 area at each end. This was done, of course, since we are interested in rejecting our hypothesis if the sample mean is either extremely large or small relative to the population mean. This type of hypothesis test is often referred to as a *two-tailed* or *two-sided* *hypothesis test*. The hypothesis tests that were previously discussed are called *one-tailed* or *one-sided hypothesis tests*.

To complete the present example, assume that the mean for our 36 girls is $\bar{X} = 8.6$. Since 8.6 is in the critical region of the sampling distribution, we

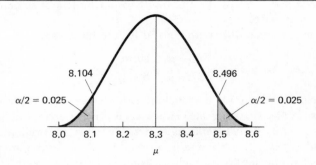

FIGURE 9.6

Sampling distribution of $\bar{X}$'s with critical regions $\bar{X} > 8.496$ and $\bar{X} < 8.104$

reject H_0: $\mu = 8.3$ and conclude that girls at Roosevelt High are significantly slower than the norm group in the 50-yd dash.

Hypothesis testing, in general, may be summarized by using the following outline* of steps:

1. State the goal or purpose of the experiment.
2. State the hypothesis to be tested and its alternative(s).
3. Decide on the level of significance α, reflecting the risk of rejecting a true hypothesis.
4. Select a sample, collect the necessary data, and compute the appropriate statistics.
5. Determine the critical region, or values, in the sampling distribution which cause the rejection of the hypothesis.
6. Make a statement of acceptance or rejection of the hypothesis, including the level of α.
7. State the resultant conclusion in terms of the experiment.

Basically, we have applied these steps in the one-sided and two-sided hypothesis tests discussed thus far. To summarize, one-sided hypothesis testing we have, in general form:

Hypothesis: Population mean is equal to a specified number, σ is known. One-sided test, alternative $\mu < \mu_0$.

1. State the goal or purpose of the experiment.
2. State the hypothesis and its alternative(s).

   H_0: $\mu \geqslant \mu_0$
   H_A: $\mu < \mu_0$

* The idea for this basic outline was obtained from Wilfrid J. Dixon and Frank J. Massey, *Introduction to Statistical Analysis*. New York: McGraw-Hill, 1969.

3. Decide on the level of significance α. Choose α after careful consideration.
4. Select a sample, collect the necessary data, and compute the statistics needed. Compute $\bar{X}$.
5. Determine the critical region, or values, in the sampling distribution which cause the rejection of the hypothesis. If we use

$$Z = \frac{\bar{X} - \mu_0}{\sigma/\sqrt{n}}$$

any value of Z less than the value for Z_α or $Z < Z_\alpha$ will cause rejection of the hypothesis, or in terms of a critical region, if $\bar{X} < \mu_0 + Z_\alpha(\sigma/\sqrt{n})$, we will reject the hypothesis.
6. Make a statement of acceptance or rejection of the hypothesis, including the level of α. State either acceptance or rejection of H_0.
7. State the resultant conclusion in the terms of the experiment.

For any one-tailed hypothesis with the alternative $\mu > \mu_0$, we need only change steps 2 and 5 as follows:

2. H_0: $\mu \leqslant \mu_0$

   H_A: $\mu > \mu_0$

5. If we use

$$Z = \frac{\bar{X} - \mu_0}{\sigma/\sqrt{n}}$$

any value of $Z > Z_{1-\alpha}$ will cause rejection of the hypothesis.

Summarizing two-tailed hypothesis tests in the established format, we have:

Hypothesis: Population mean is equal to a specified number, σ is known. Two-tailed test alternatives are $\mu > \mu_0, \mu < \mu_0$, or simply $\mu \neq \mu_0$.

1. State the goal or purpose of the experiment.
2. State the hypothesis and its alternatives(s)

   H_0 $\mu = \mu_0$

   H_A: $\mu \neq \mu_0$

3. Decide on the level of significance α which is the probability of rejecting a true hypothesis.

   Choose α after careful consideration.
4. Select a sample, collect necessary data, and compute the appropriate statistic(s). Compute $\bar{X}$.
5. Determine the critical region, or values, in the sampling distribution which cause the rejection of the hypothesis. After finding $Z = (\bar{X} - \mu_0)/(\sigma/\sqrt{n})$, we will reject the hypothesis if Z is greater than $Z_{(1-\alpha/2)}$ or less than $Z_{\alpha/2}$. When we write this as one statement, we can say reject H_0 if $Z_{\alpha/2} > Z > Z_{(1-\alpha/2)}$.

6. Make a statement of acceptance or rejection of the hypothesis, including the level of α.
7. State the resultant conclusion in the terms of the experiment.

9.3 HYPOTHESIS TESTING OF μ: σ UNKNOWN

In the examples presented thus far, we assumed that the population variance σ was known and as a result we could find $\sigma_{\bar{X}}$. There are many problems where the value of σ is unknown and must be estimated. In these cases, the estimate we use is s, the sample standard deviation, and with it we determine $s_{\bar{X}}$, the corresponding estimate of $\sigma_{\bar{X}}$. As with the confidence interval estimation, explained in Chapter 8, when we use $s_{\bar{X}}$ as an estimate of the standard error of the mean, $\sigma_{\bar{X}}$, we must use the t-distribution instead of the normal distribution when determining critical values or regions. All other procedures and concepts in testing hypotheses remain exactly the same as when we know σ. Using the steps for hypothesis testing that were previously outlined, we can summarize the one-tailed hypothesis test when σ is unknown.

Hypothesis: Population mean is equal to a specified number; σ is unknown. One-tailed test, alternative $\mu > \mu_0$.

1. State the goal or purpose of the experiment.
2. State the hypothesis and its alternative(s).

H_0: $\mu \leqslant \mu_0$
H_A: $\mu > \mu_0$

3. Decide on the level of significance α. Carefully choose α.
4. Select a sample, collect necessary data, and compute the statistics needed: $\bar{X}$ and s.
5. Determine the critical region or values of the sampling distribution which will cause the rejection of the hypothesis. After finding $t = (\bar{X} - \mu_0)/(s/\sqrt{n})$, reject the hypothesis if t is greater than $t_{(1-\alpha),(n-1)}$.
6. Make a statement of acceptance or rejection of the hypothesis, including the level of α.
7. State the resultant conclusion in terms of the experiment.

Hypothesis: Population mean is equal to a specified number, σ is unknown. One-tailed alternative $\mu < \mu_0$.

This, of course, is exactly the same as the immediately preceding hypothesis test with the following modifications:

2. H_0: $\mu \geqslant \mu_0$
H_A: $\mu < \mu_0$

5. After finding

$$t = \frac{\bar{X} - \mu_0}{s/\sqrt{n}}$$

reject the hypothesis if $t < t_{(\alpha),(n-1)}$.

Example 1

1. Assume that we have determined through experience that before learning the balance required in a handstand, an individual must be able to support his own body weight with his arms for more than 10 sec. We are interested in determining whether the eighth-grade boys (there are 500 of them) in our school are, on the average, ready to be taught the handstand. A test in which the student stands on his hands in an inverted position with the instructor providing the needed stability for as long as possible is given to 25 randomly selected eighth-grade boys. Results from that test yield $\bar{X} = 11.1$ sec and $s = 3.0$. Do we have evidence enough to conclude that, on the average, the students are ready to learn the handstand?

SOLUTION

2. H_0: $\mu \leqslant 10$ sec

   H_A: $\mu > 10$ sec

3. Since there is a safety factor involved, we would want our type I error to be rather small, so we choose $\alpha = 0.025$.
4. For the sample of size $n = 25$,

$$\bar{X} = 11.1 \quad \text{and} \quad s = 3.0$$

5. The calculated

$$t = \frac{(11.1 - 10.0)}{3.0/\sqrt{25}} = \frac{1.1}{0.6} = 1.833$$

and $t_{0.975,(24)} = 2.064$.

6. Since $t < t_{0.975,(24)}$, we are unable to reject the hypothesis H_0: $\mu \leqslant 10$ at the 2.5% level of significance.
7. We conclude that our students, on the average, are not ready to be taught the handstand.

For any two-tailed hypothesis when σ is unknown we have:

Hypothesis: Population mean is equal to a specified value; σ is unknown. Two-tailed test, alternative $\mu \neq \mu_0$.

The test of this hypothesis differs from previous ones in only steps 2 and 5:

2. H_0: $\mu = \mu_0$

   H_A: $\mu \neq \mu_0$

5. After finding

$$t = \frac{\bar{X} - \mu_0}{s\sqrt{n}}$$

If $t_{(\alpha/2),(n-1)} > t > t_{(1-\alpha/2),(n-1)}$, we reject the hypothesis.

Example 2

1. We wish to check on the error of our oxygen analyzer. We have calibration gas that has an exactly known concentration of oxygen, namely 16%. During normal use of our machine over a period of time, we take readings on 16 samples of this gas. These readings are assumed to be a random sample from all possible readings from our machine. The average of these readings is 15.85% with a variance of 0.090. Does our machine have an error in the readings it gives?

2. Because we are certainly interested in errors in either direction, we form the hypotheses:

H_0: $\mu = 16.0$
H_A: $\mu \neq 16.0$

3. To be sure of the accuracy of our machine, we choose a rather large α, namely $\alpha = 0.10$.

4. For a sample size $n = 16$,

$\bar{X} = 15.85$
$s = 0.3$

5. Our calculated

$$t = \frac{(15.85 - 16)}{\sqrt{0.09/16}}$$

$$= \frac{-0.15}{0.075} = -2.000$$

and

$$t_{0.05,(15)} = -1.753$$

and

$$t_{0.95,(15)} = 1.753.$$

6. Since $t < t_{0.05,(15)}$, or $-2.000 < -1.753$, we reject the hypothesis H_0: $\mu = 16$ at the 0.10 level of significance.

7. Our oxygen analyzer gives recordings for 16% oxygen content gas which are significantly lower than 16%.

Exercises

In all of the problems below that require the test of a hypothesis, use the seven-step outline provided in the preceding section.

1. A random sample of 64 senior high school girls had a mean score of 12.5 sec and a standard deviation of 1.2 sec in the 100-yd dash.
   a. At the 5% level of significance, test the hypothesis that the mean performance of high school girls in the 100-yd dash is 12.2 sec against an alternative hypothesis that the mean is not 12.2 sec.
   b. What is the probability that you will commit a type I error?
   c. Describe what a type I error would be in this case.
   d. Describe what a type II error would be.
   e. Describe what the power of this test would mean.

2. A random sample ($n = 50$) was drawn from graduate male physical education students. The researcher was interested in determining if the reaction time of graduate male physical educators was superior to a normative group. The mean reaction time, in milliseconds, for the normative group was 13 msec and variance was 9.8. The mean performance of the graduate student sample was 12 msec.
   a. Using $\alpha = 0.01$, decide whether the reaction time of graduate male physical education students is significantly superior to the reaction time of the normative group.
   b. State the consequences of a type I error.
   c. State the consequences of a type II error.

3. Assume that the average age at the time of marriage in the United States is 22.3 yr. We would like to determine if physical educators that get married follow this same pattern. We select a random sample of 75 married physical educators and find that the average age of marriage was 24 yr with a standard deviation of 2.89. Using $\alpha = 0.10$, should we conclude that physical educators are different from the rest of the population on this variable?

4. We have carefully observed over the years that the average life of a handball for activity class use is 18 class days. A salesman for a particular company proclaims that for no extra cost he can sell us a different brand of balls that last for more than 18 days. In support of his contention he gives us two dozen of his company's handballs to test. We find that the mean life of these balls is 20 days with a standard deviation of 3.5. Assuming that the two dozen balls were randomly selected from the manufacturing line, let $\alpha = 0.05$:
   a. Determine the truth of the salesman's statement.
   b. How would the salesman set up the hypothesis if he were to test his statement? Why?

5. The average grade assigned by instructors at some university is 2.20 (A $= 4.0$). The administration has accused the Health, Physical Education, and Recreation Department of giving out higher grades than the rest of the faculty. In hopes of refuting this statement, the department selects a random sample of 20 grades given in health, physical education, and recreation classes. The grades randomly selected are listed below:

A, B, B, A, C, E, D, A, C, B,
D, A, A, B, C, A, C, B, A, A

   a. Are we able to provide evidence contrary to the administration's accusations? Use $\alpha = 0.10$.
   b. Why might we want to set α much lower, say $\alpha = 0.001$, than we did in (a)?
   c. Explain why the way we state our hypothesis is important.

6. To determine if there is an error in the recordings of a dynamometer when the recordings are close to 100 lb, we suspend a weight of precisely 100 lb from the dynamometer. We then record the weight indicated by the dynamometer on 13 separate occasions. At $\alpha = 0.01$, determine if the dynamometer gives on the average erroneous readings.

$$101, 103, 99, 100, 98, 102, 100,$$
$$101, 103, 98, 97, 100, 101$$

9.4   HYPOTHESIS TESTING OF MEANS: TWO POPULATIONS

In much of our research, we are concerned with comparing the mean of one population with the mean of another population rather than comparing the mean of one population with some specified value. For example, we need to compare two populations if we want to compare two teaching methods, the effects of two different training programs on strength, or the difference between the effects of massed practice and distributed practice in learning motor skill. These kinds of studies may have one group or sample, called the *control group*, that receives no program or treatment, and an *experimental group* or sample that receives the program or treatment of interest. Each group may receive a specified treatment if we are interested in comparing two treatments.

Procedures for testing hypotheses that are concerned with the equality of two populations are essentially the same as those used for testing hypotheses about one population. We still have one-sided and two-sided tests, and we either know the population standard deviation or have to estimate it with sample statistics. Additionally, the concepts presented earlier concerning type I and type II errors also apply to hypothesis testing when two populations are involved. However, we will discuss a few possibilities that arise when there are two groups rather than one.

The basic hypothesis tested will be $H_0: \mu_1 = \mu_2$ or the algebraic equivalent $H_0: \mu_1 - \mu_2 = 0$. The sampling distribution we use for hypothesis testing of means from two populations is the sampling distribution of the difference of sample means, $\bar{X}_1 - \bar{X}_2$, which has as its mean the difference of population means $\mu_1 - \mu_2$, and the variance $(\sigma_1^2/n_1) + (\sigma_2^2/n_2)$. We assume that this distribution is normal, either as a result of the original populations being normally distributed or, if this is not the case, as a result of our invoking the central limit theorem. We may also assume for our present discussion that the individuals composing the two groups were independently selected. This permits us to assume that the scores attained by the members of one sample have no effect on the scores attained by those in the other sample.

As before, a slight adjustment will have to be made in hypothesis statements for one-sided tests. The outline used previously will continue to serve us well in presenting the various hypotheses about two population means.

Hypothesis: The means of two populations are equal; σ_1 and σ_2 known. One-tailed test; alternative $\mu_1 > \mu_2$.

1. State the goal or purpose of the experiment.
2. State the hypothesis and its alternative(s).

H_0: $\mu_1 \leqslant \mu_2$

H_A: $\mu_1 > \mu_2$

3. Decide on the level of significance α.
4. Select two samples, collect necessary data, and compute the statistics needed:

   $\bar{X}_1$ and $\bar{X}_2$, the means of the two samples.
5. Determine the critical region or values, those values of the distribution that will cause the rejection of the hypothesis. Use the test statistic

$$Z = \frac{\bar{X}_1 - \bar{X}_2}{\sqrt{(\sigma_1^2/n_1) + (\sigma_2^2/n_2)}}$$

and reject the hypothesis if $Z > Z_{1-\alpha}$. Note that if σ_1^2 and σ_2^2 are the same, say equal to σ^2, then we can more easily obtain

$$Z = \frac{\bar{X}_1 - \bar{X}_2}{\sigma\sqrt{(1/n_1) + (1/n_2)}}$$

6. Make a statement of acceptance or rejection of the hypothesis, including the level of α.
7. State the resultant conclusion in the terms of the experiment.

It is not necessary to restate the procedures for the one-sided alternative, $\mu_1 < \mu_2$, if we adopt the convention of always identifying the population mean suspected to be larger as μ_1.

Example 3

1. We wish to determine if a new method of teaching tennis ("by discovery") is superior to traditional methods of instruction. We randomly assign 15 students to a class which we teach by "discovery" and 18 to a class which we teach "traditionally." At the end of the class, we give all students a standardized skills test, which we know has a $\sigma = 20$. We find that the "discovery" class has a sample mean $\bar{X}_1 = 78$ and the traditional class a sample mean $\bar{X}_2 = 70$. Do we have sufficient evidence to conclude that the "discovery" method is superior to the "traditional" approach?
2. So that we don't declare that the "discovery" method is superior when in fact it is not (type I error), we state the hypothesis and its alternative as:

H_0: $\mu_1 \leqslant \mu_2$

H_A: $\mu_1 > \mu_2$

where μ_1 is the population mean of the discovery group.

3. Choose $\alpha = 0.10$. (This is done to reemphasize that there is nothing sacred about 0.05 and 0.01.)
4. For the discovery class of $n_1 = 15$, $\bar{X}_1 = 78$; for the traditional class of $n_2 = 18$, $\bar{X}_2 = 70$. We are given that $\sigma_1 = \sigma_2 = 20$.
5. The critical value for $\alpha = 0.10$ is $Z_{0.10} = 1.280$. Our

$$Z = \frac{78 - 70}{20\sqrt{\frac{1}{15} + \frac{1}{18}}} = \frac{8}{20\sqrt{0.1222}}$$

$$= \frac{8}{6.992}$$

$$= 1.144$$

6. Since $Z < Z_{0.10}$, or $1.144 < 1.28$, we have insufficient evidence at the 0.10 level of significance to reject the hypothesis $H_0: \mu_1 \leqslant \mu_2$.
7. We are unable to conclude that the "discovery" method of teaching tennis is significantly superior to the "traditional" method.

For two-sided hypotheses we have:

Hypothesis: The means of two populations are equal; σ_1 and σ_2 known. Two-sided test, alternatives are $\mu_1 > \mu_2$ and $\mu_1 < \mu_2$.

All steps in our outline remain the same as before except for steps 2 and 5.

2. $H_0: \quad \mu_1 = \mu_2$

$\quad H_A: \quad \mu_1 \neq \mu_2$

5. Using the test statistic

$$Z = \frac{\bar{X}_1 - \bar{X}_2}{\sqrt{(\sigma_1{}^2/n_1) + (\sigma_2{}^2/n_2)}}$$

reject the hypothesis if

$$Z_{\alpha/2} > Z > Z_{1-\alpha/2}$$

Example 4

1. We wish to use a standardized personality test to compare the extent of "extroversion" of high school individual sport athletes with high school team-sport athletes. We randomly select 20 boys from each group and administer the test to them. (A high score indicates extroversion.) The average extroversion score for the individual sport athletes is found to be $\bar{X}_1 = 48$, while for the team-sport athletes $\bar{X}_2 = 58$. We know the population standard deviation for this measure is 16. Is there a significant difference between individual sport high school athletes and team sport high school athletes in their expressed extroversion?

2. H_0: $\mu_1 = \mu_2$

   H_A: $\mu_1 \neq \mu_2$

   with $\sigma_1 = \sigma_2 = 16$.

3. Choose $\alpha = 0.05$.

4. $\bar{X}_1 = 48$, $n_1 = 20$ (individual sport athletes)

   $\bar{X}_2 = 58$, $n_2 = 20$ (team sport athletes)

5. The critical values for $\alpha = 0.05$ are $Z_{0.025} = -1.960$ and $Z_{0.975} = 1.960$. Our calculated

$$Z = \frac{58 - 48}{16\sqrt{\frac{1}{20} + \frac{1}{20}}} = \frac{10}{16(0.31623)} = 1.976$$

6. Since $Z > Z_{0.975}$, we reject the hypothesis H_0: $\mu_1 = \mu_2$ at the 0.05 level of significance.

7. The team-sport athletes are significantly more extroverted than the individual-sport athletes.

9.5   HYPOTHESIS TESTING OF TWO POPULATION MEANS WHEN POPULATION VARIANCES ARE UNKNOWN

We often have an experimental setup that requires our testing a hypothesis about the equality of two population means when the population variances are unknown. Similar to the situation when only one population is involved, we use sample statistics to estimate the population variance. More specifically, as shown in Chapter 8, we use

$$s_p^2 = \frac{(n_1 - 1)s_1^2 + (n_2 - 1)s_2^2}{n_1 + n_2 - 2} \tag{9.4}$$

as the pooled estimate of the population variance σ^2 with s_1^2 and s_2^2 the variances of the two samples. In so doing, we assume that the variances of the two populations under consideration are equal ($\sigma_1^2 = \sigma_2^2 = \sigma^2$). If this assumption is not quite met, neither α nor β is seriously affected. We can go ahead and test our hypothesis using the procedures outlined. Being able to do this allows us to say that the hypothesis test is robust *against minor violations of the assumption of equal variances*.

When using the pooled estimate of the variance, we must use t with $(n_1 + n_2 - 2)$ d.f. instead of the normal distribution to find critical values for testing a hypothesis. Of course, we can again have one-sided or two-sided alternatives to our null hypothesis.

For a one-tailed test, we have:

Hypothesis: The means of two populations are equal; σ_1 and σ_2 are unknown, but assumed to be equal. One-tailed alternative, $\mu_1 > \mu_2$.

1. State the goal or purpose of the experiment.
2. State the hypothesis and its alternative(s).

H_0: $\mu_1 \leqslant \mu_2$

H_A: $\mu_1 > \mu_2$

3. Decide on the level of significance α.
4. Select samples, collect necessary data, and compute the statistics needed. Compute $\bar{X}_1$, $\bar{X}_2$, $s_1{}^2$, $s_2{}^2$, and

$$s_p{}^2 = \frac{(n_1 - 1)s_1{}^2 + (n_2 - 1)s_2{}^2}{- \quad n_1 + n_2\,2}$$

5. Determine the critical region or values, those values of the distribution that will cause the rejection of the hypothesis. Using the test statistic

$$t = \frac{\bar{X}_1 - \bar{X}_2}{s_p\sqrt{(1/n_1) + (1/n_2)}}$$

reject the hypothesis if $t > t_{(1-\alpha),(n_1+n_2-2)}$.
6. Make a statement of acceptance or rejection of the hypothesis, including the level of α.
7. State the resultant conclusion in the terms of the experiment.

As before, we need not discuss the other one-tailed alternative since μ_1 and μ_2 can be reversed.

Example 5

1. Assume that we are considering buying a new oxygen analyzer. The new machine supposedly reports values as rapidly as our machine, and is more accurate in determining percent of oxygen. We have been loaned this new analyzer for one week to determine whether it is more accurate than our old machine. We have 27 air bags that have predetermined percentages of oxygen; we assign 13 of these bags to our machine, the remaining 14 to the new machine, and we find the average percent of error for each of the analyzers. If the mean amount of error for our analyzer is $\bar{X}_1 = 0.060\%$, with $s_1 = 0.010$, and for the new analyzer the mean error is $\bar{X}_2 = 0.050\%$, with $s_2 = 0.015$, should we believe the purported claim?
2. Since new machines are expensive we want to be fairly certain that a new machine is superior before we spend our money on it. Thus,

H_0: $\mu_1 \leqslant \mu_2$

H_A: $\mu_1 > \mu_2$

where μ_1 is the population mean for our old analyzer, and μ_2 is the population mean for the new analyzer. Keep in mind that a large mean indicates an inaccurate analyzer.
3. Let $\alpha = 0.05$.

4. We find that for our old analyzer, $n_1 = 13$, $\bar{X}_1 = 0.060$, and $s_1 = 0.010$. For the new analyzer, $n_2 = 14$, $\bar{X}_2 = 0.050$, $s_2 = 0.015$, and

$$s_p^2 = \frac{(n_1 - 1)s_1^2 + (n_2 - 1)s_2^2}{n_1 + n_2 - 2}$$

$$= \frac{12(0.0001) + 13(0.000225)}{13 + 14 - 2} = \frac{0.004125}{25} = 0.000165$$

$$s_p = \sqrt{0.000165} = 0.012845$$

5. The critical value for $\alpha = 0.05$ is $t_{0.95,(25)} = 1.708$. Our

$$t = \frac{0.06 - 0.05}{0.012845\sqrt{\frac{1}{13} + \frac{1}{14}}}$$

$$= \frac{0.01}{0.012845\sqrt{0.148352}} = \frac{0.01}{0.004947} = 2.021$$

6. Since $t > t_{0.95,(25)}$, or $2.021 > 1.708$, we reject the hypothesis at the 0.05 level of significance.

7. We conclude that our machine has a significantly greater average error than the new machine. Therefore, we should consider buying the new machine.

For two-tailed tests we have the following:

Hypothesis: The means of two populations are equal; σ_1 and σ_2 are unknown, but assumed to be equal. Two-tailed alternative is $\mu_1 \neq \mu_2$.

The only changes in procedure from the previous hypothesis are in steps 2 and 5.

2. H_0: $\mu_1 = \mu_2$

  H_A: $\mu_1 \neq \mu_2$

5. Using the test statistic

$$t = \frac{\bar{X}_1 - \bar{X}_2}{s_p\sqrt{(1/n_1) + (1/n_2)}}$$

reject the hypothesis if

$$t_{(\alpha/2),(n_1 + n_2 - 2)} > t > t_{(1 - \alpha/2),(n_1 + n_2 - 2)}$$

Example 6

1. We want to determine if 40–45-year-old men who have exercised regularly for at least five years have a lower serum cholesterol count than men of the same age who have been sedentary for at least five years. We randomly select 25 adult males from each of the populations identified and find the means and variances of cholesterol count for each population.

2. Since we are interested in a difference of cholesterol count favoring either group, our hypothesis and its alternatives are:

H_0: $\mu_1 = \mu_2$

H_A: $\mu_1 \neq \mu_2$

3. Choose $\alpha = 0.01$.
4. Assume that we find:

$$\bar{X}_1 = 244, \quad s_1 = 30 \quad \text{(exercise group, } n_1 = 25\text{)}$$
$$\bar{X}_2 = 236, \quad s_2 = 40 \quad \text{(nonexercise group, } n_2 = 25\text{)}$$

We calculate

$$s_p{}^2 = \frac{[(24)900] + [24(1600)]}{48} = 1250$$

$$s_p = 35.214$$

Note that when we have equal size samples, $s_p{}^2$ is the average of the two sample variances or

$$s_p{}^2 = \frac{s_1{}^2 + s_2{}^2}{2}$$

5. The critical values for $\alpha = 0.01$ are $t_{0.005, (48)} = -2.681$ and $t_{0.995, (48)} = 2.681$. Our calculated

$$t = \frac{236 - 244}{35.214\sqrt{\frac{1}{25} + \frac{1}{25}}}$$

$$= \frac{-8}{35.214(0.6325)}$$

$$= -0.3591$$

6. Since $t_{0.995} > t > t_{0.005}$, or $-0.3591 > -2.681$, we cannot reject the hypothesis at the 0.01 level of significance.
7. We are unable to conclude that any significant difference exists in cholesterol count between exercising and nonexercising adult males, ages 40–45.

Exercises

7. We want to establish whether alcohol affects a driver's braking time. We randomly select 24 drivers and assign 12 to an experimental group and the remaining 12 to a control group. Each member of the experimental group is given a small amount of alcohol intravenously and then is given a response-time test on a simulated car apparatus. The control group is given the test at approximately the same time. The mean performances of the two groups are:
Experimental group

$$\bar{X}_1 = 132 \text{ msec}$$

Control group

$$\bar{X}_2 = 120 \text{ msec}$$

It is known from previous work that the population variance for performance on the machine is 27.

  a. Is there evidence that alcohol adversely affects one's braking response time? (Use $\alpha = 0.001$.)

  b Why is the way we state our hypothesis important?

  c. What are the practical consequences of a type I error? Of a type II error?

  d. Was the level of α reasonable? Why or why not?

8. To determine if men and women health, physical education, and recreation majors at our institution perform differently on the quantitative portion of the Graduate Record Exam, we select a random sample of 15 men and 10 women. Their average GRE scores are found to be:

$$\text{Men } \bar{X}_1 = 512$$
$$\text{Women } \bar{X}_2 = 516$$

(The population standard deviation of the GRE is 100.) If we let $\alpha = 0.05$, what conclusion can be made?

9. The following are the riding times, in seconds, of all-out efforts on a bicycle ergometer of two groups of male subjects. The two randomly selected groups have just completed different training programs.

Group A				Group B			
179	121	115	268	136	194	99	161
83	124	99	193	62	81	76	143
198	52	104	119	133	58	214	101
129	59	76	190	76	77	94	74
204	103	123	55	134	91	152	57

Can either program be deemed superior? Use $\alpha = 0.05$.

10. We are thinking about incorporating an isometric program in our football program. We randomly assign 10 of our players to the isometric program and randomly select 10 other players to serve as controls. The results of a player rating scale determined by the coaching staff at the end of the season are listed below.

Isometric Group	Control Group
80	84
65	75
85	81
75	67
91	86
88	90
69	72
83	82
77	63
86	78

Is there evidence enough for us to include the isometric program for the whole team next year? Use $\alpha = 0.025$.

9.6 HYPOTHESIS TESTING OF TWO MEANS WHEN OBSERVATIONS ARE DEPENDENT

In an experiment involving two populations when we select two samples and give the experimental treatment to one sample and assign the other sample to be the control group, there is always the danger that a difference, whether found or not found, may be affected by certain extraneous factors. For example, suppose we select two groups of adult males for the purpose of comparing the cardiovascular effects of a fitness program with the effects of a sedentary life. We may find a significant difference between the two groups, but it is possible that this difference is caused by something other than the effects of the two programs. If the two groups were dissimilar in terms of their ages, their smoking habits, their physical condition, or any other extraneous factors, then the difference between the two groups might not be due to the difference between the two programs. The reverse situation is also possible; that is, there could be a significant difference in the effects of the two programs, but this difference could be counterbalanced by one of the factors described above.

To overcome this problem, we could select subjects in pairs and make sure that the members of each pair were matched on one, two, or many of these factors. These pairs would then be split, with one individual placed in the control group and his match placed in the experimental group. Thus our two groups would be dependent and we could be relatively sure that extraneous factors would not affect our findings at the conclusion of the experiment. This kind of experiment or design is referred to by a number of names, such as *matched groups design*, *paired comparisons*, and *dependent groups*.

When this kind of design is necessary for a study or experiment, our hypothesis remains exactly the same as when we have two independent samples. A disparity exists in the analysis of data leading to the test of the hypothesis. A difference score is obtained for each pair of subjects or objects. The method of analyzing these difference scores is the same as we would use when working with one population. More specifically, letting $d_i = X_{1i} - X_{2i}$ represent the difference between any pair of scores, we use the statistics d and s_d in testing $H_0: \mu_1 = \mu_2$, where

$$d = \frac{\sum\limits_{i=1}^{n} d_i}{n} \tag{9.5}$$

and

$$s_d{}^2 = \frac{\sum\limits_{i=1}^{n} (d_i - d)^2}{n - 1} \tag{9.6}$$

where n = number of pairs. We use

$$t = \frac{d}{s_d / \sqrt{n}} \tag{9.7}$$

as our test statistic and compare it with a t-distribution with $n - 1$ degrees of freedom (d.f.). It should be noted that when we work with differences in scores, there are only $(n - 1)$ d.f. instead of $n + n - 2 = (2n - 2)$ d.f. The latter is what we would have if we were working with independent samples. Therefore, in our test of the null hypothesis, fewer degrees of freedom are available in the paired comparisons design than would be available with the two independent groups design.

Example 7

1. In the adult fitness example cited above, assume that we have 10 pair of men who have been matched in age and smoking habits. One of the variables of interest is resting heart rate. The resting heart rates taken after the conclusion of the program for the two groups are listed below:

Pair No.	Fitness Group	Sedentary Group	Difference
1	65	71	6
2	72	72	0
3	78	76	−2
4	60	71	11
5	77	65	−12
6	74	88	14
7	65	79	14
8	70	75	5
9	58	68	10
10	76	76	0

Since we would expect our program to decrease heart rate, we will use a one-sided alternative hypothesis.

2. H_0: $\mu_1 \geqslant \mu_2$
   H_A: $\mu_1 < \mu_2$

   where μ_1 represents the population mean for the fitness group.
3. Let $\alpha = 0.05$.
4. From the table above

$$d = \frac{6 + 0 + (-2) + 11 + (-12) + 14 + 14 + 5 + 10 + 0}{10}$$

$$= \frac{46}{10}$$

$$= 4.6$$

$$s_d = \sqrt{\frac{\sum_{i=1}^{10} d_i^2 - [(\sum d_i)^2/n]}{n-1}}$$

$$= \sqrt{\frac{828 - 2116/10}{9}}$$

$$= \sqrt{\frac{828 - 211.6}{9}} = \sqrt{68.489} = 8.276$$

and

$$s_d = \frac{8.276}{\sqrt{10}}$$

$$= 2.617$$

5. The critical value for $\alpha = 0.05$ is $t_{0.95, (9)} = 1.833$. Our calculated $t = 4.6/2.617 = 1.758$.

6. Since $t < t_{0.95, (9)}$ or $1.758 < 1.833$, we are unable to reject the hypothesis at the 0.05 level of significance.

7. We are unable to conclude that the training program had a significant effect on the resting heart rate of adult men.

Another method commonly used to control extraneous variables is to allow subjects (or objects) to serve as their own controls. For example, if we are interested in finding out the immediate effect that smoking a cigarette has on systolic blood pressure, we might measure subjects' blood pressure while they are sitting, have them smoke a cigarette at a predetermined rate, and then measure their blood pressure again. We would be interested in the difference between the pretreatment and posttreatment systolic blood pressure. This method is sometimes called the *pre–post* or *before–after* design.

This kind of experiment is analyzed in precisely the same way as the paired comparisons. Obviously, there are many situations where this kind of study would not be feasible, such as in animal studies where the measured variables are determined after destroying the animal, studies in which two actual treatments are to be compared, studies where maturation plays an important role in scores obtained on the variable, and those studies where seasonal effects may occur. However, for an experiment in which only one treatment is of interest, this design does provide an excellent control of extraneous variables.

Example 8

1. Suppose we want to determine the immediate effect a one-day workshop on mental retardation has on participants' attitudes toward retardation. We select a random sample of 15 participants during registration at the workshop and administer to them an inventory designed to measure

attitude toward retardation. We administer an alternate form of the same inventory to the 15 subjects at the end of the workshop. Given the scores below, can we conclude that our workshop had an effect on the participants' attitudes? (Assume that a high score indicates a positive attitude.)

Selected Participant	Attitude Inventory Scores Before Workshop	Attitude Inventory Scores After Workshop	Difference
1.	77	80	3
2.	88	102	14
3.	90	90	0
4.	65	70	5
5.	69	75	6
6.	89	84	−5
7.	105	104	−1
8.	60	60	0
9.	82	90	8
10.	79	82	3
11.	79	86	7
12.	82	80	−2
13.	71	88	17
14.	68	78	10
15.	92	85	−7

2. Since we are interested in either a positive or negative change in attitude,

H_0: $\mu_1 = \mu_2$

H_A: $\mu_1 \neq \mu_2$

3. Chose $\alpha = 0.10$, since a type I error is not considered serious.
4. From our data, $\bar{d} = {}^{58}\!/_{15} = 3.867$,

$$s_d = \sqrt{\frac{856 - {}^{3364}\!/_{15}}{14}}$$

$$= \sqrt{45.124}$$

$$= 6.717$$

and

$$s_{\bar{d}} = \frac{6.717}{\sqrt{15}}$$

$$= 1.734$$

5. When $\alpha = 0.10$, the critical values are $t_{0.95,(14)} = \pm 1.761$ and $t_{0.05,(14)} = -1.761$. Our calculated $t = 3.867/1.734 = 2.230$.
6. Since $t > t_{0.95,(14)}$, or $2.230 > 1.761$, we reject the hypothesis at the 0.10 level of significance.
7. We conclude that there is evidence that the workshop had a significantly positive effect on the participants' attitudes toward mental retardation.

9.7   ESTIMATING NEEDED SAMPLE SIZE

Earlier in this chapter, it was stated that the only means for controlling α and β simultaneously was to increase the size of the sample. A logical question to ask is, "How large a sample is sufficient for a given situation?" While there is no simple or concrete answer to this question, some direction can be given for answering the question.

Before this question can be answered, however, you must know the desired hypothesis and its alternative(s) and you must be able to answer one or more of the questions below.

1. What significance level do you plan to choose?
2. What size of β do you feel can be tolerated?
3. What is the population variance(s)? If the variance is unknown, what is your estimate of the variance?
4. How large a difference do you consider to be of practical value?

The first two questions are rather straightforward since the values of α and β may be chosen. The population variance(s) may not be immediately known. However, quite good estimates can be obtained from the professional literature and/or a well-planned pilot study. The last question poses the greatest difficulty for the researcher since it involves a considerable amount of professional judgment. Note that question 4 emphasizes the importance of practicality. We need to determine the difference between pairs of population means or between the hypothesized population mean and one of its alternate values that is of "practical significance." That is, we must specify a value Δ such that

$$\Delta = \mu_1 - \mu_2 \tag{9.8}$$

or

$$\Delta = \mu_0 - \mu_A \tag{9.9}$$

Be cautioned here not to think that we are predetermining the results of our experiment. Remember we do not know what actually exists in the population(s) of interest. For example, following the seven-step approach for hypothesis testing, if

$$\bar{X}_1 - \bar{X}_2 \geqslant \Delta$$

we have assurance that the probability of observing these sample mean differences is no larger than the value of α selected. If, however,

$$\bar{X}_1 - \bar{X}_2 < \Delta$$

we have no way of knowing the probability that the results occurred by chance. We can provide assurance that the probability is no larger than the value of β selected if we apply the rules given in this section.

We are attempting to get the most information out of a study or experiment for the least amount of cost in terms of sample size.

Once the four questions above are answered, we have the information necessary for *approximating* the size of sample we should have. Table V, Appendix B, provides sample size estimates, given the information above. It is beyond the scope of this text to explain the derivation of the values given in these tables. If values for α and β other than those given are of interest, a professional statistician should be consulted.

Example 9 Consider the testing of $H_0: \mu \leqslant \mu_0$ against $H_A: \mu > \mu_0$ at the 1% level of significance. If we determine that the difference

$$\Delta = \mu_0 - \mu_A$$
$$= 4$$

is of practical significance for this study, σ is known or estimated to be 8, and we wish to set $\beta = 0.25$, then we have the information necessary to find the approximate sample size that is needed. In order to use the table, we need to find

$$D = \frac{\sigma}{\Delta} \tag{9.10}$$

which in this case is $D = 8/4 = 2$. From Table V, Appendix B we find that we need approximately 36 observations for a difference as large as 4 to be declared significant at the 0.01 level. We emphasize that this sample size is only an estimate and that the actual difference has yet to be found. However, if a difference of $(\bar{X} - \mu_0) \geqslant 4$ is observed, we have provided evidence that the risk of rejecting a true H_0 is no more than 1%. Conversely, if $(\bar{X} - \mu_0) < 4$, we have also provided evidence that the sample size selected will ensure a risk of no more than 25% of accepting a false H_0.

This technique has not been widely used in physical education, recreation, or health research. However, it is an extremely useful device if the necessary information is already available or if it can be intelligently estimated.

Example 10 Suppose we wish to compare the effects of two different teaching methods on rate of learning a fine motor task. From the literature and past experience, we estimate σ to be 0.7 and we feel that any difference greater than 1.3 sec is of practical importance. We choose $\alpha = 0.05$ to test $H_0: \mu_1 = \mu_2$ against $H_A: \mu_1 > \mu_2$, and can tolerate a β of only 0.01. Approximately what size sample for each group should we select?

The answers to the four questions asked previously are:

1. Our significance level is $\alpha = 0.05$.
2. We can tolerate a $\beta = 0.01$.
3. We estimate $\sigma_1 = \sigma_2 = \sigma$ to be 0.7.
4. The practical difference $= 1.3$.

Finding $D = \sigma/\Delta = 0.7/1.3 = 0.55$ we determine from Table V, Appendix B, that samples of at least 11 should be obtained for *each* teaching method. This procedure provides some assurance that the sample selected will adequately answer the question of interest with 5% and 1% risks of making type I and II errors, respectively.

9.8 RELATIONSHIP BETWEEN CONFIDENCE INTERVALS ON MEANS AND HYPOTHESIS TESTING OF MEANS

By now you may have noticed a great deal of similarity between the material presented in Chapter 8, "Confidence Intervals," and in the present chapter on hypothesis testing. Since these similarities often confuse the beginning student, the relationship and differences between these two procedures will be shown. All points will be illustrated with the simplest case, namely a case where there is one population and σ is known. The concepts presented here can be applied to other situations with relative ease.

In both hypothesis testing and the establishment of confidence intervals, we use the same sampling distribution, the sampling distribution of means. This distribution is represented with 95% of the area shaded in Figure 9.7.

The knowledge that 95% of all means will fall within the shaded area of the distribution and 5% outside provides the basis for both determining a 95% confidence interval and testing a hypothesis at $\alpha = 0.05$. In hypothesis testing, we know that a sample mean can be expected to fall outside the shaded area only 5% of the time, and thus when we have an $\bar{X}$ which does fall outside the shaded area we conclude that this $\bar{X}$ is not from the sampling distribution shown with population mean μ and we reject our hypothesis.

Taking the reverse of this, since we know that 95% of the sample means fall in the shaded area of the distribution, we know that 95% of the time when we establish the confidence interval around a sample mean $\bar{X}$, this interval will include the value of μ. We can see that although we do use the same

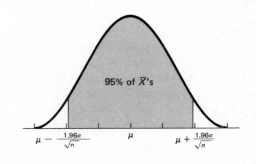

FIGURE 9.7

Sampling distribution of means

sampling distribution in confidence intervals and tests of hypotheses, our purposes for performing the two procedures differ. In establishing a confidence interval, we wish to *estimate a population parameter* using a sample statistic. In hypothesis testing, we wish to *make a decision about a population parameter*, using a sample statistic.

The direct connection between confidence intervals and tests of hypothesis explains why you will see in some research reports, and occasionally even in a basic statistics book, the statement that something is significant at a particular level of confidence. As we can now see, this is a technically incorrect statement since establishment of confidence intervals and the procedures of hypothesis testing, while using the same distribution, are different in their intent and values.

Exercises

11. Ten pairs of brothers, randomly selected, made the following scores on an achievement test. Do these results indicate that in general the older of two brothers will make a higher score? Let $\alpha = 0.05$.

Brother:	1	2	3	4	5	6	7	8	9	10
Older	86	79	67	92	65	75	61	77	91	68
Younger	80	81	60	87	71	71	56	75	93	67

12. The directors of a small private college find it necessary to increase the size of classes. A special film, utilizing advanced propaganda techniques, presents the advantages of larger-size classes. The attitude toward large classes of a randomly selected group of ten students is assessed before and after the presentation of this film. It is anticipated that more favorable attitudes (i.e., higher scores) will result from exposure to the film. Do the data below provide evidence of this? Let $\alpha = 0.10$.

Subject	Before	After
1	25	28
2.	23	19
3	30	34
4	7	10
5	3	6
6	22	26
7	12	13
8	30	47
9	5	16
10	14	9

13. The following data pertain to the increase in dynamic strength under two training conditions, A and B.

	Treatment A	Treatment B
Number of subjects	11	10
Mean increase in strength	7.04	8.80
Variance	73	64

    a. At the 5% level, is there a significant difference between these two mean increases in strength?

    b. Establish a 95% confidence interval for the difference between the two sample means.

    c. Describe the similarities and differences in the procedures (a) and (b).

14. After remedial work, a randomly selected group of 11 pupils showed the following changes in scores on a test:

$$+6, +1, +10, -2, +3, -1, +5, +2, -6, +8, +3$$

Is the claim justified that this remedial work is beneficial? Let $\alpha = 0.05$.

15. An attempt is made to compare the effectiveness of two teachers in a physical education class. Pairs of pupils are selected who are as nearly alike as possible in previous preparation and in other pertinent attributes. The data below are from a test given after completion of the class. Test the hypothesis that the teachers are, essentially, equally effective.

Pair:	1	2	3	4	5	6	7	8	9	10	11	12
Teacher A	41	35	28	39	40	24	26	32	29	41	36	34
Teacher B	36	37	32	38	43	20	22	32	25	42	30	35

Let $\alpha = 0.01$.

16. We are interested in determining whether the population of physical education, health, and recreation majors at our university differ in grade point average from the total student body average. We know that the university GPA $\sigma = 0.5$. If we choose $\alpha = 0.01$ and $\beta = 0.20$, and feel that a difference in GPA of 0.15 or more is of practical importance, how many majors should we randomly select to accomplish our purpose?

17. Suppose we are planning a study to determine how a two-year program affects intelligence. We will have a randomly selected control and experimental group. We would like to have an estimate of how large these groups must be to show a significant difference in the event that there is at least a 10-point difference between the two groups on an IQ test. We know that the population standard deviation for IQ is 16 and we are willing to accept errors of the magnitude $\alpha = 0.05$ and $\beta = 0.1$. What is the minimal number of subjects we should randomly select for each treatment group?

18. Using Exercise 1 of this chapter, construct:

    a. A 95% confidence interval for 100-yd dash performance of senior high school girls.

    b. How do the limits of this confidence interval compare to the critical values found previously? Indicate the similarities and differences between the two.

19. Repeat (a) and (b) of Exercise 18 with the information given in Exercise 3 of this chapter.

COMPUTER APPLICATION

From the fitness data on high school students recorded in Chapter 2, Exercise 14, assume that all data are from a random sample. Run a *t*-test program to determine if a significant difference exists on each of the fitness items:

20. between boys and girls.

21. between left-handed and right-handed students.

FORTRAN IV PROGRAM

t- Test for Difference Between Two Means

Col. 7
↓

```
      DIMENSIØN FMT(80)
      READ (5,100) M, N
      READ (5,101) H, T
      READ (5,102) FMT
      SUMX = 0.0
      SUMXSQ = 0.0
      DØ 50 J = 1, M
      READ (5,FMT) X
      SUMX = SUMX + X
  50  SUMXSQ = SUMXSQ + X**2
      L = M + N
      SUMY = 0.0
      SUMYSQ = 0.0
      DØ 60 J = M+1, L
      READ (5,FMT) X
      SUMY = SUMY + X
  60  SUMYSQ = SUMYSQ + X**2
      A = M
      B = N
      C = L
      XBAR = SUMX/A
      VARX = (SUMXSQ - (A*XBAR**2))/(A-1)
      SDX = SQRT(VARX)
      YBAR =   SUMY/B
      VARY = (SUMYSQ - (B*YBAR**2))/(B-1)
      SDY = SQRT(VARY)
      VARSP = ((A-1)*VARX + (B-1)*VARY)/(C-2)
      SEDSQ = VARSP*(1/A + 1/B)
      SEDIFF = SQRT(SEDSQ)
      DIFBAR = XBAR - YBAR
      CR = DIFBAR/SEDIFF
      WRITE (6,103) XBAR, VARX, SDX
      WRITE (6,104) YBAR, VARY, SDY
      WRITE (6,105) DIFBAR, SEDIFF
      WRITE (6,106) CR
      IF (H-2) 85, 80, 80
  80  CR = ABS(CR)
  85  IF (CR.GE.T) GØ TØ 86
      WRITE (6,107) T
      GØ TØ 110
  86  WRITE (6,108) T
      GØ TØ 110
 100  FØRMAT (2I2)
 101  FØRMAT (F1.0,F3.2)
 102  FØRMAT (80A1)
 103  FØRMAT (' ','MEANX =',F10.3,'VARX =',F10.3,'SDX =',F10.3)
 104  FØRMAT (' ','MEANY =',F10.3,'VARY =',F10.3,'SDY =',F10.3)
 105  FØRMAT (' ','MEAN DIFF =',F10.3,'STD ERR ØF DIF =',F10.3)
 106  FØRMAT (' ','ØBSERVED T =',F10.3)
 107  FØRMAT (' ','ACCEPT NULL HYPØ, ØBS T IS LESS THAN T =',F10.3)
 108  FØRMAT (' ','REJECT NULL HYPØ, ØBS T IS GREATER THAN T =',F10.3)
 110  STØP
      END
```

Order of cards:

1. System cards
2. Program deck
3. Sample sizes card
    Cols. 1, 2: Sample size for first group
       3, 4: Sample size for sec   d group
4. Alternative hypothesis and critic   value card
       Col. 1: Keypunch 1 if one-tail test
          Keypunch 2 if two-tail test
    Cols. 2–4: Keypunch critical t-value according to format statement 102
5. Data format card
6. Data cards for first group
7. Data cards for second group
8. Job termination card

Regression and Correlation Analysis

10.1 INTRODUCTION

The concept of estimation discussed in Chapter 8 may be employed to introduce the idea of regression and correlation analysis. Suppose we wish to estimate the grade point averages (GPA) of four individuals selected at random from the student body of a large university. Without any information about these individuals the most logical predictive GPA value, for each, is the value typically received by students at this university. For example, if the mean GPA is $\mu = 2.4$, then, in the absence of other information, the best guess for each student's GPA is 2.4.

Since this is an estimate, we recognize that the value 2.4 may be in error. The standard deviation of the population determines the degree of variability among individual GPA scores and is a logical measure of the error associated with using the mean as an estimate of each individual's GPA. If $\sigma = 0.7$, then we can be 95% confident that each individual's GPA is between 1.0 and 3.8. Of course, the reason we may make this statement is the fact that 95% of all students' GPA's are between these two limits. Thus the statement actually represents a confidence interval for the estimate of an individual's GPA score. Certainly, this statement provides us with little information beyond the recognizable fact that those individuals whose GPA's we requested are members of the student body at the university in question.

Suppose we determine that among the four students we selected, two were freshmen, one was a sophomore, and one a senior. What effect does this knowledge have on the estimated GPA's? We might now argue that the best guess for each individual is the GPA typically achieved by students with the same classification as the individual in question. For example, the best guess for a freshman is the GPA typically achieved by freshmen.

A pictorial representation of this situation is given in Figure 10.1. The graph portrays the probability distribution of the total student body and the probability distribution for each subgroup, freshmen through seniors. The best estimate and confidence intervals for each individual's GPA may now be given as:

Estimated GPA $= 2.1$ for freshmen 1 & 2: $\qquad P(1.3 \leqslant \text{GPA} \leqslant 2.9) = 95\%$

Estimated GPA $= 2.3$ for sophomore 1: $\qquad P(1.5 \leqslant \text{GPA} \leqslant 3.1) = 95\%$

Estimated GPA $= 2.7$ for senior 1: $\qquad P(1.9 \leqslant \text{GPA} \leqslant 3.5) = 95\%$

Notice that as we learn each student's classification, we shorten each confidence interval from 2.8 to 1.6 points. The reason, of course, is that for the university population $\sigma = 0.7$ while σ_F, σ_{So}, σ_J, and σ_S are all equal to only 0.4. Thus, the fact that different classifications of students have different mean GPA's "explains" part of the variability in GPA's observed for the total group.

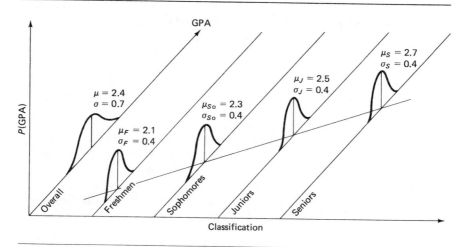

FIGURE 10.1

Distributions of university students' GPA's by classification

Suppose we assign numerals to the student classifications as follows: freshman $= 1$, sophomore $= 2$, junior $= 3$, senior $= 4$, and pair each classification numeral with its corresponding mean. This gives:

$$(1, 2.1); \quad (2, 2.3); \quad (3, 2.5); \quad (4, 2.7)$$

If these points are plotted in an (X, Y)-plane (Figure 10.2), we see that they all lie in a straight line. When the (X, Y) points lie in a straight line, we say

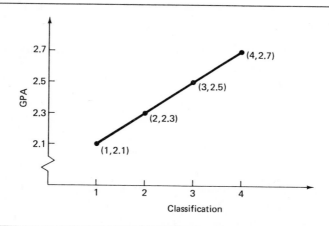

FIGURE 10.2

Graph of GPA means by classification

the variables X and Y are linearly related. Thus, the mean GPA's are linearly related to student classifications. This implies that part of the total variability in GPA's is explained by this linear relationship. We will return to the concept of "explained variance" later.

10.2 REGRESSION ANALYSIS

Regression analysis is the process of finding a line or curve that represents the functional relationship between two variables X and Y. In this chapter, we consider only the special case where a linear function may be used to describe the relationship.

We hypothesize that the following equation for a straight line describes the relationship between the variables X and Y.

$$Y = A + BX \tag{10.1}$$

Where A is the Y-intercept (i.e., the value of Y when $X = 0$) and B is the slope of the line (i.e., the ratio that indicates the unit change in Y corresponding to a unit change in X). Equation (10.1) provides a mathematical model describing the relationship between two variables. For example, the mathematical model describing the relationship between average GPA (μ_{GPA}) and student classification (C) is given by the equation

$$\mu_{GPA|C} = 1.9 + 0.2C$$

and simply indicates that the average GPA is expected to increase by 0.2 point with each change in student classification.

In general, we will not know the population parameters A and B in Eq. (10.1). Our problem is to use information from individual (X, Y) points to find the values of A and B.

The point (X_i, Y_i) will lie on the straight line defined by Eq. (10.1) if, and only if, its coordinates satisfy the equation of the line. That is, if (X_i, Y_i) lie on the line, then

$$Y_i = A + BX_i$$

or

$$Y_i - (A + BX_i) = 0$$

In general, all (X_i, Y_i) points will not lie on the line defined by Eq. (10.1). (Note, for example, that a distribution of GPA scores existed for each mean GPA–student classification coordinate.) The vertical distance from the line to any point P_i, defined by the coordinates (X_i, Y_i), will be denoted by e_i and may be determined by the equation

$$e_i = Y_i - (A + BX_i)$$

Graphically, this may be shown as in Figure 10.3. We may say that e_i represents the difference between the *observed* value Y_i and its *expected* value, $Y_i = A + BX_i$. In the context of estimation, the quantity e_i is often referred to as an *error of estimation* or *error of prediction*.

In view of the fact that, generally, not all (X, Y) points will lie in a straight line, the selection of a linear equation between X and Y, and therefore the

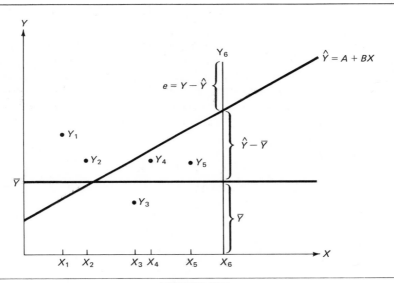

FIGURE 10.3

The partitions of an observed score

appropriate A and B values, may be made by "fitting the straight line" that is "nearest" every (X, Y) point. Another way of saying this is that we desire a straight line such that each e_i is as small as possible. A mathematically acceptable definition of the "nearest" line is provided by the *method of least squares*. This method chooses as the "nearest" line that one such that the sum of squares, $\sum_{i=1}^{n} e_i^2$, is a minimum. That is, the best fitted straight line is given when

$$\sum_{i=1}^{n} e_i^2 = \text{SSE}$$

$$= \sum_{i=1}^{n} [Y_i - (A + BX_i)]^2$$

$$= \text{minimum} \tag{10.2}$$

To minimize SSE giving appropriate values of A and B requires the use of differential calculus or at least some detailed algebra. We avoid this by simply stating that the values of A and B that minimize SSE are:

$$A = \bar{Y} - B\bar{X} \tag{10.3}$$

$$B = \frac{\sum (X - \bar{X})(Y - \bar{Y})}{\sum (X - \bar{X})^2}$$

$$= \frac{\sum XY - [(\sum X)(\sum Y)/N]}{\sum X^2 - [(\sum X)^2/N]} \tag{10.4}$$

Equations (10.3) and (10.4) provide the exact values of A and B when N represents the whole population. Because data from the whole population will seldom be available, we have to use a sample to provide estimates of A and B. We denote these estimates as a and b, respectively. Thus, employing techniques similar to those used to derive estimates of μ and σ, we find estimates of A and B based on a sample of size n.

$$a = \bar{Y} - b\bar{X} \tag{10.5}$$

$$b = \frac{\sum (X - \bar{X})(Y - \bar{Y})}{\sum (X - \bar{X})^2}$$

$$= \frac{\sum XY - [(\sum X)(\sum Y)/n]}{\sum X^2 - [(\sum X)^2/n]}$$

$$= \frac{\sum xy}{\sum x^2} \tag{10.6}$$

where $x = X - \bar{X}$ and $y = Y - \bar{Y}$.

Equations (10.5) and (10.6) provide the best fitting straight line to the sample data which represents an unbiased estimate of the population's best fitting straight line. That is,

$$\hat{Y} = a + bX \tag{10.7}$$

represents an unbiased estimate of Eq. (10.1). You will note that Eqs. (10.5) and (10.6) differ from Eqs. (10.3) and (10.4) only by the substitution of n for N.

Example 1   Determine the linear regression equation between maximal workload (X) in kpm/minute performed on the bicycle ergometer and maximal oxygen intake (Y) in millimeters/minute employing data obtained from the following 10 subjects:

Subjects:	1	2	3	4	5	6	7	8	9	10
Workload	1300	1700	1900	1700	1200	1500	1800	1500	1300	1700
Max VO_2	3400	3800	4400	4000	2900	3800	4200	3300	3000	4100

SOLUTION   For this set of data

$$n = 10$$

$\sum X = 15{,}600$	$\sum Y = 36{,}900$	$\sum XY = 58{,}600{,}000$
$\sum X^2 = 24{,}840{,}000$	$\sum Y^2 = 138{,}550{,}000$	$\sum xy = 1{,}036{,}000$
$\sum x^2 = 504{,}000$	$\sum y^2 = 2{,}389{,}000$	
$\bar{X} = 1560$	$\bar{Y} = 3690$	

giving

$$b = \frac{1{,}036{,}000}{504{,}000} = 2.0556$$

$$a = 3690 - (2.0556)(1560) = 483.26$$

and

$$\hat{Y} = 483 + 2.06X$$

The y-intercept $a = 483$, in practical terms, represents a correction factor needed because maximal workload and Max $\dot{V}O_2$ possess different scale metrics. The slope $b = 2.06$ may be interpreted as follows: For every 100 kpm/min increase in maximal workload there is an increase in Max $\dot{V}O_2$ of 206 ml/min.

The graph of the regression line describing the relationship is given in Figure 10.4.

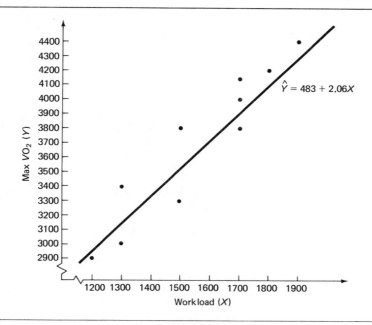

FIGURE 10.4

Scatterplot for Max VO_2–workload relationship

10.3 PARTITIONING THE TOTAL SUM OF SQUARES OF Y

Students of physical education, health, and recreation sometimes have difficulty in interpreting the linear relationship provided by a regression line. This section is presented to help ease that difficulty.

Graphically, an observed value of Y_i may be partitioned as shown previously in Figure 10.3 to give:

$$Y_i = \bar{Y} + (\hat{Y}_i - \bar{Y}) + (Y_i - \hat{Y}_i) \qquad (i = 1, 2, \ldots, n) \qquad (10.8)$$

where $\hat{Y}_i = A + BX_i$, the estimated Y_i value corresponding to the value X_i. In words, Eq. (10.8) states: The magnitude of the observed value Y_i may be explained by: (1) a part due to the mean, (2) an additional part due to the relationship between X and Y, and (3) a part that cannot be explained with the information given. For example, if the senior student's GPA was 3.0, see Figure 10.5, an explanation of this score using Eq. (10.8) gives:

2.4 points due to the overall mean GPA (i.e., $\bar{Y}$)

0.3 point due to the relationship between GPA and student's classification (i.e., $\hat{Y} - \bar{Y}$)

0.3 point which cannot be explained (i.e., $Y - \hat{Y}$, or e_i)

Suppose we rewrite Eq. (10.8) as follows:

$$Y_i - \bar{Y} = (\hat{Y}_i - \bar{Y}) + (Y_i - \hat{Y}_i) \qquad (10.9)$$

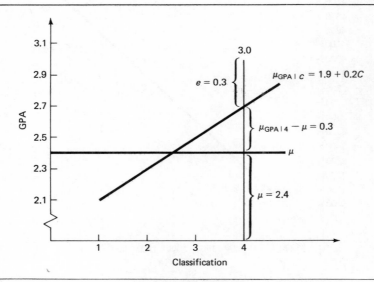

FIGURE 10.5

The partitions of GPA $= 3.0$ for a senior student

This gives the deviations of each observed Y-value from its mean on the left-hand side of the equation. Now, let us square both sides of Eq. (10.9) for every value Y_i and obtain the sum of these squares. This gives

$$\sum (Y_i - \bar{Y})^2 = \sum (\hat{Y}_i - \bar{Y})^2 + \sum (Y_i - \hat{Y}_i)^2 + 2 \sum (\hat{Y}_i - \bar{Y})(Y_i - \hat{Y}_i)$$

The quantity $\sum (\hat{Y}_i - \bar{Y})(Y_i - \hat{Y}_i)$ can be shown to be zero. This leaves

$$\sum (Y_i - \bar{Y})^2 = \sum (\hat{Y}_i - \bar{Y})^2 + \sum (Y_i - \hat{Y}_i)^2 \qquad (10.10)$$

In words, we have partitioned the total sum of squares for Y, $\sum (Y_i - \bar{Y})^2$, a measure of variability, into that source of variation in Y explained by the relationship between X and Y, $\sum (\hat{Y}_i - \bar{Y})^2$, and that part which still remains unexplained, $\sum (Y_i - \hat{Y})^2$. Stated another way, we can say that the variability of the Y-scores can be reduced by extracting the variability due to the relationship between X and Y. The reader should note that this is precisely what we did in the GPA–student classification example.

For convenience we may represent Eq. (10.10) as

$$\text{SST} = \text{SSR} + \text{SSE}$$

where SST is the total sum of squares, SSR is the sum of squares due to a linear relationship or regression, and SSE is the sum of squares due to error.

Figure 10.6(a), (b), and (c) provides graphic illustrations of the partitioning effect for no linear relationship, a perfect linear relationship, and a linear relationship when all (X, Y) points do not lie in a straight line. Figure 10.6(a) exhibits (X, Y) points showing no upward or downward trend. This indicates that the values of Y are not influenced by the values of X. Thus,

$$\text{SSR} = \sum (\hat{Y}_i - \bar{Y})^2 = 0$$

and

$$\text{SST} = \text{SSE}$$

or none of the variability of the Y-values can be explained by the relationship between X and Y.

In Figure 10.6(b), all the (X, Y) points lie in a straight line giving

$$\text{SSE} = 0$$

and

$$\text{SST} = \text{SSR}$$

implying that all the variability in the Y-values is explained by the relationship between X and Y. Finally, Figure 10.6(c), reproducing the data from Figure 10.3, provides the more general case. Since SSR and SSE are both

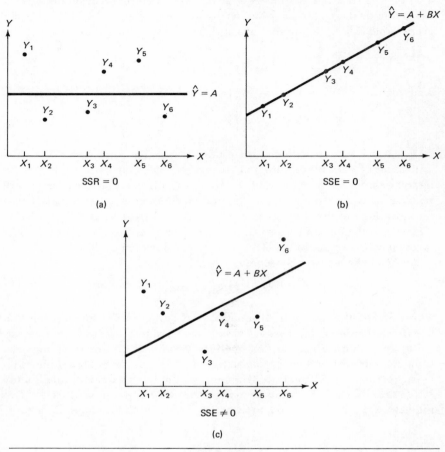

FIGURE 10.6

(a) SSR $= 0$. (b) SSE $= 0$. (c) SSE $\neq 0$ and SSR $\neq 0$

nonzero, we note that the linear relationship between X and Y permits us to reduce the total sum of squares by SSR; that is,

$$SSE = SST - SSR$$

The degrees of freedom for the total sum of squares, SST, is $n - 1$. Since SST was partitioned into SSR and SSE, it follows that its degrees of freedom should also be partitioned. This is precisely the case giving

$$n - 1 = 1 + (n - 2)$$

which denotes that SSR has 1 d.f. and SSE has $(n - 2)$ d.f. The importance of this partitioning in the analysis of the relationship between X and Y will be discussed later.

10.4   VARIANCES OF Y, a, AND b

The regression problem considers that for a given value of X, there is some particular distribution of Y-values. Our interest in estimating Y leads us to seek that linear relationship between X and Y which reduces the variability of Y-values among individuals or objects possessing a given value of X. We denote this variability by the term $\sigma_{Y|X}^2$. Note, for the GPA example, that $\sigma_{Y|X}^2 = 0.16$. The problem becomes simpler if the following assumptions are met:

1. The distribution of Y is normal for a given value of X.
2. The variance of the distribution of Y is the same for any given value of X.

The former assumption permits us to more easily derive confidence intervals on Y using $\hat{Y}$, and permits exact tests for some hypotheses of interest. The latter assumption simplifies the problem encountered when we estimate variances of the sampling distributions for $\hat{Y}$, a, and b.

Unlike the GPA example of Section 10.1, in general, we will not know the value of $\sigma_{Y|X}^2$. An estimate of $\sigma_{Y|X}^2$ provided from the sample data must be obtained. We logically label its estimate as $s_{Y|X}^2$. Since the regression line describing the relationship between X and Y "explains" part of the variability in Y, the part that is left "unexplained" should serve as the estimate of $\sigma_{Y|X}^2$. Thus,

$$s_{Y|X}^2 = \frac{\sum_{i=1}^{n} e_i^2}{n-2}$$

$$= \frac{\sum_{i=1}^{n} (Y_i - \hat{Y}_i)^2}{n-2} \tag{10.11}$$

should provide a good estimate of $\sigma_{Y|X}^2$. The logic for dividing the sum of squares of deviations by $n-2$ rather than n or $(n-1)$ is that use of the former makes Eq. (10.11) an unbiased estimate of $\sigma_{Y|X}^2$.

The reader will note that calculating the numerator of Eq. (10.11) requires computation of each $\hat{Y}_i$, using $\hat{Y}_i = a + bX_i$, which promises to be a very tedious procedure. A simpler approach is to use the formula

$$s_{Y|X}^2 = \frac{1}{n-2} \left[\sum_{i=1}^{n} (Y_i - \bar{Y})^2 - b \sum_{i=1}^{n} (X_i - \bar{X})(Y_i - \bar{Y}) \right]$$

$$= \frac{1}{n-2} \left[\sum y^2 - b \sum xy \right] \tag{10.12}$$

It should be easily recognized by now that the estimators a and b will vary depending on the particular random sample of size n selected. Suppose we denote the sample variances of a and b as $s_a{}^2$ and $s_b{}^2$, respectively. Then the formulae for computing these variances are given here without proof

$$s_a{}^2 = s_{Y|X}^2 \left(\frac{1}{n} + \frac{\bar{X}^2}{\sum x^2} \right) \tag{10.13}$$

and

$$s_b{}^2 = \frac{s_{Y|X}^2}{\sum x^2} \tag{10.14}$$

Example 2   Suppose we assume the data employed in Example 1 represent a random sample of college-age males from a large university. Then, employing the data given in that example, we find

$$s_{Y|X}^2 = \frac{1}{8}[(2,389,000) - (2.0556)(1,036,000)]$$
$$= 32,424.8$$

$$s_a{}^2 = 32,424.8 \left[\frac{1}{10} + \frac{(1560)^2}{504,000} \right]$$

$$= 159,805.63$$

and

$$s_b{}^2 = \frac{32,424.8}{504,000}$$

$$= 0.0643$$

A practical interpretation of each sample variance is best achieved by taking the square root of each.

This gives:

$$s_{Y|X} = 180.07$$
$$s_a = 399.7$$

and

$$s_b = 0.2536$$

The sample value $s_{Y|X} = 180.07$ indicates the magnitude $\hat{Y}$ is likely to be in error as an estimate of the true value Y. Since $s_Y = 515.21$, we see that the range of values likely to contain one's true Max $\dot{V}O_2$ value is considerably reduced by the knowledge of one's maximal workload.

Similarly, $s_a = 399.7$ provides a measure useful in deriving a confidence interval for the parameter A. Subjectively, it appears that s_a is quite large in comparison with the magnitude of the sample value a. In retrospect, it should be noted that if the estimation of A is of prime importance, the values of X should be selected during the planning stage so that $\bar{X} = 0$. In this way, more observations are used to estimate $Y = A$, and $s_a{}^2$ is as small as possible. (The latter may be verified by referring to Eq. (10.13).)

Finally, $s_b = 0.2536$ also indicates the degree of variability in the statistic b as an estimate of the parameter B. In our example, we may say with 95% confidence that for every 100 kpm/min increase in one's maximal workload there exists a corresponding increase in his Max $\dot{V}O_2$ between 147 and 264 ml.

INFERENCES ABOUT B, THE SLOPE OF THE REGRESSION LINE

The primary interest in studying the relationship between X and Y is to first determine if a relationship exists. It is only when a relationship exists that variability in Y can be reduced and in particular permit close estimates of random values of Y. Thus, we attempt to determine if the data selected present sufficient evidence to indicate that X and Y are, in fact, linearly related. If no relationship exists, then knowing an individual's score on X will not contribute any information toward an estimate of his score on Y. To show how this influences the equation for our regression line, let us use the fact that $a = \bar{Y} - b\bar{X}$ to rewrite Eq. (10.12) as

$$\hat{Y} = \bar{Y} + b(X - \bar{X}) \tag{10.15}$$

When no relationship exists, the estimated value of Y (i.e., $\hat{Y}$) should be the same regardless of the particular value of X, which implies that B must be zero. This gives

$$\hat{Y} = \bar{Y} + 0(X - \bar{X})$$

or

$$\hat{Y} = \bar{Y} \tag{10.16}$$

which is precisely the estimate used in the GPA example when no information on student classification was available. Thus, when no relationship between X and Y exists, Eq. (10.16) states that the estimated value of Y will be the estimated value of the population mean ($\bar{Y}$), regardless of the given value of X. An example of $\hat{Y} = \bar{Y}$ is given in Figure 10.6(a).

Since b is a random variable dependent on the sample points (X_i, Y_i) $(i = 1, 2, \ldots, n)$, we recognize that b may not be zero when the population value B is zero. A logical estimate of the variability in b is given by the sample variance s_b^2. If we assume that the variable Y is normally distributed, it follows that b is normally distributed (b is a linear function of the variable Y and a linear function of a normal variable is also normally distributed). Then the ratio

$$t = \frac{b - B}{s_b} \tag{10.17}$$

has a t-distribution with $n - 2$ degrees of freedom (d.f.) and may be used to test the hypothesis $H_0 : B = 0$. The $(n - 2)$ d.f. results because s_b^2 is based on SSE which has $(n - 2)$ d.f. In general, we note that any value B_0 may be hypothesized and a test of significance run. A particular B_0 should be suggested by the professional literature or, at least, selected in advance of selecting the sample data on which testing the hypothesis will be based.

The alternative hypothesis on B may be $H_A: B \neq B_0$, $H_A: B \leqslant B_0$, or $H_A: B \geqslant B_0$. When $H_A: B \neq B_0$ is specified, we use the two-tailed test as specified in Chapter 9. The basis for $H_A: B \neq 0$ is that, if a relationship exists, we have no prior basis for suggesting that B will be positive or negative. The other two alternative hypotheses suggest that we have some prior information regarding the slope of the regression line. For example, when $B = 0$ is hypothesized we may be interested in determining if a particular trend in the data exists, that is, if a positive or a negative relationship exists between X and Y. When $B > 0$ we note that the straight line describing the relationship between X and Y slants upward from left to right. This indicates that as values of X increase, values of Y also increase. When $B < 0$, the straight line slants downward from left to right, indicating that as values of X increase, values of Y decrease. These results are shown graphically In Figure 10.7. The relationship between vertical jump and the 50-yd dash provides an example of $B < 0$, while the relationship between oxygen intake and steady-state workload provides an example of $B > 0$.

Test of hypotheses may also be made on the y-intercept, A, using the ratio

$$t = \frac{a - A}{s_a} \tag{10.18}$$

which has a t-distribution with $(n - 2)$ d.f. for the same reasons given for (10.17).

Example 3   Test the hypothesis $H_0: A = 0$ and $H_0: B = 0$ for the data of Example 1.

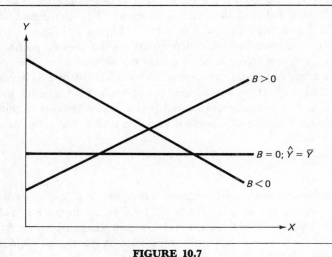

FIGURE 10.7

Regression lines for various values of B

SOLUTION With $H_0: A = 0$, we set $H_A: A > 0$, since negative Max $\dot{V}O_2$ values are not possible. Then, with $a = 483.26$ and $s_a = 399.7$, we find

$$t = \frac{483.26 - 0}{399.7} = 1.209$$

Using $\alpha = 0.05$ and $n = 10$ or d.f. $= 8$, we find from Table II, Appendix B, that

$$t_{0.95,8} = 1.860$$

and since $t < 1.860$, we accept the hypothesis $H_0 : A = 0$. It should be noted that this test is not very powerful due to the wide range of X-values considered in this example. Thus, as previously noted, s_a is inflated. This example should caution the reader not to draw conclusions before having carefully evaluated the total test situation. Subjectively, one would argue that the value $a = 483$ does contribute significantly to the estimate of Y, since to omit it, as suggested by accepting H_0, will reduce each Max $\dot{V}O_2$ by 483 ml.

To test the hypothesis $H_0 : B = 0$, we recall that $b = 2.0556$ and $s_b = 0.2536$, giving

$$t = \frac{2.0556}{0.2536}$$

$$= 8.106$$

and since $t > 1.860$ we reject $H_0 : B = 0$. We may then conclude that a positive linear relationship exists between maximal workload and Max $\dot{V}O_2$.

10.5 CORRELATION ANALYSIS

We recall from Eq. (10.7) that the quantity

$$\text{SSE} = \sum_{i=1}^{n} (Y_i - \hat{Y}_i)^2 \tag{10.19}$$

represented the unexplained portion of the total sum of squares in the Y variable. Thus, if SSE is large, we assume a weak relationship between X and Y because many individual Y-values apparently lie far from the regression line $\hat{Y} = a + bX$. Conversely, a small SSE implies that most Y-values lie close to the regression line.

This suggests that the quantity SSE may be used as an indication of the strength of the relationship between X and Y. The one drawback to this suggestion is the fact that SSE is expressed in the units of measurement on the variable Y. For example, a quantity measured in feet will produce one value for SSE, while the same measurements expressed in meters will produce another. Thus, no rule of thumb can be given for using SSE to interpret the strength of the relationship.

Suppose we divide SSE by SST, giving

$$\frac{\text{SSE}}{\text{SST}} = \frac{\sum (Y_i - \hat{Y}_i)^2}{\sum (\bar{Y}_i - \bar{Y})^2} \tag{10.20}$$

Then, because both SSE and SST have the same units of measurement, the units cancel out when the ratio of the two is taken. Notice that the ratio formed in Eq. (10.20) will always have a value between zero and one, for SSE can never be less than zero nor greater than SST. When SSE/SST is zero, all the points in the (X, Y)-plane lie on the line $\hat{Y} = a + bX$, indicating a perfect relationship between X and Y. When SSE/SST is one, the points form no pattern with the line $\hat{Y} = a + bX$, implying that no linear relationship exists between X and Y. Thus, as the ratio SSE/SST increases from zero to one, the relationship between X and Y decreases. To make this statement less confusing, let us subtract the quantity SSE/SST from one. This gives

$$r^2 = 1 - \frac{\text{SSE}}{\text{SST}} \tag{10.21}$$

where r^2 is used simply to denote the quantity on the right-hand side of Eq. (10.21). This equation gives us the strength of the linear relationship between the variables X and Y. When $r^2 = 0$, there is no relationship, and when $r^2 = 1$, a perfect relationship exists. Thus,

$$0 \leqslant r^2 \leqslant 1 \tag{10.22}$$

To provide a formula that is useful in calculating the value of r^2 from sample values, and to obtain a practical interpretation of r^2, let us rewrite Eq. (10.21) as follows:

$$r^2 = \frac{\text{SST} - \text{SSE}}{\text{SST}} \tag{10.23}$$

Recall from Eq. (10.7) that

$$\text{SST} - \text{SSE} = \text{SSR}$$

Making this substitution in Eq. (10.23) gives

$$r^2 = \frac{\text{SSR}}{\text{SST}} \tag{10.24}$$

Equation (10.24) permits us to interpret r^2 as *the amount of variation in the variable Y (SST) that can be explained by the linear relationship between the variable Y and the variable X (SSR)*. In addition to this description of r^2, by using previous values outlined for SSR and SST, we may show that

$$r^2 = b^2 \frac{\sum (X - \bar{X})^2}{\sum (Y - \bar{Y})^2}$$

$$= b^2 \frac{\sum x^2}{\sum y^2} \tag{10.25}$$

and that

$$r = b \sqrt{\frac{\sum x^2}{\sum y^2}} \qquad (10.26)$$

The quantity r defined by Eq. (10.26) is popularly referred to as the *coefficient of linear correlation* between X and Y. The fact that the quantity under the radical is always positive implies that r has the same sign as b. Thus, when r is negative, a negative relationship exists between X and Y, and when r is positive, a positive relationship exists between X and Y. The range of values for r may be summarized as follows:

$$-1 \leqslant r \leqslant 1 \qquad (10.27)$$

where $r = -1$ represents a perfect negative linear relationship and $r = +1$ represents a perfect positive linear relationship.

Quite frequently we may wish to compute the value of r before determining the value of b. In particular, when $r = 0$, we would not have need for the regression line, since it contributes nothing to the estimation of Y. Thus, we may substitute in Eq. (10.26) the value for b given by Eq. (10.11). This gives the computational formula for r as:

$$\begin{aligned} r &= \frac{\sum (X - \bar{X})(Y - \bar{Y})}{\sqrt{\sum (X - \bar{X})^2 \sum (Y - \bar{Y})^2}} \\ &= \frac{\sum XY - n\bar{X}\bar{Y}}{\sqrt{(\sum X^2 - n\bar{X}^2)(\sum Y^2 - n\bar{Y}^2)}} \\ &= \frac{\sum xy}{\sqrt{\sum x^2 \sum y^2}} \end{aligned} \qquad (10.28)$$

Example 4 Compute the correlation between maximal workload and Max $\dot{V}O_2$ for the data in Example 1.

SOLUTION From Example 1 we know that $\sum xy = 1{,}036{,}000$, $\sum x^2 = 504{,}000$, and $\sum y^2 = 2{,}389{,}000$. We find

$$r = \frac{1{,}036{,}000}{\sqrt{(504{,}000)(2{,}389{,}000)}}$$

$$= 0.9441 \qquad (10.29)$$

10.6 HYPOTHESIS TESTING OF THE POPULATION CORRELATION COEFFICIENT

The reader will observe that the sample correlation coefficient, r, is an estimator of a population correlation coefficient, which we label as ρ (the Greek letter rho).

If we wish to test the hypothesis that $\rho = 0$, we use the equation

$$t = r\sqrt{\frac{n-2}{1-r^2}} \tag{10.30}$$

which has the t-distribution with $(n - 2)$ d.f. We emphasize that Eq. (10.30) is useful for testing *only* the hypothesis $H_0 : \rho = 0$ against one of the alternative hypotheses, $H_A : \rho \neq 0$, $H_A : \rho > 0$, or $H_A : \rho < 0$. The reason for this limitation is that with $\rho \neq 0$ the distribution of r is not normally distributed and, therefore, Eq. (10.30) will not hold. Thus, the sample correlation coefficient, r, has the t-distribution only when ρ is equal to zero, provided that we may assume that the variable Y is normally distributed and possesses equal variance across the range of X-values of interest. As with previous hypothesis tests, Eq. (10.30) is robust against minor departures from these assumptions. To test $H_0 : \rho = 0$ against one of the alternative hypotheses above, we merely evaluate Eq. (10.30) and compare its value with the tabular value of t for a given type I error.

Example 5 Test the hypothesis that $\rho = 0$ for the data of Example 1.

SOLUTION First we set $H_0 : \rho = 0$ and $H_A : \rho > 0$, and recall from Example 4 that $r = 0.9441$. Then

$$t = 0.9441\sqrt{\frac{8}{1-(0.9441)^2}}$$

$$= 8.1030$$

and since $t > t_{0.95,\,8} = 1.860$, we reject $H_0 : \rho = 0$ and conclude that a positive linear relationship exists between maximal workload and Max $\dot{V}O_2$.

The reader will note that the conclusion of Example 3 to reject $H_0 : B = 0$ is identical to the conclusion to reject $H_0 : \rho = 0$. This is logical because a value of $B = 0$ implies that no relationship exists between X and Y, giving $\rho = 0$; when $B \neq 0$, ρ should also be nonzero. A minimum amount of algebra will show that

$$t = \frac{r\sqrt{n-2}}{\sqrt{1-r^2}}$$

$$= \frac{r}{s_r}$$

$$= \frac{b}{s_b}$$

when $H_0 : \rho = 0$ and $H_0 : B = 0$ are hypothesized. Thus the two tests given by Eqs. (10.16) and (10.30) are identical.*

* The slight discrepancy between t-values computed in Examples 3 and 5 is due to rounding error.

10.7 CAUTION WITH THE INTERPRETATIONS OF CORRELATION AND REGRESSION COEFFICIENTS

Regression and correlation analyses are quite useful tools for the study of functional relationships among variables. Some caution in their use, however, is warranted.

The techniques considered in this chapter are for the special case of a hypothesized *linear* relationship between two variables. Reasons for this limited viewpoint include: (1) Many relationships are linear in nature; (2) the methods to be presented may be easily extended to include other functional forms; (3) even when the relationship is nonlinear, the linear equation may give an acceptable approximation to the actual relationship; and (4) within a limited range of scores the relationship may be linear.

The fact that a linear relationship cannot be established between two variables does not necessarily imply that a relationship does not exist. For example, it may be shown that when $Y = X^2$, r will be zero. When this second-degree or nonlinear relationship exists, $Y = \bar{Y}$ is the best estimate of the linear equation describing the linear relationship between two variables X and Y for the full range of X-values. This is shown in Figure 10.8. Thus the correlation coefficient r, when zero, more appropriately demonstrates that no *linear* relationship exists between the two variables X and Y.

However, if we determine the best straight line describing all points in Figure 10.8 greater than $X = 0$, we find $r = 0.96$ and $\hat{Y} = -1.375 + 3.0X$. The graph of Y and $\hat{Y}$ is shown in Figure 10.9.

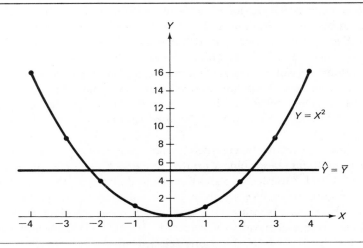

FIGURE 10.8

Linear regression equation when $Y = X^2$

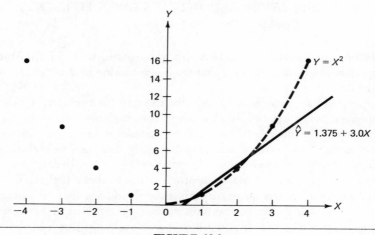

FIGURE 10.9

Linear regression equation for $X > 0$ when $Y = X^2$

Figure 10.9 and the magnitude of r indicate that a limited range of X-values may permit a reasonable straight line fit to nonlinear data. Thus, we must further clarify the interpretation of r^2 based on a linear relationship when studying nonlinear data. Since the data in Figures 10.8 and 10.9 can be completely explained by the equation $Y = X^2$, we must interpret r^2 as providing a measure of the amount of variation in the variable Y that can be explained by the *linear relationship* between X and Y. It should be noted that a popular interpretation for r^2 is: The amount of variation in Y that is explained by the variation in X. Two reasons exist for this usage. First, when Y and X are jointly normally distributed and $\rho = 0$, no relationship of any kind exists between X and Y. This statement cannot be made for nonnormal data. Second, r^2 values may be determined for nonlinear equations such as $Y = X^2$, $Y = e^z$, etc. Thus, the reader should note that when the functional relationship is not given, it should be understood that an interpretation of r^2 is made with respect to the functional equation hypothesized to fit the sample data.

Care must be taken when interpreting linear relationships established on the basis of data describing a limited range of X-values. Suppose we have values of X and Y limited to a small range as denoted by the dotted vertical lines in Figure 10.10. We see from this graph that a straight line fits the plotted (X, Y) points quite well within the range considered. However, outside the range of X-values considered we note that the straight line no longer fits the plotted (X, Y) points (circled data). This implies that it is hazardous to extrapolate the relationship between X and Y beyond the range of X-values used to establish the relationship, because there is no

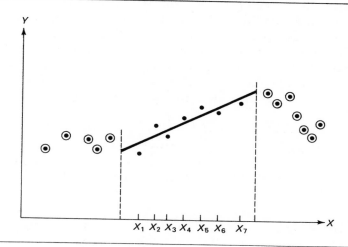

FIGURE 10.10

Data depicting extrapolating risks

guarantee that the relationship will continue to hold. For example, a linear relationship exists between oxygen intake and heart rate for steady-state work that produces heart rate values between 120 and 170 beats per minute. The relationship becomes nonlinear for heart rate values above 170 beats (in particular the heart rate–oxygen intake values approach their maximum values asymptotically). The relationship changes to a low linear relationship for heart rate values below 120 beats per minute due to the influence of many extraneous factors.

Two problems arise when we restrict the range of scores for the independent variable X. First, the range of scores selected for X defines the population of individuals or objects to which inferences concerning the X, Y relationship may be made. Thus, reducing the range of X-values reduces the range of inference. Second, reducing the range of X-values increases the standard error of estimate for b (i.e., s_b). That is, when s_X^2 is small, the variability of b as an estimate of B is large and vice versa. The reader may verify the latter concept by noting that when s_X^2 is large, $\sum (X_i - \bar{X})^2$, the denominator of the right side of Eq. (10.14) giving s_b^2, is large—thereby reducing s_b^2.

Finally, the interpretation of a correlation coefficient as a measure of the linear relationship between two variables is a purely mathematical one. That is, just because a linear equation has been fitted to a set of data yielding a high correlation coefficient, it may not be assumed that a cause and effect relationship exists between the variables. The fact that two variables tend to increase or decrease together does not imply that one has any direct or indirect effect on the other. We cannot overemphasize this final point. Regression and correlation analysis may greatly aid the researcher in his search for cause and effect relationships. However, he can only claim that changes in X-values cause changes in Y-values after he has demonstrated by experimentation that altering an attribute X in a particular way results in an altering of attribute Y. For example, a positive relationship exists between $X =$ number of fire engines at a fire, and $Y =$ amount of damage done by the fire. However, it would be wrong to conclude that the way to minimize damage is to have fewer fire engines at the fire.*

Exercises

1. Determine the linear relationship between the following 10 golfers' average score (Y) and the number of 18-hole rounds played per week.

Golfer:	1	2	3	4	5	6	7	8	9	10
Average score (Y)	75	90	88	80	92	86	90	95	84	80
Number of rounds (X)	4	1	1	2	2	3	2	1	3	4

   a. Find s_e, s_b, s_a.
   b. Find the average score a golfer can expect if he plays three rounds per week.
   c. Test the hypothesis that the slope of the regression line is zero.
   d. Compute the correlation between X and Y.
   e. Calculate the explained and unexplained variances of the Y's.
   f. Interpret the relationship obtained.

2. When the temperatures, X, in Fahrenheit were plotted against steady-state heart rates, Y, for 600 kpm/min of work, a linear trend was indicated. The equation of the best fitting line was found to be $Y = -24 + 2X$.
   a. How does an increase in temperature affect steady-state heart rate? What is the magnitude of this effect?
   b. Interpret the Y-intercept.
   c. Assume that it is known that optimum steady-state heart rates are achieved at $62°$ and a given individual's assayed value of 135 was recorded at $70°$. Estimate his optimum steady-state value?

3. The following data represent average performance scores for a gross motor novel skill (Y) assessed following eight practice trials (X):

Practice Trial:	1	2	3	4	5	6	7	8
Performance Score:	5	23	26	29	31	32	33	33

   a. Plot the data in an (X, Y) coordinate system.
   b. Find a, b, s_e, s_a, s_b.
   c. Draw the best fitted straight line on your graph.
   d. Test the hypothesis that A and B are each zero. Interpret your results.
   e. Compute the correlation coefficient r. Calculate r^2 and interpret.
   f. Using the equation of the best fitted straight line, calculate predictive performance scores for each practice trial. Compare these predictive values with the values observed.

4. Compare the concepts of explained variance and conditional probability.

---

* Example suggested to the authors by Professor Virgil Anderson, Purdue University, Lafayette, Indiana.

5. Show that s_d^2, the variance for paired comparisons, is given by the formula

$$s_d^2 = s_x^2 + s_y^2 - 2r_{xy}s_x s_y$$

In view of this relationship, under what conditions is the paired comparisons technique more sensitive as a test of the hypothesis $H_0 : \mu_Y = \mu_X$ than the t-test using independent samples? Less sensitive?

6. The following correlation coefficients and sample sizes were obtained. Can each be regarded as significantly different from zero at the 5% level of significance?
   a. $r = 0.20, n = 100$ b. $r = 0.30, n = 20$
   c. $r = -0.50, n = 27$ d. $r = 0.10, n = 1000$
   e. $r = -0.80, n = 5$ f. $r = 0.40, n = 50$

7. How large must the correlation coefficient be for a sample size of 11 to permit one to conclude that a linear relationship exists at the 0.05 level?

8. A correlation coefficient of 0.6 is found not significant at the 0.01 level. What sample size was the basis for the coefficient?

9. Suppose a high school football coach has a set number of plays that each player must learn. He wishes to conduct an experiment to determine the number of trials necessary to learn and execute the set of plays when zero, one, two, and three audibles called at the line of scrimmage are added to the set. Eight subjects were selected for each set of audible conditions. The following data were obtained:

NUMBER OF AUDIBLES

0	1	2	3
4	12	16	19
9	7	12	17
3	9	7	19
7	14	15	18
5	11	14	12
10	8	13	16
8	9	9	20
4	10	15	17

   a. Determine the linear regression line between the number of trials (Y) and the number of audibles (X) for the data given.
   b. Test $H_0 : A = 0$ vs. the alternate hypothesis $H_A : A > 0$, and $H_0 : B = 0$ vs. $H_A : B > 0$.
   c. Interpret your results.
   d. How many trials are expected to learn the set of plays when two audibles are added to the set?

COMPUTER APPLICATION

10. Determine the linear relationship and correlation between the following variables for the total group employing the fitness data of Chapter 2 and the computer program given below:
    a. height and weight
    b. 50- and 100-yd dashes
    c. 50-yd dash and standing long jump

11. Repeat the computer analysis employing the simple linear regression program (BMD 01V) from BMD series published by the Health Sciences Computing Facility, BMD: Biomedical Computer Programs, University of California, Los Angeles.

FORTRAN IV PROGRAM
Regression and Correlation

Col. 7

```
      DIMENSIØN FMT (80)
      READ (5,100) N
      READ (5,101) FMT
      SUMX = 0.0
      SUMXSØ = 0.0
      SUMY = 0.0
      SUMYSØ = 0.0
      SUMXY = 0.0
      DØ 50 J = 1, N
      READ (5,FMT) X, Y
      SUMX = SUMX + X
      SUMXSØ = SUMXSØ + X**2
      SUMY = SUMY + Y
      SUMYSØ = SUMYSØ + Y**2
   50 SUMXY = SUMXY + X*Y
      S = N
      XBAR = SUMX/S
      VARX = (SUMXSØ - S*XBAR**2)/(S-1)
      SDX = SØRT(VARX)
      YBAR = SUMY/S
      VARY = (SUMYSØ - S*YBAR**2)/(S-1)
      SDY = SØRT(VARY)
      B = (SUMXY - S*XBAR*YBAR)/(SUMXSØ - S*XBAR**2)
      A = YBAR - B*XBAR
      SESØ = (SUMYSØ - S*YBAR**2-B*(SUMXY - S*XBAR*YBAR))/(S-1)
      SE = SØRT(SESØ)
      SDASØ = (1/S + XBAR**2/(SUMXSØ - S*XBAR**2))*SE
      SDA = SØRT(SDASØ)
      SDBSØ = SESØ/(SUMXSØ - S*XBAR**2)
      SDB = SØRT(SDBSØ)
      TA = A/SDA
      TB = B/SDB
      RSØ = (SUMXY-S*XBAR*YBAR)**2/(SUMYSØ-S*YBAR**2)*(SUMXSØ-S*XBAR**2)
      R = SØRT(RSØ)
      FRSØ =(S - 2)/(1 - RSØ)
      FR = SØRT(FRSØ)
      TR = R*FR
      WRITE (6,102) S
      WRITE (6,103) SUMX, SUMXSØ
      WRITE (6,104) SUMY, SUMYSØ
      WRITE (6,105) SUMXY
      WRITE (6,106) XBAR, VARX, SDX
      WRITE (6,107) YBAR, VARY, SDY
      WRITE (6,108) A, SDA, TA
      WRITE (6,109) B, SDB, TB
      WRITE (6,110) RSØ
      WRITE (6,111) R
      WRITE (6,112) TR
  100 FØRMAT (I2)
  101 FØRMAT (80A1)
  102 FØRMAT (' ','N =',F10.3)
  103 FØRMAT (' ','SUMX =',F10.3,'SUMXSØ =',F10.3)
  104 FØRMAT (' ','SUMY =',F10.3,'SUMYSØ =',F10.3)
  105 FØRMAT (' ','SUMXY =',F10.3)
  106 FØRMAT (' ','MEANX =',F10.3,'VARX =',F10.3,'SDX =',F10.3)
  107 FØRMAT (' ','MEANY =',F10.3,'VARY =',F10.3,'SDY =',F10.3)
  108 FØRMAT (' ','A =',F10.3,'SDA =',F10.3,'T VALUE FØR A =',F10.3)
  109 FØRMAT (' ','B =',F10.3,'SDB =',F10.3,'T VALUE FØR B =',F10.3)
  110 FØRMAT (' ','R SQUARED =',F5.4)
  111 FØRMAT (' ','R =',F5.4)
  112 FØRMAT (' ','T VALUE FØR R =',F10.3)
      STØP
      END
```

Order of cards:

1. System cards
2. Program deck
3. Sample size card
     Col. 1, 2: keypunch sample size according to format statement 100
4. Format card
5. Data cards
6. Job termination card

11

Analysis of Variance

11.1 INTRODUCTION

In Chapter 9 we proposed test statistics for testing $H_0 : \mu_1 = \mu_2$ when $\sigma_1^2 = \sigma_2^2$ for the two special cases when samples were selected from two normal populations defined by the parameters μ_1 and μ_2 and when paired comparisons data existed. This chapter introduces the idea of analysis of variance to permit the restrictive two-population comparison to be expanded to any number of populations.

Specifically, the general hypothesis referred to above may be stated as

$$H_0 : \quad \mu_1 = \mu_2 = \cdots = \mu_k \tag{11.1}$$

Equation (11.1) may be restated in words as the hypothesis that the means of k normal populations are equal. The alternative hypothesis to H_0 is

$$H_A : \quad \mu_i \neq \mu_j \tag{11.2}$$

where $i \neq j$ $(i, j = 1, 2, \ldots, k)$. In words, H_A states that at least two of the k means are not equal. Thus, we reject H_0 if sample data for any two sample means $\bar{X}_i$ and $\bar{X}_j$ provide sufficient evidence that the corresponding μ_i and μ_j are not equal.

The problem suggests that, logically, each sample mean $\bar{X}_i$ should be compared with all other $\bar{X}_j$'s by means of a series of t-tests outlined in Chapter 9. This approach, in fact, could be followed and a decision, to accept or reject H_0, could be made on the basis of the repeated t-test results. For example, suppose we wish to compare mean health knowledge scores of students enrolled in three basic health classes. We might establish the following hypotheses:

$$H_{01} : \quad \mu_1 = \mu_2, \qquad H_{02} : \quad \mu_1 = \mu_3, \qquad H_{03} : \quad \mu_2 = \mu_3$$

and independently test each H_{0i} using the appropriate t-test. Then, if any one H_{0i} $(i = 1, 2, 3)$ is rejected, it would seem that the general hypothesis

$$H_0 : \quad \mu_1 = \mu_2 = \mu_3$$

could also be rejected in view of the way H_A in (11.2) was stated.

The problem with this approach, however, is that the decision to reject $H_0 : \mu_1 = \mu_2 = \mu_3$ may possess a type I error which is in fact larger than the level we think we have set and are willing to assume. For example, we note that by following the repeated t-test rule for our health knowledge problem, we reject H_0 if any one of the following three decisions is reached:

$$\mu_1 \neq \mu_2, \qquad \mu_1 \neq \mu_3, \quad \text{or} \quad \mu_2 \neq \mu_3$$

But, what is the probability of this event occurring when, in fact, $\mu_1 = \mu_2 = \mu_3$? The answer is a function of the type I errors that can be made for any one of the three t-tests. We may derive this overall type I error by noting that the probability that at least one mean difference $(\bar{X}_i - \bar{X}_j)$ is judged significant when in fact no difference exists is equal to one minus the probability that all three mean differences are judged nonsignificant. For example, if $\alpha = 0.05$ in each case, then,

P(overall type I error using repeated t-tests)

$$= 1 - P(\text{accepting } H_{0_1}, H_{0_2}, \text{ and } H_{0_3})$$
$$= 1 - P(\text{accepting } H_{0_1})P(\text{accepting } H_{0_2})P(\text{accepting } H_{0_3})$$

which gives

$$1 - (0.95)^3 = 1 - 0.857375 = 0.142625$$

This shows that using a repeated t-test approach to test $H_0 : \mu_1 = \mu_2 = \cdots = \mu_k$ leads to a greater chance of rejecting H_0—when in fact it is true—than the individual type I errors used.

Exercises

1. The hypothesis $H_0 : \mu_1 = \mu_2 = \mu_3$ is tested using repeated t-tests. If $\alpha = 0.01$ in each case, determine the overall type I error of rejecting H_0. How does this value compare with the type I error derived using $\alpha = 0.05$? How will the type II errors compare for the two situations?
2. Review two articles in a professional journal that employ repeated t-tests to test multiple hypotheses. Assume independent applications of the t-test; determine the overall type I error for each article.

11.2 THE PARTITIONING OF VARIANCES

In view of the generally larger type I error demonstrated in Section 11.1, we must select some alternative approach for testing the hypothesis that means of k normal populations are equal. In particular, we need some method that permits the combination of all k means into the same test statistic.

We note that if $H_0 : \mu_1 = \mu_2 = \cdots = \mu_k$ is true, then each population mean μ_i is equal to a constant mean μ. That is,

$$\mu_i = \mu \qquad (i = 1, 2, \ldots, k) \tag{11.3}$$

It follows that the sample means $\bar{Y}_1, \bar{Y}_2, \ldots, \bar{Y}_k$ should each be equal, within sampling error, to a constant mean $\bar{Y}$. This concept is graphically portrayed in Figure 11.1.

Thus, even though each population mean μ_i is equal to a constant mean μ, the sample means $\bar{Y}_i$ may vary about a common mean $\bar{Y}$ and a measure of variability in $\bar{Y}_i$'s can be computed.

In addition to the variability of sample means, we still have the usual variability of sampled individual scores about their respective group mean. This implies that two kinds of variability exist: one due to variability among sample means and one due to variability among individuals. This concept

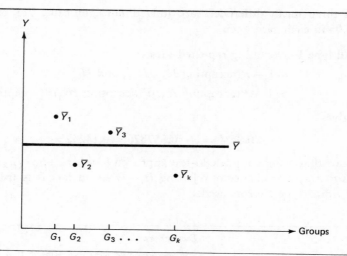

FIGURE 11.1

Scatterplot of group means

is shown in Figure 11.2. From this figure, we see that an individual's score, Y_{ij}, can be partitioned as follows:

$$Y_{ij} = \bar{Y} + (\bar{Y}_i - \bar{Y}) + (Y_{ij} - \bar{Y}_i) \qquad \begin{array}{l} (i = 1, 2, \ldots, k) \\ (j = 1, 2, \ldots, n) \end{array} \qquad (11.4)$$

In words, Eq. (11.4) states that the Y-value for the jth individual in the ith group is explained by: (1) a part due to the mean $\bar{Y}$; (2) an additional part

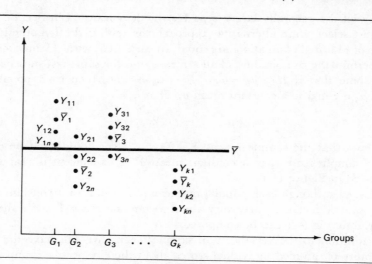

FIGURE 11.2

Among individuals within group variability

due to the variability of the ith group's sample mean, $\bar{Y}_i$; and (3) a part due to the variability of the jth individual from his group mean $\bar{Y}_i$.

Now if we rewrite Eq. (11.4) and find the sum of squares for $(Y_{ij} - \bar{Y})$, we obtain:

$$(Y_{ij} - \bar{Y}) = (\bar{Y}_i - \bar{Y}) + (Y_{ij} - \bar{Y}_i)$$

and

$$\sum (Y_{ij} - \bar{Y})^2 = \sum (\bar{Y}_i - \bar{Y})^2 + \sum (Y_{ij} - \bar{Y}_i)^2 \qquad (11.5)*$$

The sum of squares, $\sum (Y_{ij} - \bar{Y})^2$, may be referred to as the *total sum of squares (SST)* since it represents the amount of variability among individuals whom we do not identify with a particular group. The sum of squares, $\sum (\bar{Y}_i - \bar{Y})^2$, may also be referred to as the *among means sum of squares (SSA)*, since it represents the amount of variability existing among group means. Finally, the sum of squares, $\sum (Y_{ij} - \bar{Y}_i)^2$, may be referred to as the *within group sum of squares (SSW)*, since it represents the amount of variability existing among individuals within each group. Using the abbreviations for the appropriate sum of squares, we have

$$\text{SST} = \text{SSA} + \text{SSW} \qquad (11.6)$$

The reader will recall that SST has $(N-1)$ degrees of freedom (d.f.) where N represents the total number of individuals in the k groups. SSA is computed by summing the squared values of

$$(\bar{Y}_i - \bar{Y}), (\bar{Y}_2 - \bar{Y}), \ldots, (\bar{Y}_k - \bar{Y})$$

which represents k deviations. Then, the degrees of freedom for SSA must be $(k-1)$. Since the total sum of squares, SST, has been partitioned into the two parts SSA and SSW, it follows that the total degrees of freedom $(N-1)$ should also be partitioned. Following this approach, we may determine the degrees of freedom of SSW by subtraction. That is,

$$\text{d.f.}_{\text{SST}} = \text{d.f.}_{\text{SSA}} + \text{d.f.}_{\text{SSW}}$$

or

$$N - 1 = k - 1 + \text{d.f.}_{\text{SSW}}$$

giving

$$\text{d.f.}_{\text{SSW}} = N - k \qquad (11.7)$$

The partitioned sum of squares and degrees of freedom obtained above are conveniently summarized in Table 11.1, which is referred to as an *analysis of variance (ANOV) table*. All entries in Table 11.1 were derived from the discussion above except entries in the column labeled "Mean Squares." We can derive a purely computational definition of mean squares from

---

* The reader should note the similarity between Eq. (11.5) and Eq. (10.10).

TABLE 11.1

Analysis of Variance Table

Source of Variation	d.f.	Sum of Squares	Mean Squares
Among means	$k-1$	SSA	MSA
Within groups	$N-k$	SSW	MSW
Totals	$N-1$	SST	

Table 11.1 by noting that each mean square is obtained by dividing each sum of squares by its respective degrees of freedom. Thus,

$$\text{Among groups mean squares} = \frac{\text{SSA}}{k-1}$$

and

$$\text{Within groups mean squares} = \frac{\text{SSW}}{N-k}$$

11.3   THE F-TEST

The reader will note that the among and within groups mean squares resemble formulae used previously to compute estimates of population measures of variability. For example, the unbiased estimate of $\sigma_y{}^2$ is given by the formula

$$s_y{}^2 = \frac{\text{SST}}{N-1} \tag{11.8}$$

because

$$E\left(\frac{\text{SST}}{N-1}\right) = \sigma_y{}^2$$

It is logical then to ask what is the expected value of the among and within groups mean squares? The answer to this question is given here without proof for the situation where we specify the k populations under study and where the sample size for each group is equal to a constant n.*

$$E(\text{MS among groups}) = \sigma_e{}^2 + \frac{n}{k-1} \sum_{i=1}^{k} (\mu_i - \mu)^2 \tag{11.9}$$

$$E(\text{MS within groups}) = \sigma_e{}^2 \tag{11.10}$$

---

* The reader may note that we might also select populations at random prior to selecting individuals within each population. This situation is not considered here for the sake of simplicity. The requirement of a constant n is also used for simplicity, but in general, it need not be.

Notice that the quantity

$$\sum_{i=1}^{k} (\mu_i - \mu)^2$$

will be equal to zero if H_0 is true. That is, if each population mean μ_i is equal to a constant mean μ,

$$\sum_{i=1}^{k} (\mu_i - \mu)^2 = 0$$

Thus, when $H_0 : \mu_1 = \mu_2 = \cdots = \mu_k$ is true, the expected mean squares for among groups becomes

$$E(\text{MS among groups}) = \sigma_e^2 + 0 = \sigma_e^2$$

which implies that when H_0 is true the expected values of MS among and MS within are the same.

Suppose we form the ratio

$$F = \frac{\text{EMS(Among)}}{\text{EMS(Within)}} = \frac{\sigma_e^2 + n/(k-1)\sum_{i=1}^{k}(\mu_i - \mu)^2}{\sigma_e^2} \qquad (11.11)$$

then if H_0 is true, the value of F should be

$$F = 1$$

Also, if H_0 is not true, then, since $\sum_{i=1}^{k}(\mu_i - \mu)^2$ can never be negative, the value of F should be greater than 1. Thus, the quantity

$$F = \frac{\text{MS(Among)}}{\text{MS(Within)}} \qquad (11.12)$$

based on the sample data selected at random from the k normal populations, appears to be a reasonable function that can be used to test the general hypothesis that the means of k normal populations are equal. From this discussion, we may form the following decision rule:

Result	Decision
If observed $F = 1$	Accept H_0
If observed $F > 1$	Reject H_0

It has been observed that the variable F defined by Eq. (11.12) has a distribution function as given in Figure 11.3 when the variable Y is normally distributed and the population variances are all equal (i.e., when $\sigma_1^2 = \sigma_2^2 = \cdots = \sigma_k^2$). The F-distribution depends only on the degrees of freedom v_1 and v_2 where v_1 is the degrees of freedom of the numerator mean square and v_2 is the degrees of freedom of the denominator mean square. In line

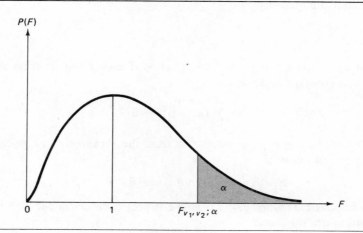

FIGURE 11.3

The F-distribution

with our previous concept of sampling variability, we recognize that the observed F may be greater than one when, in fact, H_0 is true. Thus, we reject H_0 only if the observed F is greater than a value we feel cannot be explained by chance or random sampling variation. Table III of Appendix B provides upper percentage points for various values of v_1 and v_2 of the F-distribution.

Example 1 Suppose the following ANOV table was computed for the health knowledge example:

Source	d.f.	Mean Squares
Among groups	2	44.6
Within groups	27	10.2
Total	29	

The observed F for testing the hypothesis $H_0 : \mu_1 = \mu_2 = \mu_3$ is

$$F_{\text{observed}} = 4.37$$

If we select a type I error of $\alpha = 0.05$, then from Table III, Appendix B we find

$$F_{2, 27; (0.05)} = 3.35$$

by referring to the 5 percentage point table and extracting the F-value in the column labeled "$v_1 = 2$" and the row labeled "$v_2 = 27$." Since

$$F_{\text{observed}} > F_{2, 27; (0.05)}$$

we reject H_0 and conclude that at least two means are not equal. An answer to the question of which mean difference(s) account(s) for the significant F will be given later.

The t-test for comparing two means is equivalent to the F-test when two population means are involved, because an F-value with 1 d.f. in the numerator is equal to t^2 for a two-tailed test. Thus, referring to Tables II and III, Appendix B we note for verification that

$$t_{0.025,\ (15)} = 2.13$$

and

$$t^2_{0.025,\ (15)} = 4.537 = F_{1,\ 15;\ (0.05)}$$

The discussion above provides evidence that the F-distribution may be used to compare the means of several normal populations. We note that these means may arise as a result of our classifying a population according to some common characteristic such as age, grade level, structural measures, or functional measures. In addition, we note that several means may result from our comparing several groups after the completion of some experimental conditions (called _treatments_) when the groups' means were initially known to be equal. Of course, in the latter example, we wish to determine if the treatments assigned to groups are equally effective, which is equivalent to testing the hypothesis that k means are equal.

The idea that treatments are associated with population means sometimes is a difficult concept for beginning students of statistics to understand. To help you understand this concept, suppose all individuals or objects in a defined population are taught tennis by the method of " discovery of exploration" (treatment 1). After the course of instruction, a valid measure of tennis skill is applied to determine the effectiveness of the course of instruction. The resulting measurements may be used to determine the parameters μ_1 and σ_1 for the population of tennis skill scores following instruction by treatment 1. Now suppose, instead, that we taught all individuals in the population by the method of "demonstration–imitation" (treatment 2). Following the same steps as for treatment 1, we see that corresponding to each treatment there is a potential population that exists if that treatment were applied to all members of the population. The number of potential populations will be equal to the number of treatments applied. Appropriately, then, the among groups sum of squares may be referred to as the _treatment sum of squares_. The nature of the analysis will determine which terminology is appropriate.

We may make similar comments about the within groups sum of squares. Suppose we begin with a group of subjects that are identical in every way according to some specified criterion. From this group, we assign two individuals to receive the same treatment. It is logical to expect that these two identically treated subjects will not respond identically to the effect of the treatment. For example, two individuals equal in initial muscular strength who complete a six-weeks strength training program according to the same method of strength development will likely exhibit different post-training muscular strength. We may formally define this unexplained difference as due to experimental error. In general, we may define *experimental error as the failure of two identically treated experimental units (subjects or objects) to yield identical responses*. We note that this difference includes measurement error plus other extraneous variables that influence the measured variable or the treatment applied.

11.4   THE COMPLETELY RANDOMIZED DESIGN

When subjects are selected completely at random from several populations or from a single population and when these subjects are assigned completely at random to several groups, we have a statistical analysis called the *completely randomized (CR) design*. The CR design results when the number of subjects to be assigned to each group is the only restriction imposed on the selection and/or assignment of subjects to treatments or groups.

Suppose that the means of k populations are to be compared based on sample data collected from n individuals or objects selected at random from the k populations. The data may be symbolically represented as shown in Table 11.2.

TABLE 11.2

Data Layout for k Groups Each of Size n

		GROUPS			
	1	2	$\cdots$	k	
	Y_{11}	Y_{21}		Y_{k1}	
	Y_{12}	Y_{22}		Y_{k2}	
	$\vdots$	$\vdots$		$\vdots$	
	Y_{1n}	Y_{2n}		Y_{kn}	
Sum	G_1	G_2	$\cdots$	G_k	G
Mean	$\bar{Y}_1$	$\bar{Y}_2$	$\cdots$	$\bar{Y}_k$	$\bar{Y}$

We need the following computations to obtain an analysis of variance of the type presented in Table 11.1.

$$G = \sum_{i=1}^{k} G_i = \sum_{i=1}^{k} \sum_{j=1}^{n} Y_{ij} \tag{11.13}$$

$$\sum Y^2 = \sum_{i=1}^{k} \sum_{j=1}^{n} Y_{ij}^2 \tag{11.14}$$

$$\text{SSG} = \frac{G^2}{kn} \tag{11.15}$$

$$\mathrm{SSA} = \frac{1}{n} \sum_{i=1}^{k} G_i{}^2 - \mathrm{SSG} \tag{11.16}$$

$$\mathrm{SSW} = \sum Y^2 - \mathrm{SSG} - \mathrm{SSA} \tag{11.17}$$

$$\mathrm{SST} = \sum Y^2 - \mathrm{SSG} \tag{11.18}$$

The assumptions underlying the analysis of variance for a CR design may be given as follows:

1. We assume the observations Y_{ij} are explained by the mathematical model

$$Y_{ij} = \mu + T_i + E_{ij} \tag{11.19}$$

which states that any observed Y_{ij}-value is equal to the overall mean μ for all the populations plus the deviation T_i produced by the ith mean, μ_i, deviating from the overall mean; that is, $T_i = \mu_i - \mu$ plus a random deviation E_{ij} from the ith mean μ_i.
2. The Y_{ij}'s are normally and independently distributed.
3. The variances of each population are equal; that is, $\sigma_1{}^2 = \sigma_2{}^2 = \cdots = \sigma_k{}^2$.

Once the foregoing assumptions are met, the expected mean squares derived in Section 11.4 are valid and the resulting F-test may be made for the hypothesis $H_0 : \mu_1 = \mu_2 = \cdots = \mu_k$. When the Y_{ij}'s are not normally distributed, the central limit theorem may be applied to assume that the $\bar{Y}_i$'s are approximately normally distributed when n is large. When the variances $\sigma_i{}^2$ are not equal, the expected mean squares for SSA and SSW are not true and tend to bias the F-tests that are computed. It should be noted, as pointed out for the two-means analysis in Chapter 9, that the F-test is also robust against minor violations of the above assumptions.

An assumption must also be made about the k treatments included in the experiment. If K treatments are potentially possible, then it may be assumed that (1) $k = K$, which implies that only the k treatments are of interest to the researcher; or (2) $k < K$, which implies that the study includes only a sample of all possible treatments for which inferences are to be made. When case (1) is assumed, we say we have a *fixed model*, while case (2) is referred to as a *random model*. The distinction between the two models may be seen in Table 11.3.

The effect of the assumption of a fixed or random model when the CR design is employed lies in the interpretation of the results or inferences made. When a fixed model is assumed the hypothesis of interest is

$$H_0 : \quad T_i = 0 \qquad (i = 1, 2, \ldots, k)$$

This implies that we are interested only in the k treatments included in the analysis and that we hypothesize that each treatment (T_i) has the same effect on the variable of interest (Y_{ij}).

Had a random model been assumed, the hypothesis to be tested would be

$$H_0 : \quad \sigma_T{}^2 = 0$$

TABLE 11.3

ANOV for Data of Table 11.2 Showing Expected Mean Squares (EMS) for Fixed and Random Models

Source of Variation	d.f.	SS	MS	EMS Fixed Model	EMS Random Model
Treatment	$k-1$	SSA	$\dfrac{SSA}{(k-1)}$	$\sigma_e^2 + \dfrac{n\sum_{i=1}^{k} T_i^2}{(k-1)}$	$\sigma_e^2 + n\sigma_T^2$
Experimental error	$k(n-1)$	SSW	$\dfrac{SSW}{k(n-1)}$	σ_e^2	σ_e^2
Totals	$kn-1$	SST			

Restated verbally, the latter hypothesis indicates that "There are no differences among the effects of *all* treatments in the population from which the k treatments included in the experiment are a random sample."

We note in each case that the computations and test procedures for the two stated hypotheses are the same. We have two motives for including a seemingly trivial matter: (1) The inferences to be made by the two models are about entirely different populations, and (2) in more complex analyses, the test procedures vary depending on the model used.

Example 2 Consider an experiment to see how training affects the capacity of the coronary tree in wistar rats. One group of rats trained under aerobic conditions, a second trained under anaerobic conditions, while a third served as a control and did no training. The data in Table 11.4 were obtained.

TABLE 11.4

Coronary Tree Weights, in Grams, of 10 Wistar Rats Following Training Under Three Conditions

	Aerobic	Anaerobic	Control	Total
	2.8	2.6	2.5	
	2.9	2.9	2.0	
	3.0	3.0	2.4	
	3.3	2.5	2.3	
	3.2	2.8	2.1	
	3.1	3.2	2.0	
	3.5	2.7	1.9	
	3.6	2.8	2.1	
	3.2	3.1	2.5	
	3.4	2.4	2.2	
Sum	32.0	28.0	22.0	82.0
Means	3.2	2.8	2.2	2.73

Following Eqs. (11.13) through (11.17), we can make the necessary calculations

$$G = (2.8 + 2.9 + \cdots + 2.2) = 82.0$$

$$\sum Y^2 = (2.8^2 + 2.9^2 + \cdots + 2.2^2) = 230.82$$

$$\text{SSG} = \frac{(82.0)^2}{(3)(10)} = 224.13$$

$$\text{SSA} = \tfrac{1}{10}(32.0^2 + 28.0^2 + 22.0^2) - 224.13 = 5.0667$$

$$\text{SSW} = 1.62$$

$$\text{SST} = 6.6867$$

The analysis of variance appears in Table 11.5. Since there are three groups or treatments, the degrees of freedom for treatments are $3 - 1 = 2$. Ten rats were included in each training group. Hence, $N = n_1 + n_2 + n_3 = 30$ and SSW has $30 - 3 = 27$ d.f.

TABLE 11.5

Summary of Analysis of Variance for Example 2

Source of Variation	d.f.	SS	MS	F
Treatments	2	5.0667	2.5333	42.2222
Experimental	27	1.62000	.060000	

The F-value for $v_1 = 2$ and $v_2 = 27$ is found, by interpolation, from Table III, Appendix B to be 3.35. Since the observed F from Table 11.5 is greater than 3.35, we reject the null hypothesis of equality of mean coronary tree weights produced by the three conditions. It must be concluded that at least two means are significantly different.

UNEQUAL SAMPLE SIZES

When there are a disproportionate number of individuals in each population, it is not feasible for the researcher to obtain equal sample sizes from all populations of interest. Typical examples include comparisons among levels of fitness, athletic and nonathletic groups, personality types, and interest groups. When the sample sizes employed are proportional to the number of individuals or objects in each population, then an analysis is possible by using a *least-squares solution*. The symbolic representations of the data and computational formulae for this analysis are:

TABLE 11.6

Data Layout for k Groups Each of Size n_i

	GROUPS			
	1	2	$\cdots$	k	Total
	Y_{11}	Y_{21}		Y_{k1}	
	Y_{12}	Y_{22}		Y_{k2}	
	$\vdots$	$\vdots$		$\vdots$	
	Y_{1n1}	Y_{2n2}		Y_{knk}	
Sum	G_1	G_2	$\cdots$	G_k	G
n_i	n_1	n_2	$\cdots$	n_k	N
Means	$\bar{Y}_1$	$\bar{Y}_2$	$\cdots$	$\bar{Y}_k$	$\bar{Y}$

$$G = \sum_{i=1}^{k} G_i = \sum_{i=1}^{k} \sum_{j=1}^{n_i} Y_{ij} \tag{11.20}$$

$$\sum Y^2 = \sum_{i=1}^{k} \sum_{j=1}^{n_i} Y_{ij}^2 \tag{11.21}$$

$$SSG = \frac{G^2}{\sum_{i=1}^{k} n_i} = \frac{G^2}{N} \tag{11.22}$$

$$SSA = \sum_{i=1}^{k} \frac{G_i^2}{n_i} - SSG \tag{11.23}$$

$$SSW = \sum Y^2 - SSG - SSA \tag{11.24}$$

The resulting analysis of variance table is presented as Table 11.7.

TABLE 11.7

Analysis of Variance Table for CR Design with Unequal Groups

Source of Variation	d.f.	SS	MS	EMS Fixed Model	EMS Random Model[a]
Treatment	$k-1$	SSA	$\dfrac{SSA}{(k-1)}$	$\sigma_e^2 + \dfrac{\sum_{i=1}^{k} n_i T_i^2}{(k-1)}$	$\sigma_e^2 + n_0 \sigma_T^2$
Experimental error	$\sum_{i=1}^{k}(n_i - 1)$	SSW	$\dfrac{SSW}{\sum_{i=1}^{k}(n_i - 1)}$	σ_e^2	σ_e^2
Total	$N-1$				

[a] The constant n_0 is similar to an average n_i.

Unequal sample sizes have a complex effect on the statistical analyses of a completely randomized experiment. A thorough discussion of this subject is beyond the scope of these introductory remarks. We note, however, that if we assume the variances are equal, we must have equal sample sizes if we are to have comparable precision in evaluating the treatment effects. Thus, if the experiment plan calls for an equal number of observations under each treatment, but unequal sample sizes exist due to circumstances not related to the experimental treatments, the computational formulae outlined above are inappropriate. When this condition occurs, the appropriate computations are obtained by employing an *unweighted-means analysis*. The details of this analysis are not presented here and the interested reader is referred to Winer* for additional details.

Example 3 Kenyon's ATPA Scale† was used to compare the perceived values of physical activity held by collegiate athletes participating in four varsity sports. The data given in Table 11.8 were recorded for the scale

TABLE 11.8

Data Layout for Perceived Values Study

	Golf	Basketball	Tennis	Track & Field	Total
	1.8	1.0	2.0	0.3	
	1.0	0.6	2.3	1.0	
	1.4	1.1	1.5	0.8	
	1.6	2.0	1.2	1.2	
	2.4	1.2	1.9	1.4	
	2.0	0.8		0.9	
		1.4		0.6	
		1.5		1.1	
		0.5		1.5	
		1.4		0.4	
		1.2		0.7	
		1.1		1.1	
				0.8	
				0.5	
				1.2	
Sum	10.2	13.8	8.9	13.5	46.4
n_i	6	12	5	15	38
Mean	1.7	1.15	1.78	0.9	1.22

* B. J. Winer, *Statistical Principles in Experimental Design.* New York: McGraw-Hill Book Company, 1971.

† G. S. Kenyon, "A Conceptual Model for Characterizing Physical Activity," *Research Quarterly*, **39**: 98–101, 1968.

identifying the perceived value of physical activity as a social experience.

$$G = (1.8 + 1.0 + \cdots + 1.2) = 46.4$$

$$\sum Y^2 = (1.8^2 + 1.0^2 + \cdots + 1.2^2) = 66.78$$

$$\text{SSG} = \frac{(46.4)^2}{38} = 56.6568$$

$$\text{SSA} = \left(\frac{10.2^2}{6} + \frac{13.8^2}{12} + \frac{8.9^2}{5} + \frac{13.5^2}{15}\right) - 56.6568 = 4.5452$$

$$\text{SSW} = 66.78 - 4.5452 - 56.6568 = 5.5780$$

The resulting analysis of variance is summarized in Table 11.9. The F-value with $v_1 = 3$ and $v_2 = 34$ is not included in Table III, Appendix B. We may select the value corresponding to $v_1 = 3$ and $v_2 = 30$ (the nearest v_2-value),

TABLE 11.9

ANOV for Perceived Values Study

Source of Variation	d.f.	SS	MS	F Ratio
Sports	3	4.5453	1.5151	9.235
Within sports	34	5.5780	0.1641	
Totals	37	10.1233		

which is 3.32 for $\alpha = 0.05$, and compare this value with the observed F reported in Table 11.9. Since $F_{\text{observed}} > 3.32$, we reject $H_0: \text{T}_i = 0$ $(i = 1, 2, 3, 4)$. We conclude from these results that athletes participating in different sports do not have the same perception of physical activity as a social experience.

11.5   COMPARISON AMONG TREATMENT MEANS

Once the null hypothesis $H_0: \mu_1 = \mu_2 = \cdots = \mu_k$ has been rejected, the researcher is faced with the problem of deciding which of the two or more means are responsible for producing the significant F ratio. Several approaches are available. One might examine the sample means and decide which of the means appear to subjectively differ. This approach should not be ruled out entirely for the opinion of the researcher is a valuable ingredient in decision making. The approach must be ruled out in general, however, because the reliability of conclusions drawn by subjective methods cannot be determined. We previously provided reasons why repeated application of the t-test is undesirable. Basically, this latter approach produces a larger than desirable type I error. This results in more mean differences between two populations taken at a time being judged significantly different than is the true state of affairs.

Several attempts have been made to derive test statistics that can be used in making multiple comparisons among treatment means that possess desirable statistical properties. For a general discussion of this problem, the reader is referred to Ostle* or Winer.† We present here only one method favored by the authors. The method about to be described is known as the *Newman–Keuls test.* This method keeps the level of significance at the value α for sets of ranges within an overall inclusive range. Thus, the method is more powerful for each individual comparison between two means than the repeated *t*-tests. In practical terms, if a given mean difference is judged significant by the Newman–Keuls test, one can feel safer in concluding that a true difference exists than would be the case if the repeated *t*-tests were employed. In passing, it may be noted that, of the multiple-comparisons tests, the Newman–Keuls test is neither the most conservative (i.e., it doesn't have a tendency to yield few significant differences) nor the most liberal (i.e., it doesn't have a tendency to yield a large number of significant differences).

Once an overall F ratio from the analysis of variance table has been shown to be significant, the treatment means are then arranged in ascending order of magnitude. For example, the means for k treatments included in an analysis of variance for a CR designed experiment should be ordered according to the following arrangement:

$$\begin{array}{c|cccc} \text{Order} & 1 & 2 & \cdots & k \\ \hline \text{Means} & \bar{Y}_1 & \bar{Y}_2 & \cdots & \bar{Y}_k \end{array} \qquad (11.25)$$

The ordering of means given assumes that the following inequality chain holds:

$$\bar{Y}_1 < \bar{Y}_2 < \cdots < \bar{Y}_k$$

Tests of significance for the difference between two means are then computed using the studentized range statistic (q)

$$q_r = \frac{\bar{Y}_j - \bar{Y}_i}{\sqrt{\text{MSW}/n}} \qquad (11.26)$$

where MSW is the within groups (experimental error) mean squares, n is the number of individuals or objects making up each group, and r is the number of steps between two means on the ordered scale (11.25). For example, $r = 4$ when $\bar{Y}_4$ and $\bar{Y}_1$ are inserted in (11.26), $r = 3$ when $\bar{Y}_5$ and $\bar{Y}_3$ or $\bar{Y}_4$ and $\bar{Y}_2$ are inserted in (11.26), and $r = k$ when $\bar{Y}_k$ and $\bar{Y}_1$ are

---

* B. Ostle, *Statistics in Research.* Ames: The Iowa State University Press, 1963.
† B. J. Winer, *Statistical Principles in Experimental Design.* New York: McGraw-Hill Book Company, 1971.

inserted in (11.26). Critical values for q_r are obtained from Table IV, Appendix B. The critical value for q_r is $q_{1-\alpha}(r, s)$, where r and α are as defined above and s is the degrees of freedom for MSW. Thus, entries in Table IV are read in the same way as entries in the F table.

To facilitate multiple comparisons, it is more convenient to obtain a critical value for the difference between two means. This is accomplished by noting that Eq. (11.26) may be written as:

$$q_r \sqrt{\frac{\text{MSW}}{n}} = \bar{Y}_j - \bar{Y}_i$$

That is, since $q_{1-\alpha}(r, s)$ is the critical value for q_r, the critical value for $\bar{Y}_j - \bar{Y}_i$ will be $q_{1-\alpha}(r, s)\sqrt{\text{MSW}/n}$. In addition, systematic tests are more conveniently achieved by recording mean differences in tabular form. The procedure is best illustrated by an example.

Example 4   Suppose five methods of developing upper arm and shoulder strength were included in a CR designed experiment. Assume the variable of interest was maximum number of chins. Assume further that a significant F ratio suggests we reject H_0: $\mu_1 = \mu_2 = \mu_3 = \mu_4 = \mu_5$. Our next step is to order the five means from lowest to highest. Suppose the following results were obtained:

Order	1	2	3	4	5
Mean	6	7	12	15	17

We now compute all possible mean differences among the five ordered means and record our findings in Table 11.10. Included in Table 11.10 is the

TABLE 11.10

Order:	1	2	3	4	5			
								$q_{0.95}(r. 60)$
Means	6	7	12	15	17	r	$q_{0.95}(r. 60)$	$\sqrt{\text{MSW}/n}$
6	—	1	6	9	11	5	3.98	7.96
7		—	5	8	10 — — 4	4	3.74	7.48
12			—	3	5 — — —3	3	3.40	6.80
15				—	2— — —2	2	2.83	5.66
17					—			

MSW = 52; $n = 13$; $\alpha = 0.05$

appropriate critical value for each mean difference recorded. All mean differences that are the same number of steps apart are connected by dotted lines identifying a diagonal for each r-value. The tests of significance are conducted along one diagonal beginning from the upper left-hand corner.

Each entry is compared with its corresponding critical value and judged significant if

$$\bar{Y}_j - \bar{Y}_i \geqslant q_{1-\alpha}(r, s) \sqrt{\frac{MSW}{n}}$$

and not significant if

$$\bar{Y}_j - \bar{Y}_i < q_{1-\alpha}(r, s) \sqrt{\frac{MSW}{n}}$$

Thus, all entries lying on the first diagonal from the left are to be compared with the critical value corresponding to $r = 2$. In our example, this value is 5.66. We see from Table 11.10 that none of the entries along the first diagonal exceed 5.66. Therefore, the hypotheses $\mu_2 - \mu_1 = 0$, $\mu_3 - \mu_2 = 0$, $\mu_4 - \mu_3 = 0$, and $\mu_5 - \mu_4 = 0$ are accepted. Tests are now made for all differences corresponding to $r = 3$. These values are found along the second diagonal from the left. The appropriate critical value is 6.80. Only the mean difference between $\bar{Y}_4$ and $\bar{Y}_2$ is greater than 6.80, leading us to reject the hypothesis that $\mu_4 - \mu_2 = 0$ and to accept the hypotheses $\mu_3 - \mu_1 = 0$ and $\mu_5 - \mu_3 = 0$. In addition, without further comparisons we may immediately reject the hypothesis that $\mu_5 - \mu_2 = 0$. The implication is that with μ_4 judged significantly greater than μ_2, μ_5 must also be significantly greater than μ_2 because $\bar{Y}_5 > \bar{Y}_4$.

Mean differences corresponding to $r = 4$ that were not previously ruled on are now compared with their appropriate critical value. The critical value is 7.48. The observed differences are found along the third diagonal line. In our example, only the first value is considered. Since the observed difference (9) is greater than the critical value (7.48), we reject the hypothesis that $\mu_4 - \mu_1 = 0$. It also immediately follows that $\mu_5 - \mu_1 = 0$ must be rejected for reasoning similar to that given above. This completes the test.

For convenience, a summary table may be developed denoting significance and nonsignificance as concluded above. This gives

Order:	1	2	3	4	5
Means	$\bar{Y}_1$	$\bar{Y}_2$	$\bar{Y}_3$	$\bar{Y}_4$	$\bar{Y}_5$
$\bar{Y}_1$	−			*	*
$\bar{Y}_2$		−		*	*
$\bar{Y}_3$			−		
$\bar{Y}_4$				−	
$\bar{Y}_5$					−

where an asterisk denotes statistical significance at the 0.05 level.

The Newman–Keuls test may be employed with unequal sample sizes provided the number of observations does not differ markedly from group to group. The procedure is the same as for equal sample sizes except that the harmonic mean of the sample sizes, n_j's, is employed in place of the equal sample size, n, assumed previously. The harmonic mean $\bar{n}$ is defined as

$$\bar{n} = \frac{k}{(1/n_1) + (1/n_2) + \cdots + (1/n_k)} \tag{11.27}$$

11.6 THE RANDOMIZED COMPLETE BLOCK DESIGN

A key concept describing the CR design is that no restrictions were placed on the sampling procedures. We now discuss a design known as the *randomized complete block (RCB) design*, whereby a restriction is placed on the sampling procedure. An important concept we wish to convey in this section is that restrictions placed on the sampling and/or assignment of subjects to groups (commonly called *randomization procedure*) completely determines the appropriate analysis for hypothesis testing. Although we discuss only two basic designs in this chapter, a number of other designs exist for multiple-group analyses.

Chapter 4 defined a random sample as one in which every individual or object in the population has an equal chance of selection. An alternate definition is that no restrictions are placed on the sampling procedures.

Suppose we have a population of subjects classified according to tennis skill level (high, medium, and low). Then, suppose we wish to select three groups from each classification for the purpose of studying the effectiveness of three methods of teaching tennis. We may represent the resulting nine groups selected as follows:

Skill Level	Sample Group
High	G_{H1}, G_{H2}, G_{H3}
Medium	G_{M1}, G_{M2}, G_{M3}
Low	G_{L1}, G_{L2}, G_{L3}

Now let us assign one method of tennis instruction at random to each of the three groups in each skill level category. If we begin with the high-skilled level, we may assign at random, say, group G_{H2} to method 1. As a result of this assignment, groups G_{H2} and G_{H3} must receive one of the remaining two methods. Thus, a restriction has been imposed on the randomization of groups to methods. The reader will note that the same restriction exists for the medium- and low-skilled levels. This restriction must be considered in the analysis of mean differences. The RCB design does just that, as we will see shortly.

Basically, the RCB design is a group of CR designs. A *block* consists of a CR design and the group of blocks make up the design called the RCB design. These blocks are called " complete " because all methods (treatments) appear in each block.

The advantages of an RCB design over the CR design may be stated as follows: (1) Greater inference is possible since several classifications (blocks) of subjects are included in the analysis; (2) the within groups sum of squares should be smaller since the variability due to skill has been isolated and removed from the within groups sum of squares; (3) the effectiveness of the treatments studied can be compared with respect to the classification levels; and (4) the RCB design prevents subjects or objects of a particular classification from being assigned only to a few treatments at the exclusion of others.

Greater inference is provided when the blocks represent different school districts, sex, race, or physical and/or motor characteristics. Advantage number two is true since the classification of subjects should make the variability of subjects within each classification level smaller than the total group considered without classification. Advantage number three is true because all treatments are assigned to each classification. The importance of this approach is that one treatment may be effective at one classification level while another is more effective at a second classification level. The justification for number four is recognized when it is noted that often we cannot depend on the process of randomization to evenly distribute subjects with varying levels of a particular characteristic across the treatments under study.

TABLE 11.11

Symbolic Representation of Data for an RCB Design[a]

Blocks	TREATMENTS 1	2	$\cdots$	j	$\cdots$	k	Sum	Mean
1	Y_{11}	Y_{12}	$\cdots$	Y_{1j}	$\cdots$	Y_{1k}	B_1	$\bar{Y}_{1.}$
2	Y_{21}	Y_{22}	$\cdots$	Y_{2j}	$\cdots$	Y_{2k}	B_2	$\bar{Y}_{2.}$
$\vdots$	$\vdots$	$\vdots$		$\vdots$		$\vdots$	$\vdots$	$\vdots$
i	Y_{i1}	Y_{i2}	$\cdots$	Y_{ij}	$\cdots$	Y_{ik}	B_i	$\bar{Y}_{i.}$
$\vdots$	$\vdots$	$\vdots$		$\vdots$		$\vdots$	$\vdots$	$\vdots$
m	Y_{m1}	Y_{m2}	$\cdots$	Y_{mj}	$\cdots$	Y_{mk}	B_m	$\bar{Y}_{m.}$
Sum	G_1	G_2	$\cdots$	G_j	$\cdots$	G_k	G	—
Mean	$\bar{Y}_{.1}$	$\bar{Y}_{.2}$	$\cdots$	$\bar{Y}_{.j}$	$\cdots$	$\bar{Y}_{.k}$	—	$\bar{Y}_{..}$

[a] The dot notation indicates that the appropriate mean value has been obtained by summing over the dimension replaced by one dot.

The data layout and resulting analysis for an RCB design (Tables 11.11 and 11.12) may now be given. Suppose that k treatments are to be assigned to km subjects that are classified in m blocks.

$$G = \sum_{i=1}^{m} B_i = \sum_{j=1}^{k} G_j = \sum_{i=1}^{m} \sum_{j=1}^{k} Y_{ij} \qquad (11.28)$$

$$\sum Y^2 = \sum_{i=1}^{m} \sum_{j=1}^{k} Y_{ij}^2 \tag{11.29}$$

$$\text{SSG} = \frac{G^2}{mk} \tag{11.30}$$

SSG = Sum of squares among blocks

$$= \sum_{i=1}^{m} \frac{B_i^2}{k} - \text{SSG} \tag{11.31}$$

SSA = Sum of squares among treatments

$$= \sum_{j=1}^{k} \frac{G_j^2}{m} - \text{SSG} \tag{11.32}$$

$$\text{SSW} = \sum Y^2 - \text{SSB} - \text{SSA} - \text{SSG} \tag{11.33}$$

TABLE 11.12

ANOV for RCB Design Experiment

Source of Variation	d.f.	SS	MS
Blocks	$m-1$	SSB	$\dfrac{\text{SSB}}{(m-1)}$
Treatments	$k-1$	SSA	$\dfrac{\text{SSA}}{(k-1)}$
Experimental error	$(m-1)(k-1)$	SSW	$\dfrac{\text{SSW}}{(m-1)(k-1)}$
Totals	$mk-1$	SST	

The assumptions underlying the analysis of variance for an RCB design may be given as follows:

1. We assume the observations Y_{ij} may be explained by the mathematical model

$$Y_{ij} = \mu + \mathrm{B}_i + \mathrm{T}_j + E_{ij} \tag{11.34}$$

which states that any observed Y_{ij}-value is equal to the overall mean μ for all populations *plus* the deviation B_i produced by the ith block's mean $\mu_{i.}$ deviating from the overall mean (i.e., $\mathrm{B}_i = \mu_{i.} - \mu$) *plus* the deviation T_j produced by the jth mean, $\mu_{.j}$, deviating from the overall mean (i.e., $\mathrm{T}_j = \mu_{.j} - \mu$) *plus* the random factor E_{ij} due to the combined influence of many unidentified sources.
2. The Y_{ij}'s are normally and independently distributed.
3. The variances of the E_{ij}'s should all be equal.

TABLE 11.13

Source of Variation and Expected Mean Squares (EMS) for an RCB Design

Source of Variation	d.f.	EMS Fixed Treatments	EMS Random Treatments
Blocks	$m - 1$	$\sigma_e{}^2 + \dfrac{k \sum_{i=1}^{m} B_i{}^2}{(m-1)}$	$\sigma_e{}^2 + \dfrac{k \sum_{i=1}^{m} B_i{}^2}{(m-1)}$
Treatments	$k - 1$	$\sigma_e{}^2 + \dfrac{m \sum_{j=1}^{k} T_j{}^2}{(k-1)}$	$\sigma_e{}^2 + m\sigma_T{}^2$
Experimental error	$(m-1)(k-1)$	$\sigma_e{}^2$	$\sigma_e{}^2$
Total	$km - 1$		

As in Section 11.3, either a fixed or random model may be assumed with respect to treatments. In this discussion, blocks are assumed only to be fixed. The expected mean squares under these conditions are given in Table 11.13.

The primary interest in the analysis of variance for the RCB design given above lies in the elimination of block effects from experimental error. In view of this purpose, statistical tests of hypotheses should be restricted only to treatments. The authors recognize that this restriction may confuse some readers in view of the expected mean squares outlined in Table 11.13. (They seem to suggest that a test of hypothesis of equality of blocks can be formulated.) There is a very sound mathematical basis for the restriction. Intuitively, we justify the decision by noting that while treatments are assigned at random to experimental units within blocks, the blocks are *not* formed in a random fashion. In particular, employment of blocks generally connotes that before the experiment is conducted there are considerable differences among the blocks.

A special case of the RCB design occurs when the same experimental unit is observed under more than one treatment level. The special case is referred to as a *repeated measures design*. When people represent experimental units, the responses of people to a given treatment may show large variability due to differences between people that existed prior to the experiment. When it is possible to observe the same individual under each experimental treatment, this latter source of variability can be separated from the uncontrolled sources of variability that are collectively included as the experimental error. Repeated measures designs permit subjects to serve as their own control.

The repeated measures design may be employed in physical education, health, and recreation in a number of ways. For example, in motor learning, subjects may be observed over time so that learning curves can be established. Additionally, the effect of drugs on physical performance and/or health parameters may be more efficiently studied by observing each subject under the influences of each drug (provided no carry-over effects exist).

Within the context of the RCB design, each experimental unit is considered as a separate block. For example, subjects' endurance performances studied under normoxic and varying hyperoxic conditions prior to the performance gives the following data format:

Blocks	NORMOXIC 21%	31%	HYPEROXIC 41%	51%
Subject 1	$Y_{1N(21)}$	$Y_{1h(31)}$	$Y_{1h(41)}$	$Y_{1h(51)}$
Subject 2	$Y_{2N(21)}$	$Y_{2h(31)}$	$Y_{2h(41)}$	$Y_{2h(51)}$
$\vdots$	$\vdots$	$\vdots$	$\vdots$	$\vdots$
Subject m	$Y_{mN(21)}$	$Y_{mh(31)}$	$Y_{mh(41)}$	$Y_{mh(51)}$

The number of blocks considered in the experiment is equal to the number of subjects included in the study. Following this format, we can use Eqs. (11.28) to (11.33) to calculate the appropriate sum of squares for subjects, treatments, and experimental error.

Example 5 Six subjects of varying badminton ability competed against high, medium, and low competition while telemetry heart rate was assessed. Table 11.14 shows the data for average match heart rate.

TABLE 11.14

Data for Telemetry Heart Rate During Badminton Competition

Subject	COMPETITION High	Medium	Low	Total	Mean
1	176	144	137	457	152.33
2	170	154	147	471	157
3	135	137	128	400	133.33
4	132	135	121	388	129.33
5	150	163	160	473	157.67
6	168	171	169	508	169.33
Sum	931	904	862	2697	–
Mean	155.17	150.67	143.67	–	149.83

$$G = 2697$$

$$\sum Y^2 = 409{,}069$$

$$\text{SSG} = \frac{(2697)^2}{18} = 404{,}100.50$$

$$\text{SSB} = \frac{(457^2 + 471^2 + \cdots + 508^2)}{3} - 404{,}100.5 = 3575.17$$

$$\text{SSA} = \frac{(931^2 + 904^2 + 862^2)}{6} - 404{,}100.5 = 403.0$$

$$\text{SSW} = 409{,}069 - 3575.17 - 403.00 - 404{,}100.5 = 990.33$$

TABLE 11.15

Analysis of Variance for Telemetry Heart Rate Data

Source	d.f.	SS	MS	F Ratio
Subjects	5	3575.17	715.03	—
Competition	2	403.00	201.50	2.03
Experimental error	10	990.33	99.03	
Total	17			

The resulting analysis of variance is summarized in Table 11.15. Since six subjects are included in the study, $m = 6$ and the degrees of freedom for blocks (i.e., subjects) is $6 - 1 = 5$. Similarly, with three competition levels included, the treatment (i.e., competition) degrees of freedom are $3 - 1 = 2$. Finally, the degrees of freedom for experimental error are

$$(6-1)(3-1) = 5 \times 2 = 10$$

The F ratio for competition is less than the critical value ($F_{(0.05), (2), (10)} = 4.10$) needed for significance. We conclude from these results that subjects of varying badminton ability exhibit similar average match heart rates while competing against varying levels of competition.

You should note that more confidence can be placed in the conclusion drawn with the repeated measures design (i.e., RCB) employed as opposed to the conclusion drawn from the completely randomized design. For example, if the subjects factor were not included in the analysis described in Example 5, the sum of squares presently assigned to subjects would be included with that identified as experimental error. Assuming this to be the case gives

$$SSW_{CR} = SSW_{RCB} + SSB$$

Then, for Example 5,

$$SSW_{CR} = 990.33 + 3575.17 = 4565.50$$

which is substantially larger than the 990.33 that was recorded for the experimental error source of variation in Table 11.15. Notice that using SSW_{CR} inflates the experimental error mean square and subsequently reduces the F ratio for competition. That is, under the completely randomized design, the F ratio for competition would be

$$F = \frac{MS \text{ competition}}{SSW_{CR}/15}$$

$$= \frac{201.90}{304.36} = 0.663$$

In this example, we purposely violated the design procedures to illustrate a point. That is, since the sources of variation all have positive values, employing the inappropriate design will always produce an inflated experimental error mean square. This, in turn, will lead to smaller F-values than will be the case when the correct design is employed. Thus, if a significant F-value occurs for treatments, then significant differences in treatment means definitely exist at the α-level chosen. If, however, treatments turn out to be *not* significant, one cannot safely say that this describes the true state of the population. From this discussion, one realizes the importance of employing the correct design for testing hypotheses. As a warning sign, we note that if the F ratio is substantially less than one, then one should suspect that an inappropriate design has been employed. Included in this concept is the idea that one or more assumptions underlying the design may have been violated. When an inappropriate design is suspected, one should check these assumptions to make sure that each has been satisfied.

Exercises

3. Employ the Newman–Keuls test for individual means comparison to determine which means accounted for the significant F-value reported in Examples 2 and 3.
4. Users of marijuana claim that physical performance is enhanced by Delta-9 Tetrahydrocannabinal (THC), an active ingredient in marijuana. To test this claim, 35 college males were selected at random from a large university and assigned to four groups. One group is given a placebo and serves as the control while the others are given either 25, 50, or 75 mg of THC. Thirty minutes following ingestion of the placebo or THC, each subject's maximal leg extensor strength was assessed. The following scores were recorded:

LEG STRENGTH

Control	25-mg dose	50-mg dose	75-mg dose
691	650	679	649
604	666	612	681
647	674	646	634
643	677	645	623
668	678	691	637
698	681	654	676
674	674	657	645
652	602		671
687			686
603			683

Compute an appropriate analysis of variance among the mean performances of the four groups. Is your F significant at the 0.05 level? Does the data suggest additional analysis?

5. While studying the influence of muscular fatigue, patterns of the intercontraction rest interval, Clarke* suspected that the initial strength recorded would be a function of the rate of contractions undertaken. To test this hypothesis, he recorded the initial strengths of 30 subjects at the onset of undertaking rhythmic maximal contractions

---

* David H. Clarke, "The Influence on Muscular Fatigue Patterns of the Intercontraction Rest Interval." *Medicine and Science in Sports*. Vol. 3, No. 2 pp. 83–88, Summer, 1971.

of the elbow flexor muscles at rates of contraction of 15/min, 30/min, 45/min, and 60/min. The following data, in kilograms, were recorded:

Subject	RATE OF CONTRACTION 15/min	30/min	45/min	60/min
1	52.7	48.5	53.9	46.7
2	62.5	56.0	61.3	56.9
3	60.6	53.7	46.2	53.4
4	41.0	42.9	41.3	41.1
5	54.1	49.5	57.1	48.7
6	49.4	54.4	48.8	43.1
7	52.3	57.4	56.0	56.2
8	31.7	39.7	32.9	31.2
9	67.2	59.2	56.4	54.6
10	64.4	70.0	68.8	54.4
11	58.8	60.4	57.9	54.6
12	67.2	59.3	60.7	58.8
13	51.6	52.5	53.9	51.5
14	58.5	55.0	62.7	39.0
15	80.0	78.1	81.7	64.4
16	67.9	77.0	88.9	82.1
17	54.4	57.2	55.5	50.4
18	62.1	62.0	59.5	59.5
19	69.5	58.6	53.9	56.0
20	38.9	36.2	36.9	38.2
21	67.6	62.3	64.9	63.9
22	57.6	49.7	58.3	50.8
23	56.0	54.6	59.7	52.3
24	70.4	69.7	68.4	66.7
25	77.5	69.3	69.7	71.9
26	52.5	53.4	44.3	47.1
27	67.4	64.4	64.8	63.5
28	55.3	56.2	55.7	53.9
29	44.6	39.4	39.6	36.6
30	58.1	65.3	57.6	56.2

Compute an appropriate analysis of variance among the mean strength scores. If a significant F-test for treatments is indicated, employ the Newman–Keuls test to isolate the mean(s) accounting for the significance.

COMPUTER APPLICATION

6. Compute the appropriate analysis of variance for data given in Exercises 4 and 5 using computer programs selected from BMD series.

12

Alternative Methods in Tests of Hypotheses

12.1   INTRODUCTION

This text has emphasized the estimation of population parameters and tests of hypotheses about these parameters. This is why the subdiscipline involving these procedures is referred to as *parametric statistics*. In the last few decades, there has been concern over the fact that in parametric statistics we make certain assumptions about the distributions from which the parameters come (such as normality and homogeneity of variance) that are not always met.* Thus, another branch or subdiscipline of statistics has been developed in which distributions are considered in lieu of parameters. This subdiscipline is referred to as *nonparametric statistics*. Since in this area we work with entire distributions and there are no assumptions made about the distribution of scores, another name sometimes given to this branch of statistics is *distribution-free statistics*. When testing hypotheses using these techniques, we talk about *nonparametric or distribution-free tests of hypotheses*.

In addition to the advantage of not having to meet assumptions about the distribution of scores, one of the other reasons usually given for the use of nonparametric techniques is that

nonparametric tests focus on the rank of scores or even on scores that involve classification rather than the "numerical value" of scores.

To give you a more complete understanding of the implications of this statement, a distinction among scales of measurement needs to be made.

SCALES OF MEASUREMENT

The four scales of measurement usually identified are nominal, ordinal, interval, and ratio. The *nominal* scale can be used only to identify an object or person. An example of this kind of scale would be sex. A person belongs to either the male sex or the female sex. We could indicate that all those who are male are to be assigned the numeral 1 and those who are female are to be assigned the numeral 2. These numbers or scores indicate identity only and cannot be interpreted as connoting order or amount. Therefore, we are able to determine only if various frequencies of observations are equal ($=$) or not equal ($\neq$) to one another.

The *ordinal* scale allows us to indicate the rank or order of various scores. For example, we record the results in the various events in a track meet by stating the order of finish. We might say that in the 100-yd dash Joe finished first, Jack second, Don third, and Bill fourth. We would assign the numerals 1, 2, 3, and 4, respectively, to the four participants above. In this example, the scores do not imply meaning beyond identification and the rank-order

---

* It must be reiterated that the parametric tests are many times robust to these assumptions and when the assumptions are moderately violated, our type I error is changed very little.

finish of the race for each individual. Not only can we determine if our observations are $=$ or $\neq$, but also if any observation is less than $(<)$ or greater than $(>)$ any other observation. However, these scores do not permit us to determine the amount of difference between 1 and 2, 2 and 3, 3 and 4. These scores indicate position only.

Interval and *ratio* scales are the highest levels of measurement. These scales are truly quantitative and therefore indicate amount. They also permit the use of arithmetic operations of addition, subtraction, multiplication, and division. These scales have all the properties inherent in the ordinal scale, but have a very important additional property in that they do measure the amount associated with an observation. Thus, differences between points on any part of the scale are equal. If student A is able to successfully do five chins, student B seven chins, and student C nine chins, then we know that the difference in performance between students A and B is the same as the difference in performance between students B and C, namely, two chins. By the same token, if student D does ten chins, then he is only one chin better than student C. Many of the measurements we use in health, physical education, and recreation are of this nature.

The only difference between the interval and ratio scales is that the interval scale utilizes an arbitrary zero point while the ratio scale employs an absolute zero point. In the ratio scale, zero indicates the absence of the phenomenon measured, while in the interval scale it does not. Therefore, we can talk about ratios of numbers in the ratio scale, but cannot do so with the interval scale. An example which illustrates this point rather well is measuring the height of individuals. The usual method is to measure one's height from the floor. Therefore, if you are 70 in. tall and your little brother is 35 in. tall, it can be said that not only are you 35 in. taller than your brother, but also that you are twice as tall as he is. This is an example of a ratio scale with zero indicating the absence of height. Had we made our measurements from the top of a desk that is 30 in. high, then you would be given a score of 40 in. and your brother a score of 5 in. We could still say that you are 35 in. taller than your brother, but it would be erroneous to say that on the basis of this measurement you are eight times taller than your brother. This latter measurement is an example of an interval scale where 0 is only an arbitrary point of reference.

The scales of measurement in descending order, according to how much information is given by them, are ratio, interval, ordinal, and nominal. In other words, the ratio and interval scales give us more information than do the ordinal or nominal scales.

Nonparametric techniques, then, deal with scores that attain only ordinal or nominal scaling. This would seem to indicate that parametric statistics are appropriate tools only if we are working with scores or measurements that attain interval or ratio scaling. However, even when we have nominal scales, the sampling distribution of means is approximately normal. Thus, some statisticians would argue that we may still use the parametric methods.

Two other reasons that are often cited for the use of nonparametric statistics tests are that *they are useful when sample sizes are quite small ($n < 6$) and they are computationally simpler than the parametric statistical tests.* The former reason may be valid even though there are those who would argue that with such small samples it is not practical to even attempt inferring to a population. With the availability of modern digital computers the question of computational difficulties is moot.

A disadvantage in using nonparametric techniques with scores that are originally numerical in nature is that we lose a considerable amount of numerical information. For example, if three boys run the 100-yd dash in 10.4, 10.6, and 11.2 sec, we lose information when we record their scores as simply 1st, 2nd, and 3rd, respectively. A final disadvantage is that in everyday life we usually think in terms of comparing averages instead of comparing distributions; thus, nonparametric tests may be more difficult to conceptualize.

This section is not intended to convince you to use or not to use nonparametric statistics. Instead, the authors have presented some of the advantages and disadvantages of their use. You must be the final judge. It does appear to the authors that unless there is evidence that phenomena greatly violate the parametric assumptions, the researcher might do well to stick with the parametric techniques that have already been presented.

Only a few of the more commonly used nonparametric techniques will be presented in this introductory text. For a more thorough coverage of nonparametric techniques, it is recommended that the reader consult a text that is devoted to this subject. The techniques to be presented here are the chi-square tests, Man–Whitney U-test, sign test, Wilcoxon matched-pairs signed-rank test, and the Spearman rank order correlation coefficient.

12.2   CHI-SQUARE (χ^2) TESTS*

The family of nonparametric hypothesis tests called chi-square (denoted by the Greek letter χ with superscript ^{2}) tests are best suited for use when we have categorical (nominal) or ordered (ordinal) data. We may concurrently consider one or more variables with these procedures.

THE χ^2 TEST FOR ONE SAMPLE

Suppose we want to determine if the time of day our city pool is open to housewives is important. After having selected 600 housewives at random, we ask them to indicate their choice of pool hours. The choices given are: 8–10 A.M., 10–12 A.M., 1–3 P.M., and 3–5 P.M. The results obtained are:

---

* A χ^2-distribution is actually a distribution of sample variances. The derived χ^2 in this chapter is only approximately distributed as the tabled χ^2 which will be used.

	TIME OF DAY			
	8–10	10–12	1–3	3–5
Number of housewives selecting	100	300	150	50

The hypothesis that we will test is whether the observed distribution of housewives' preference differs significantly from the expected distribution when no preference exists. If no preference exists, we expect the distribution of 600 women to be:

	TIME OF DAY			
	8–10	10–12	1–3	3–5
Number of housewives selecting	150	150	150	150

Therefore, is the difference between the expected distribution (sometimes called the *theoretical distribution*) and the observed distribution great enough for us to conclude at, say, the 5% level of significance that the distribution of preferences in the population of housewives is different from what we hypothesized? We could also express this hypothesis in terms of proportions: H_0: $p_1 = p_2 = p_3 = p_4$ (where p_1 is the proportion of housewives preferring 8–10, and so on) against the alternative that not all the proportions are equal.

The hypothesis is tested by calculating:

$$\chi^2 = \sum_{i=1}^{K} \frac{(f_o - f_e)^2}{f_e} \tag{12.1}$$

where f_o is the observed number in a given category, f_e is the expected number in a given category, and K is the number of categories.

This is compared with the χ^2-distribution (Table VI, Appendix B), which has $(k-1)$ d.f. For our example:

$$\chi^2 = \frac{(100-150)^2}{150} + \frac{(300-150)^2}{150} + \frac{(150-150)^2}{150} + \frac{(50-150)^2}{150}$$

$$= \frac{2500 + 22{,}500 + 0 + 10{,}000}{150}$$

$$= \frac{35{,}000}{150}$$

$$= 233.33$$

Since we chose $\alpha = 0.05$, when we compare this obtained χ^2 with $\chi^2_{(4-1=3\,\text{d.f.})} = 7.81*$ (found in Table VI, Appendix B) we reject our hypothesis and conclude that housewives do prefer certain times of the day for the pool to be open.

---

* Note that the tabled values are $\chi^2_{1-\alpha,(K-1)}$.

In applications with a single variable, such as the example above, the χ^2-test is sometimes referred to as a "goodness of fit" test. In all one-variable χ^2-tests we determine how "good" some sample distribution fits an expected or theoretical distribution.

We could have an expected or theoretical distribution with something other than equal proportions. For example, suppose we hypothesize that the incidence of initial heart attack among men is in the ratio $2:3:5$ for the respective age groups of 30–40, 40–50, and 50–60. The respective population proportions hypothesized would then be $\frac{1}{5}$, $\frac{3}{10}$, and $\frac{1}{2}$. Let $\alpha = 0.01$. Assume that we observed a sample of 200 cardiac patients and found the age distribution that is presented in Table 12.1.

TABLE 12.1

Observed and Expected Frequencies of Initial Heart Attacks by Age

	AGE RANGE		
	30–40	40–50	50–60
Number in sample (f_o)	55	45	110
Expected (f_e)	(40)	(60)	(100)

The expected values in parentheses are found by multiplying the expected or hypothesized proportion ($\frac{1}{5}$, $\frac{3}{10}$, or $\frac{1}{2}$) by the number in our sample (200). For example, in the first category 40 is found by multiplying $\frac{1}{5} \times 200$. The calculated

$$\chi^2 = \sum_{i=1}^{3} \frac{(f_o - f_e)^2}{f_e}$$

$$= \frac{(55-40)^2}{40} + \frac{(45-60)^2}{60} + \frac{(110-100)^2}{100}$$

$$= \frac{225}{40} + \frac{225}{60} + \frac{100}{100}$$

$$= 5.625 + 3.75 + 1$$

$$= 10.375$$

Since we chose $\alpha = 0.01$, $\chi^2_{0.99,2} = 9.21$ and our obtained value is larger than the critical value $(10.375 > 9.21)$. Thus we reject the hypothesized proportions of heart attacks for the three age groups.

Note that when finding critical values we considered only the upper end of the χ^2-distribution. This was done because as sample frequencies deviate further from the hypothesized frequencies, our calculated χ^2 will become larger. Thus, only significantly large χ^2 values suggest we reject the null hypothesis.

THE χ^2 TESTS WHEN TWO OR MORE SAMPLES ARE CONSIDERED

We often want to compare the distributions of two or more samples. We hypothesize that the sample distributions come from populations with the same distribution, or in other words, from the same population. The procedures for testing these types of hypotheses are basically an extension of the one-sample case. The χ^2-tests may be appropriately applied to two or more samples only if the samples were selected independently of one another. This same assumption is made in many of our parametric tests.

Example 1   To see how physical education background affects attitude toward physical activity, we gave four samples of college freshmen an inventory that purported to measure attitude toward physical activity. The four samples of students were:

1. 50 students who had 12 years of physical education instruction in the public schools,
2. 100 students who had physical education instruction in elementary school only,
3. 100 students who had physical education instruction in high school only, and
4. 50 students who never had physical education instruction.

As a result of the attitude inventory, the students were classified into categories listed from 1 to 5, with (1) indicating a very negative attitude toward physical activity and (5) indicating a very positive attitude toward physical activity. The results obtained from the 300 students are presented in Table 12.2.

TABLE 12.2

Results of Physical Education Attitude Inventory

Physical Education Background	ATTITUDE CATEGORY					Total
	1	2	3	4	5	
Twelve years	(a)8[a]	8	9	7	18	50
Elementary	15	15	22	20	28	100
High school	10	17	(b)30[a]	36	7	100
None	7	15	9	12	7	50
Totals	40	55	70	75	60	300

[a] (a) and (b) used only to identify two tabular entries in illustrative example.

There is no immediately obvious procedure for determining the expected values in the various categories. Let us look at tabular entry (a). If our hypothesis is true, we would expect an equal proportion of *each* of the "background" groups to fall into category 1. Since there are 40 students out of a total of 300 in category 1, we would expect that $^{40}\!/_{300} \times 50 = 6.67$ of the "twelve years" group would be in category one. Thus, the expected frequency for cell (a) would be 6.67.

We determine the other expected frequencies in the same way. For instance, the expected frequency for cell (b) is $^{70}\!/_{300} \times 100 = 23.33$. Table 12.3 contains the observed data with the expected frequencies in parentheses.

TABLE 12.3

Attitude Frequencies with Expected Frequencies

Physical Education Background	ATTITUDE CATEGORY					
	1	2	3	4	5	Total
Twelve years	$8_{(6.67)}$	$8_{(9.17)}$	$9_{(11.67)}$	$7_{(12.5)}$	$18_{(10)}$	50
Elementary	$15_{(13.33)}$	$15_{(18.33)}$	$22_{(23.33)}$	$20_{(25)}$	$28_{(20)}$	100
High school	$10_{(13.33)}$	$17_{(18.33)}$	$30_{(23.33)}$	$36_{(25)}$	$7_{(20)}$	100
None	$7_{(6.67)}$	$15_{(9.17)}$	$9_{(11.67)}$	$12_{(12.5)}$	$7_{(10)}$	50
Totals	40	55	70	75	60	300

Our hypothesis then is that the observed distribution of scores is the same as the expected distribution of scores or, in terms of the experiment, that the students' attitudes are not affected by their physical education background.

To calculate χ^2, we use

$$\chi^2 = \sum_{r=1}^{r} \sum_{c=1}^{c} \frac{(f_o - f_e)^2}{f_e} \tag{12.2}$$

where r is the number of rows, and c is the number of columns.

In our example,

$$\chi^2 = \frac{(8 - 6.67)^2}{6.67} + \frac{(8 - 9.17)^2}{9.17} + \cdots + \frac{(7 - 10)^2}{10}$$

$$= 36.31$$

In the two sample problems, there are $(r-1)(c-1)$ cells free to vary. Thus, in our present example, we have

$$(5-1)(4-1) = 4 \times 3 = 12 \text{ d.f.}$$

If we set $\alpha = 0.01$, then $\chi^2_{0.99,12} = 26.22$. Since the observed χ^2 is greater than the tabled χ^2, or $36.31 > 26.22$, we reject the hypothesis that students' attitudes are not affected by their physical education background. Data presented as nominal or ordinal create difficulty when we attempt to form functional relationships among variables. Since students' physical education backgrounds were basically classified into nominal categories, we cannot determine how students' attitudes vary according to exposure to physical education. Thus, we are limited in the amount of information we can extract from a study like the present one. It does appear that those who have physical education backgrounds have more favorable attitudes toward physical activity than those who have no background, but nothing definite beyond that conclusion can be stated.

PRECAUTIONS IN THE APPLICATION OF χ^2

Since the hypothesis tests which utilize χ^2-distributions are approximate in nature, there are a few precautions that should be taken when applying these tests.

Whenever 1 d.f. exists for the χ^2-test, a correction should be made for continuity (much like that used when we use the normal distribution as an approximation to the binomial). This is accomplished by reducing each absolute difference $f_o - f_e$ by 0.5 before computing χ^2. In the one-sample case, if $k = 2$ and therefore d.f. $= 1$,

$$\chi^2 = \sum_{i=1}^{k} \frac{(f_o - f_e - 0.5)^2}{f_e} \tag{12.3}$$

and in the two-or-more-sample situations when $r = 2$ and $c = 2$, d.f. $= 1$, and

$$\chi^2 = \sum_{r=1}^{r} \sum_{c=1}^{c} \frac{(f_o - f_e - 0.5)^2}{f_e} \tag{12.4}$$

In all χ^2-tests, if more than 20% of the cells in a frequency table have an expected frequency of less than five, or if any cell has an expected frequency of less than one, the application of any χ^2-test becomes rather meaningless. In a 1-d.f. situation, there should not be any cells with an expected frequency less than five. If these restrictions are not met by our data, then we must either collapse the data into fewer categories or use other procedures, which are too advanced to be presented in this text.

12.3   MANN–WHITNEY U-TEST

The Mann–Whitney U-test is one of the most powerful nonparametric tests. It is often used as an alternative to the parametric t-test when interval scaling is not attained or when it is feared that the assumptions underlying the use of the t have been grossly violated.

At least ordinal scaling is required for the application of the Mann–Whitney U-test. Assume that we have taught tennis to independent sample groups of size $n_1 = 5$ and $n_2 = 4$ by an experimental and the traditional method respectively. At the end of the unit, students in both groups compete in a single ladder tournament to determine the ranking of all $n_1 + n_2 = 4 + 5 = 9$ students according to tennis skill. We would like to know if students taught by the experimental method ($n_1 = 5$) are superior to those taught by the traditional method $(n_2 = 4)$. We hypothesize that the two groups have the same distribution of ranks. The alternative hypothesis is that the experimental group has higher ranks than those in the control group. Denoting our two groups by E (experimental) and C (control), we find the ranks in the ladder tournament for the two groups to be:

$$E - \text{group ranks:} \quad 1, 2, 4, 7, 9$$
$$C - \text{group ranks:} \quad 3, 5, 6, 8$$

TABLE 12.4

Ranks of Experimental and Control Groups

Rank	1	2	3	4	5	6	7	8	9
Group	E	E	C	E	C	C	E	C	E

Suppose we represent the group ranks as shown in Table 12.4. If the hypothesis is true, the E's and C's should be randomly distributed across the ranks. Thus, the number of C's to the right of each E should become progressively less as we move from rank 1 to rank 9. Conversely, if the hypothesis is not true, the E's and C's should form distinct clusters and the number of C's to the right of each E should not decrease as we move from rank 1 to rank 9. Of course, random fluctuations will interfere with either of these two ideal situations. To determine significant variations from the hypothesized rankings, we compute the statistic U (or U').

To find U, we determine the number of times each E precedes a C. In our example, the first E precedes all four C's; the second E also precedes all four C's, while the third E precedes three C's. The fourth E precedes one C, and the fifth E does not precede any C's. U is the sum of the number of times each E-rank precedes a C-rank. Thus, $U = 4 + 4 + 3 + 1 + 0 = 12$. Had we concentrated on the number of C's preceding E's, we would have found $U' = 3 + 2 + 2 + 1 = 8$. The problem now is to determine if the sample rankings are consistent with the hypothesized rankings.

The sampling distributions of U and U' are known when the hypothesis is true. We need know only the sample sizes n_1 and n_2 to determine critical values for U and U' recorded in Table VII, Appendix B. When the hypothesis is true, U and U' will be equal. When the hypothesis is not true, U will be small while U' will be large. Thus, we reject the null hypothesis if

$$U_{\text{observed}} < U_{n_1, n_2} \tag{12.5}$$

or

$$U'_{\text{observed}} > U'_{n_1, n_2} \tag{12.6}$$

but we accept it otherwise. Returning to the tennis methods example, let us set $\alpha = 0.05$ for a one-tail test. We find

$$U_{5,4} = 2$$

and

$$U'_{5,4} = 18$$

Since $U_{observed} > U_{5,4}$, we fail to reject the null hypothesis. Employing U' we find $U'_{observed} < U'_{5,4}$, and we reach the same conclusion. It should be noted that we need calculate only U or U', not both.

It should also be noted that both one- and two-tailed tests of hypotheses are possible with the U statistic. The only difference in procedure is the tabled values used.

12.4 NONPARAMETRIC TESTS INVOLVING RELATED SAMPLES

Thus far in our discussion of nonparametric hypothesis tests with two or more samples, we assumed that the samples were independently selected. Since it is not always feasible and often not desirable to meet this assumption, we present nonparametric methods for comparing distributions that are not independent. Two nonparametric tests which may be utilized for this purpose are the sign test and Wilcoxon matched-pairs signed-ranks tests.

SIGN TEST

Imagine that we have 14 pairs of students matched on intelligence and social acceptance, and we assign one group to an experimental program in physical education and the other group to a supervised play period in place of physical education. After one year, the students are given a leadership score on the basis of a self-answered questionnaire. We would like to determine if one or the other of the two groups shows superior leadership potential. The leadership scores are presented in Table 12.5.

The sign test considers only the sign of the difference $E - C$. Thus, anytime a student from the experimental group has a higher leadership score than his "match" in the control group, a plus is entered in the right-hand column. For example, with the first pair, the student from the experimental group has a leadership score of 40 and his control group "match" has a score of 35, so a plus is entered for the first pair. When a student from the control group obtains a higher score than his experimental group counterpart, a minus is entered for the pair (for example, see matched pair 3). When no difference exists between a matched pair, a zero is written (for example, see matched pair 2).

We hypothesize that the two programs have an equal influence on leadership scores. The alternate hypothesis may state simply that the two programs

TABLE 12.5

Leadership Scores of Experimental and Control Groups for Sign Test

Matched Pair	LEADERSHIP SCORES Experimental	Control	Sign of Difference (E — C)
1	40	35	+
2	35	35	0
3	35	40	—
4	33	30	+
5	30	20	+
6	27	27	0
7	24	25	—
8	23	22	+
9	20	15	+
10	19	8	+
11	18	20	—
12	15	12	+
13	10	3	+
14	6	7	—

do not have an equal influence on leadership, or that one is superior to the other. The reader will recognize the former as our familiar two-tailed test, while the latter suggests our one-tailed text. Symbolically, we may state the null hypothesis as

$$H_0: \quad p = q = \tfrac{1}{2}$$

where p is the probability of observing a plus and q is the probability of observing a minus difference for a given matched pair. If we disregard zero differences, then either a plus or a minus must occur. Since each matched pair represents an independent replication of the experiment, the appropriate probability distribution describing $X = $ "number of pluses" is the binomial distribution. Thus, if $X_0 = $ "number of observed pluses" among n matched pairs, then

$$p(X \geqslant X_0) = \sum_{X=X_0}^{n} \binom{n}{X_0} p^{X_0} q^{(n-X_0)} \tag{12.7}$$

where p and q are the hypothesized binomial probabilities. We reject the null hypothesis if

$$p(X \geqslant X_0) \leqslant \frac{\alpha}{2} \tag{12.8}$$

for a two-tailed test, or

$$p(X \geqslant X_0) \leqslant \alpha \tag{12.9}$$

for a one-tailed test.

Returning to our example, we set $n = 12$ since two pairs have equal scores. We find that, out of 12 pairs, 8 are plus and 4 are minus. Employing Eq. (12.7), or referring to Table VIII, Appendix B, we find

$$p(X \geqslant 8) = 1 - p(X < 8)$$
$$= 1 - .806$$
$$= .194$$

Assuming we selected $\alpha = .10$ prior to conducting the experiment, we would not be able to reject the null hypothesis since

$$p(X \geqslant 8) > .05$$

In the sign test, we assumed only ordinal scaling for the scores on the leadership questionnaire. We used only the information that two scores were different. In other words a difference of five (pair 1) was treated the same as a difference of one (pair 8), since in each case a plus was assigned to the pair. If our data permit us to assume that a difference of five is meaningfully greater than a difference of one, and so on, then we can apply a more powerful test called the Wilcoxon matched-pairs signed-rank test.

WILCOXON MATCHED-PAIRS SIGNED-RANK TEST

If we take the data from Table 12.5 and assume that the magnitude of the differences as well as the direction of differences may be validly considered, then the differences between pairs would appear as shown in Table 12.6.

The rank of each absolute difference is determined. For example, one is the smallest absolute difference existing. Since we have three differences

TABLE 12.6

Leadership Scores for Wilcoxon Matched-Pairs Signed-Rank Test

Matched Pair	LEADERSHIP SCORES Experimental	Control	Difference	Rank of Difference	Rank with Smaller Sum
1	40	35	+5	+8	
2	35	35	0	-	
3	35	40	-5	-8	-8
4	33	30	+3	+5.5	
5	30	20	+10	+11	
6	27	27	0	-	
7	24	25	-1	-2	-2
8	23	22	+1	+2	
9	20	15	+5	+8	
10	19	8	+11	+12	
11	18	20	-2	-4	-4
12	15	12	+3	5.5	
13	10	3	+7	+10	
14	6	7	-1	-2	-2

$$T = -16$$

that are one, namely -1, $+1$, and -1, these three occupy the first three ranks and are each given the average rank of two. The appropriate signs are placed in front of the ranks, giving us entries of -2, $+2$, -2 in the column entitled "Rank of Difference."

We find a statistic called T, which is the sum of the ranks that have the smaller absolute sum. Since the negative ranks have the smaller absolute sum in our problem, T is equal to 16. We compare this T with a critical value found in Table IX of Appendix B. If our obtained T *is less than* the tabled T, we reject our hypothesis. Once again, we consider $N = 12$ since we do not include scores that are equal. The critical value of T at the 0.10 level (two- tailed test) is found to be 17. Since our obtained value of $T = 16$ is less than this critical value, we are able to reject the hypothesis. Note that we did not reject the hypothesis employing the sign test. Subjectively, we feel it should be. Therefore, the Wilcoxon matched-pairs signed-rank test is suggested to be a more powerful test than the sign test. In general, this is so because more information is used when the Wilcoxon test is employed.

12.5   SPEARMAN RANK-ORDER CORRELATION COEFFICIENT (r_{rho})

One of the most widely used nonparametric techniques is the Spearman rank-order correlation coefficient, generally denoted by r_{rho}. It is a measure of association between two variables that requires that both variables attain at least ordinal scaling. The Spearman rho, as it is called, was originally derived as an estimate of the Pearson product-moment correlation coefficient r. The Spearman rho requires that we find the difference between ranks of individuals and employ that difference to determine relationships instead of obtained scores.

Suppose we desire the relationship between chinning ability of our students and their placement in a tennis ladder tournament. The results obtained for the two variables on each of 12 students are presented in Table 12.7.

Note that it is necessary to find the ranks for both the ladder tournament placement and the chinning variable. The formula for calculating r_{rho} is

$$r_{rho} = 1 - \frac{6 \sum_{i=1}^{N} D_i^2}{n(n^2 - 1)} \tag{12.10}$$

where n is the number of subjects or objects for which we have data. We use $\sum D^2$ in our formula and may logically see that if the rankings generally agree then $\sum D^2$ will be small, and consequently our correlation coefficient will be a large positive value. For our example,

$$r_{rho} = 1 - \frac{6(171)}{12(144 - 1)} = 1 - \frac{1026}{1716}$$

$$= 1 - 0.60 = 0.40$$

TABLE 12.7

Chin Scores and Ranks in Ladder Tournament

Student	Number of Chins	Rank in Chinning	Rank in Ladder Tournament	Difference D_i	D_i^2
A	12	2	1	1	1
B	9	4.5	3	1.5	2.25
C	5	9	7	2	4
D	7	6.5	6	0.5	0.25
E	2	11	12	−1	1
F	9	4.5	11	−6.5	42.25
G	1	12	8	4	16
H	7	6.5	2	4.5	20.25
I	15	1	4	−3	9
J	3	10	5	5	25
K	6	8	9	−1	1
L	10	3	10	−7	49
				Sum =	171

Therefore, the correlation between chinning ability and rankings from the tennis ladder tournament is $r_{rho} = 0.40$.

The rank-order correlation, like the Pearson r, can attain values between $+1$ and -1. An $r_{rho} = +1$ indicates perfect agreement in ranks for the two variables under consideration; while an $r_{rho} = -1$ indicates that the ranks of one variable are completely reversed to the ranks of the other variable; an $r_{rho} = 0$ indicates the absence of any association or agreement between the ranks of the two variables.

Exercises

1. Distinguish among and give an example of each of the following scales: nominal, ratio, ordinal, and interval.
2. We wish to determine if students have a preference for a color of tennis balls. The following preferences were expressed by a random sample of 65 students.

COLOR OF BALL

	Red	Green	Yellow	White
Students preferring	14	16	18	17

Is there a difference in color preference? Use $\alpha = 0.01$.
3. The following data were obtained on random samples of students with the various grades.

USE OF RECREATIONAL FACILITIES IN ONE SEMESTER

Grade Point Average	Never	Once or Twice	3–6 Times	7–12 Times	More than Twelve
3.0 or better	5	7	6	4	4
2.5–3.0	8	6	9	12	11
1.9–2.5	12	8	6	8	7
Less than 1.9	14	9	5	7	4

Is there a difference among the various grade groups? Use $\alpha = 0.05$.

4. We have two randomly selected groups, one practicing tennis in massed practices and the other in distributed practices. The results of a ladder tournament for the two groups at the conclusion of the course is given below:

Distributed practice group ranks – 2, 3, 4, 6, 8, 11

Massed practice group ranks – 1, 5, 7, 9, 10, 12

   a. Is the distributed practice superior? Use $\alpha = 0.05$.

   b. What hypothesis was tested above?

5. Two judges each ranked 10 students (labeled A, B, C, etc.) in order of gymnastics skill. The rankings are given below.

Judge I	Judge II
C	A
A	C
B	B
D	G
F	D
E	F
G	E
J	H
I	J
H	I

   a. Test the difference between the two judges' rankings assuming that the amount of difference in ranks is meaningless. Use $\alpha = 0.10$.

   b. Test the difference between the two judges' rankings assuming that the amount of difference in ranks is meaningful.

   c. What hypothesis was tested in each of the above?

6. We desire to test football teams that do knee-strengthening exercises to see if these teams tend to have fewer knee injuries than teams that do not do knee-strengthening exercises. The frequencies of knee injuries for the two random samples are presented below:

Teams	None	NUMBER OF INJURIES 1–2	3–4	5–6	Total
Did exercises	75	19	5	1	100
No exercises	95	26	19	10	150
Totals	170	45	24	11	250

Let $\alpha = 0.01$ and find the desired information.

7. We want to determine if our elementary students' "sociability" increases during a one-year period. A random sample of students is given a sociability score at the beginning and the end of the year. The scores are listed below.

	Before	After
Bill	10	10
Jane	5	7
Jean	6	3
Harold	4	8
John	2	6
Maritta	6	5

a. If only the rank between scores is valid, test the hypothesis that no change in sociability took place. Let $\alpha = 0.05$.

b. If the differences between scores may be ranked, test the hypothesis that no change in sociability took place.

8. As a measure of objectivity, find the correlation between the judges' rankings in Exercise 5 and explain what this correlation means.

9. Given the following data on two items for a group of students, find the rank-order correlation between them and interpret this correlation.

Student No.	Score on Tennis Written Test	Rank on Skill Test
1	70	10
2	82	2
3	65	15
4	90	1
5	55	14
6	75	3
7	75	9
8	93	6
9	62	13
10	74	7
11	78	4
12	98	5
13	67	12
14	41	11
15	72	8

Bibliography

Alder, H. L., and **Roessler, E. B.** 1968. *Introduction to Probability and Statistics.* San Francisco: Freeman.

Davies, Owen L. 1956. *The Design and Analysis of Industrial Experiments,* Second Edition. Edinburgh: Oliver and Boyd.

Dixon, Wilfrid J., and **Massey, Frank J., Jr.** 1969. *Introduction to Statistical Analysis,* Third Edition. New York: McGraw-Hill.

Ferguson, G. A. 1971. *Statistical Analysis in Psychology and Education.* New York: McGraw-Hill.

Hall, P. G. 1971. *Elementary Statistics.* New York: Wiley.

Hammond, K. R.; Householder, J. E., and **Castellan, N. J., Jr.** 1970. *Introduction to the Statistical Method.* New York: Knopf.

Hays, William L. 1963. *Statistics.* New York: Holt, Rinehart and Winston.

Huntsberger, D. V. 1968. *Elements of Statistical Inference.* Boston: Allyn and Bacon.

Kempthorne, Oscar. 1952. *The Design and Analysis of Experiments.* New York: Wiley.

Lohnes, Paul R., and **Cooley, William W.** 1968. *Introduction to Statistical Procedures: With Computer Exercises.* New York: Wiley.

Marascuilo, L. A. 1971. *Statistical Methods for Behavioral Science Research.* New York: McGraw-Hill.

Mendenhall, W. 1971. *Introduction to Probability and Statistics.* Belmont: Durbury Press.

Minium, Edward W. 1970. *Statistical Reasoning in Psychology and Education.* New York: Wiley.

Mode, E. B. 1966. *Elements of Probability and Statistics.* Englewood Cliffs, N.J.: Prentice-Hall.

Mosteller, F.; Rourke, Robert E. K.; and **Thomas, G. B., Jr.** 1970. *Probability with Statistical Applications.* Reading, Mass.: Addison-Wesley.

Ostle, Bernard. 1963. *Statistics in Research.* Ames: The Iowa State University Press.

Remington, R. D., and **Schork, M. A.** 1970. *Statistics with Applications to the Biological and Health Sciences.* Englewood Cliffs, N.J.: Prentice-Hall.

Runyon, R. P., and **Haber, A.** 1971. *Fundamentals of Behavioral Statistics.* Reading, Mass.: Addison-Wesley.

Siegel, Sidney. 1956. *Nonparametric Statistics for the Behavioral Sciences.* New York: McGraw-Hill.

Winer, B. J. 1971. *Statistical Principles in Experimental Design.* New York: McGraw-Hill.

Appendix A
Review of Some Basic Mathematical and Algebraic Operations

A.1 EQUATION SOLVING

The derivations of many statistical formulae require the use and understanding of algebraic equations. We should think of every algebraic equation as being a mathematical sentence with the "$=$" serving as our verb. In solving for any unknown in an equation, we only need to remember one rule. *Whatever is done on one side of the equality sign must be done on the other side of the equality sign in order to keep the sentence a true statement.* In other words, if we add or subtract something, or multiply or divide by something, on one side of the $=$, then we must, respectively, add or subtract the same thing, or multiply or divide by the same thing, on the other side of the $=$. The following examples illustrate this rule for each operation and combinations of operations.

Example 1 Given the equation $X - 8 = 2$, solve for X by adding 8 to each side of $=$.

$$X - 8 + 8 = 2 + 8$$
$$X = 10$$

Example 2 Given the equation of $X + 5 = 8$, solve for X. Subtract 5 from each side of the $=$.

$$X + 5 - 5 = 8 - 5$$
$$X = 3$$

Example 3 Given the equation $Y/6 = 3$, solve for Y. Multiply each side of the equation by 6.

$$\not{6} \cdot \frac{Y}{\not{6}} = 3 \cdot 6$$
$$Y = 18$$

Example 4 Given the equation $6Z = 26$, solve for Z. Divide each side of the equation by 6.

$$\frac{\not{6} \cdot Z}{\not{6}} = \frac{26}{6}$$

$$Z = 4.33$$

Example 5 Given $(X - 3)/5 = 4$, solve for X.

1. Multiply by 5.

$$\frac{\not{5}(X - 3)}{\not{5}} = 5 \cdot 4$$

2. Add 3.

$$X - 3 = 20$$
$$X - 3 + 3 = 20 + 3$$
$$X = 23$$

Example 6 Given $15X - 7 = 3X + 29$, solve for X.

1. Subtract $3X$.

$$15X - 7 - 3X = 3X + 29 - 3X$$
$$12X - 7 = 29$$

2. Add 7.

$$12X - 7 + 7 = 29 + 7$$
$$12X = 36$$

3. Divide by 12.

$$\frac{\not{12}X}{\not{12}} = \frac{36}{12}$$

$$X = 3$$

With the application of this rule, all equations that are solvable can be solved. If you need further review and work in this area, you should consult a basic algebra text.

A.2 FINDING THE EQUATION OF A STRAIGHT LINE

If we are given any two points on a straight line, we can find an equation that will represent the line. For example, if we have the line shown below, with indicated points P_1: (x_1, y_1) and P_2: (x_2, y_2), then the horizontal line

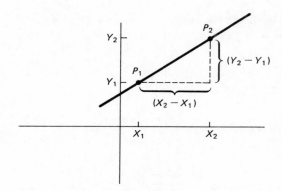

distance between these two points is $(x_2 - x_1)$ and the vertical distance is $(y_2 - y_1)$. Thus,

$$\frac{y_2 - y_1}{x_2 - x_1} = b$$

represents the proportional amount of change in y for a corresponding unit change in x. This quantity b is called the slope of the line since it indicates the degree of incline for the line with respect to the x-axis. When $x = 0$, that is, when the line intersects the y-axis, the value of y will be some value, say $y = a$. Then, in terms of the coefficients a and b, the equation for a straight line may be written as

$$y = a + bx$$

The formula necessary to determine the appropriate values for a and b is

$$\frac{y - y_1}{y_2 - y_1} = \frac{x - x_1}{x_2 - x_1}$$

when two points on the straight line are given. If, for example, two points lying on a straight line are

$$(1, 5) \quad \text{and} \quad (3, 9)$$

then the equation describing all points on that line is determined to be

$$\frac{y - 5}{9 - 5} = \frac{x - 1}{3 - 1}$$

or

$$y = 3 + 4x$$

This equation may be used to determine a y value simply by knowing its corresponding x value. Equations for straight lines are used in statistics when we wish to predict an individual's score for one variable if we know his score for a second variable.

A.3 SUMMATION NOTATION

Summation notation plays an important role in the presentation of statistical concepts. The following are typical examples of the uses made in this text. Each example is followed by a general summation rule or definition.

1. The summation of a constant number:

$$\sum_{i=1}^{3} 2 = 2 + 2 + 2$$
$$= 6$$

or

$$\sum_{i=1}^{4} C = C + C + C + C$$
$$= 4C$$

In general,

$$\sum_{i=1}^{N} C = NC$$

2. The summation of a sum or difference:

$$\sum_{i=1}^{3} (X_i + Y_i) = (X_1 + Y_1) + (X_2 + Y_2) + (X_3 + Y_3)$$
$$= \sum_{i=1}^{3} X_i + \sum_{i=1}^{3} Y_i$$

$$\sum_{i=1}^{2} (X_i - \bar{X}) = (X_1 - \bar{X}) + (X_2 - \bar{X})$$
$$= \sum_{i=1}^{2} X_i - 2\bar{X} \qquad \text{(since } \bar{X} \text{ is a constant)}$$

In general,

$$\sum_{i=1}^{N} (X_i - \bar{X}) = (X_1 - \bar{X}) + (X_2 - \bar{X}) + \cdots + (X_N - \bar{X})$$
$$= \sum_{i=1}^{N} X_i - \sum_{i=1}^{N} \bar{X}$$
$$= \sum_{i=1}^{N} X_i - N\bar{X} = 0$$

3. The summation of a product of pairs of values:

$$\sum_{i=1}^{4} X_i Y_i = X_1 Y_1 + X_2 Y_2 + X_3 Y_3 + X_4 Y_4$$

In general,

$$\sum_{i=1}^{N} X_i Y_i = X_1 Y_1 + X_2 Y_2 + \cdots + X_N Y_N$$

4. The summation of the products of a constant times each number:

$$\sum_{i=1}^{5} aX_i = aX_1 + aX_2 + aX_3 + aX_4 + aX_5$$
$$= a(X_1 + X_2 + X_3 + X_4 + X_5)$$

which also equals:

$$a \sum_{i=1}^{5} X_i$$

In general,

$$\sum_{i=1}^{N} aX_i = a \sum_{i=1}^{N} X_i$$

5. The summation of squares:

$$\sum_{i=1}^{3} X_i^2 = X_1^2 + X_2^2 + X_3^2$$

In general,

$$\sum_{i=1}^{N} X_i^2 = X_1^2 + X_2^2 + \cdots + X_N^2$$

A special application of this rule would be:

$$\sum_{i=1}^{N} (X_i - \bar{X})^2 = (X_1 - \bar{X})^2 + (X_2 - \bar{X})^2 + \cdots + (X_N - \bar{X})^2$$

6. The square of a summation:

$$\left(\sum_{i=1}^{3} X_i \right)^2 = (X_1 + X_2 + X_3)^2$$

In general,

$$\left(\sum_{i=1}^{N} X_i \right)^2 = (X_1 + X_2 + \cdots + X_N)^2$$

Note that rules 5 and 6 are not the same. Suppose $X_1 = 2$, $X_2 = 4$, and $X_3 = 5$; then from rule 5,

$$\sum_{i=1}^{3} X_i^2 = 2^2 + 4^2 + 5^2$$
$$= 4 + 16 + 25 = 45$$

and from rule 6,

$$\left(\sum_{i=1}^{3} X_i\right)^2 = (2 + 4 + 5)^2$$
$$= 11^2 = 121$$

Appendix B

Statistical Tables

TABLE I

The Normal Distribution[a]

Area under the standard normal curve from 0 to z, shown shaded, is $A(z)$.

Examples If Z is the standard normal random variable and $z = 1.64$, then

$$A(z) = P(0 < Z < z) = 0.4495$$
$$P(Z > z) = 0.0505$$
$$P(Z < z) = 0.9595$$
$$P(|Z| < z) = 0.8990$$

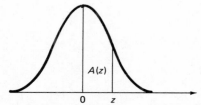

z	0.00	0.01	0.02	0.03	0.04	0.05	0.06	0.07	0.08	0.09
0.0	0.0000	0.0040	0.0080	0.0120	0.0160	0.0199	0.0239	0.0279	0.0319	0.0359
0.1	0.0398	0.0438	0.0478	0.0517	0.0557	0.0596	0.0636	0.0675	0.0714	0.0753
0.2	0.0793	0.0832	0.0871	0.0910	0.0948	0.0987	0.1026	0.1064	0.1103	0.1141
0.3	0.1179	0.1217	0.1255	0.1293	0.1331	0.1368	0.1406	0.1443	0.1480	0.1517
0.4	0.1554	0.1591	0.1628	0.1664	0.1700	0.1736	0.1772	0.1808	0.1844	0.1879
0.5	0.1915	0.1950	0.1985	0.2019	0.2054	0.2088	0.2123	0.2157	0.2190	0.2224
0.6	0.2257	0.2291	0.2324	0.2357	0.2389	0.2422	0.2454	0.2486	0.2517	0.2549
0.7	0.2580	0.2611	0.2642	0.2673	0.2704	0.2734	0.2764	0.2794	0.2823	0.2852
0.8	0.2881	0.2910	0.2939	0.2967	0.2995	0.3023	0.3051	0.3078	0.3106	0.3133
0.9	0.3159	0.3186	0.3212	0.3238	0.3264	0.3289	0.3315	0.3340	0.3365	0.3389
1.0	0.3413	0.3438	0.3461	0.3485	0.3508	0.3531	0.3554	0.3577	0.3599	0.3621
1.1	0.3643	0.3665	0.3686	0.3708	0.3729	0.3749	0.3770	0.3790	0.3810	0.3830
1.2	0.3849	0.3869	0.3888	0.3907	0.3925	0.3944	0.3962	0.3980	0.3997	0.4015
1.3	0.4032	0.4049	0.4066	0.4082	0.4099	0.4115	0.4131	0.4147	0.4162	0.4177
1.4	0.4192	0.4207	0.4222	0.4236	0.4251	0.4265	0.4279	0.4292	0.4306	0.4319
1.5	0.4332	0.4345	0.4357	0.4370	0.4382	0.4394	0.4406	0.4418	0.4429	0.4441
1.6	0.4452	0.4463	0.4474	0.4484	0.4495	0.4505	0.4515	0.4525	0.4535	0.4545
1.7	0.4554	0.4564	0.4573	0.4582	0.4591	0.4599	0.4608	0.4616	0.4625	0.4633
1.8	0.4641	0.4649	0.4656	0.4664	0.4671	0.4678	0.4686	0.4693	0.4699	0.4706
1.9	0.4713	0.4719	0.4726	0.4732	0.4738	0.4744	0.4750	0.4756	0.4761	0.4767
2.0	0.4772	0.4778	0.4783	0.4788	0.4793	0.4798	0.4803	0.4808	0.4812	0.4817
2.1	0.4821	0.4826	0.4830*	0.4834	0.4838	0.4842	0.4846	0.4850	0.4854	0.4857
2.2	0.4861	0.4864	0.4868	0.4871	0.4875	0.4878	0.4881	0.4884	0.4887	0.4890
2.3	0.4893	0.4896	0.4898	0.4901	0.4904	0.4906	0.4909	0.4911	0.4913	0.4916
2.4	0.4918	0.4920	0.4922	0.4925	0.4927	0.4929	0.4931	0.4932	0.4934	0.4936
2.5	0.4938	0.4940	0.4941	0.4943	0.4945	0.4946	0.4948	0.4949	0.4951	0.4952
2.6	0.4953	0.4955	0.4956	0.4957	0.4959	0.4960	0.4961	0.4962	0.4963	0.4964
2.7	0.4965	0.4966	0.4967	0.4968	0.4969	0.4970	0.4971	0.4972	0.4973	0.4974
2.8	0.4974	0.4975	0.4976	0.4977	0.4977	0.4978	0.4979	0.4979	0.4980	0.4981
2.9	0.4981	0.4982	0.4982	0.4983	0.4984	0.4984	0.4985	0.4985	0.4986	0.4986
3.0	0.4987	0.4987	0.4987	0.4988	0.4988	0.4989	0.4989	0.4989	0.4990	0.4990

[a] Abridged from Table 9 in *Biometrika Tables for Statisticians*, vol. 1 (3d ed.) New York: Cambridge, 1966. Edited by E. S. Pearson and H. O. Hartley. Reproduced with kind permission of E. S. Pearson for the *Biometrika* trustees.

TABLE II

The t-Distribution[a]

d.f.	$t_{0.60}$	$t_{0.70}$	$t_{0.80}$	$t_{0.90}$	$t_{0.95}$	$t_{0.975}$	$t_{0.99}$	$t_{0.995}$	$t_{0.9995}$
1	0.3250	0.7270	1.376	3.078	6.3138	12.706	31.821	63.657	636.619
2	0.2885	0.6172	1.061	1.886	2.9200	4.3027	6.965	9.9248	31.598
3	0.2766	0.5840	0.978	1.638	2.3534	3.1825	4.541	5.8409	12.924
4	0.2707	0.5692	0.941	1.533	2.1318	2.7764	3.747	4.6041	8.610
5	0.2672	0.5598	0.920	1.476	2.0150	2.5706	3.365	4.0321	6.869
6	0.2648	0.5536	0.906	1.440	1.9432	2.4469	3.143	3.7074	5.959
7	0.2632	0.5493	0.896	1.415	1.8946	2.3646	2.998	3.4995	5.408
8	0.2619	0.5461	0.889	1.397	1.8595	2.3060	2.896	3.3554	5.041
9	0.2610	0.5436	0.883	1.383	1.8331	2.2622	2.821	3.2498	4.781
10	0.2602	0.5416	0.879	1.372	1.8125	2.2281	2.764	3.1693	4.587
11	0.2596	0.5400	0.876	1.363	1.7939	2.2010	2.718	3.1058	4.437
12	0.2590	0.5387	0.873	1.356	1.7823	2.1788	2.681	3.0545	4.318
13	0.2586	0.5375	0.870	1.350	1.7709	2.1604	2.650	3.0123	4.221
14	0.2582	0.5366	0.868	1.345	1.7613	2.1448	2.624	2.9768	4.140
15	0.2579	0.5358	0.866	1.341	1.7530	2.1315	2.602	2.9467	4.073
16	0.2576	0.5358	0.865	1.337	1.7459	2.1199	2.583	2.9208	4.015
17	0.2574	0.5344	0.863	1.333	1.7396	2.1098	2.567	2.8982	3.965
18	0.2571	0.5338	0.862	1.330	1.7341	2.1009	2.552	2.8784	3.922
19	0.2569	0.5333	0.861	1.328	1.7291	2.0930	2.539	2.8609	3.883
20	0.2567	0.5329	0.860	1.325	1.7247	2.0860	2.528	2.8453	3.850
21	0.2566	0.5325	0.859	1.323	1.7207	2.0796	2.518	2.8314	3.819
22	0.2564	0.5321	0.858	1.321	1.7171	2.0739	2.508	2.8188	3.792
23	0.2563	0.5318	0.858	1.319	1.7139	2.0687	2.500	2.9073	3.767
24	0.2562	0.5315	0.857	1.318	1.7109	2.0639	2.492	2.7969	3.745
25	0.2561	0.5312	0.856	1.316	1.7081	2.0595	2.485	2.7874	3.725
26	0.2560	0.5309	0.856	1.315	1.7056	2.0555	2.479	2.7787	3.707
27	0.2559	0.5307	0.855	1.314	1.7033	2.0518	2.473	2.7707	3.690
28	0.2558	0.5304	0.855	1.313	1.7011	2.0484	2.467	2.7633	3.674
29	0.2557	0.5302	0.854	1.311	1.6991	2.0452	2.462	2.7564	3.659
30	0.2556	0.5300	0.854	1.310	1.6973	2.0423	2.457	2.7500	3.616
35	0.2553	0.5292	0.8521	1.3062	1.6896	2.0301	2.438	2.7239	3.5919
40	0.2550	0.5286	0.8507	1.3031	1.6839	2.0211	2.423	2.7045	3.5511
45	0.2549	0.5281	0.8497	1.3007	1.6794	2.0141	2.412	2.6896	3.5207
50	0.2547	0.5278	0.8489	1.2987	1.6759	2.0086	2.403	2.6778	3.4965
60	0.2545	0.5272	0.8477	1.2959	1.6707	2.0003	2.390	2.6603	3.4606
70	0.2543	0.5268	0.8468	1.2938	1.6669	1.9945	2.381	2.6480	3.4355
80	0.2542	0.5265	0.8462	1.2922	1.6641	1.9901	2.374	2.6388	3.4169
90	0.2541	0.5263	0.8457	1.2910	1.6620	1.9867	2.368	2.6316	3.4022
100	0.2540	0.5261	0.8452	1.2901	1.6602	1.9840	2.364	2.6260	3.3909
120	0.2539	0.5258	0.8446	1.2887	1.6577	1.9799	2.358	2.6175	3.3736
140	0.2538	0.5256	0.8442	1.2876	1.6558	1.9771	2.353	2.6114	3.3615
160	0.2538	0.5255	0.8439	1.2869	1.6545	1.9749	2.350	2.6070	3.3527
180	0.2537	0.5253	0.8436	1.2863	1.6534	1.9733	2.347	2.6035	3.3456
200	0.2537	0.5252	0.8434	1.2858	1.6525	1.9719	2.345	2.6006	3.3400
∞	0.2533	0.5244	0.8416	1.2816	1.6449	1.9600	2.326	2.5758	3.2905

Reproduced from *Documenta Geigy Scientific Tables*, 7th edition, Basle, Switzerland, 1970. Courtesy CIBA-GEIGY Limited, Basle, Switzerland.

TABLE III

The F-Distribution,[a] $\alpha = 0.05$

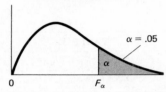

ν_1

d.f. for ν_2	1	2	3	4	5	6	7	8	9
1	161.4	199.5	215.7	224.6	230.2	234.0	236.8	238.9	240.5
2	18.51	19.00	19.16	19.25	19.30	19.33	19.35	19.37	19.38
3	10.13	9.55	9.28	9.12	9.01	8.94	8.89	8.85	8.81
4	7.71	6.94	6.59	6.39	6.26	6.16	6.09	6.04	6.00
5	6.61	5.79	5.41	5.19	5.05	4.95	4.88	4.82	4.77
6	5.99	5.14	4.76	4.53	4.39	4.28	4.21	4.15	4.10
7	5.59	4.74	4.35	4.12	3.97	3.87	3.79	3.73	3.68
8	5.32	4.46	4.07	3.84	3.69	3.58	3.50	3.44	3.39
9	5.12	4.26	3.86	3.63	3.48	3.37	3.29	3.23	3.18
10	4.96	4.10	3.71	3.48	3.33	3.22	3.14	3.07	3.02
11	4.84	3.98	3.59	3.36	3.20	3.09	3.01	2.95	2.90
12	4.75	3.89	3.49	3.26	3.11	3.00	2.91	2.85	2.80
13	4.67	3.81	3.41	3.18	3.03	2.92	2.83	2.77	2.71
14	4.60	3.74	3.34	3.11	2.96	2.85	2.76	2.70	2.65
15	4.54	3.68	3.29	3.06	2.90	2.79	2.71	2.64	2.59
16	4.49	3.63	3.24	3.01	2.85	2.74	2.66	2.59	2.54
17	4.45	3.59	3.20	2.96	2.81	2.70	2.61	2.55	2.49
18	4.41	3.55	3.16	2.93	2.77	2.66	2.58	2.51	2.46
19	4.38	3.52	3.13	2.90	2.74	2.63	2.54	2.48	2.42
20	4.35	3.49	3.10	2.87	2.71	2.60	2.51	2.45	2.39
21	4.32	3.47	3.07	2.84	2.68	2.57	2.49	2.42	2.37
22	4.30	3.44	3.05	2.82	2.66	2.55	2.46	2.40	2.34
23	4.28	3.42	3.03	2.80	2.64	2.53	2.44	2.37	2.32
24	4.26	3.40	3.01	2.78	2.62	2.51	2.42	2.36	2.30
25	4.24	3.39	2.99	2.76	2.60	2.49	2.40	2.34	2.28
26	4.23	3.37	2.98	2.74	2.59	2.47	2.39	2.32	2.27
27	4.21	3.35	2.96	2.73	2.57	2.46	2.37	2.31	2.25
28	4.20	3.34	2.95	2.71	2.56	2.45	2.36	2.29	2.24
29	4.18	3.33	2.93	2.70	2.55	2.43	2.35	2.28	2.22
30	4.17	3.32	2.92	2.69	2.53	2.42	2.33	2.27	2.21
40	4.08	3.23	2.84	2.61	2.45	2.34	2.25	2.18	2.12
60	4.00	3.15	2.76	2.53	2.37	2.25	2.17	2.10	2.04
120	3.92	3.07	2.68	2.45	2.29	2.17	2.09	2.02	1.96
∞	3.84	3.00	2.60	2.37	2.21	2.10	2.01	1.94	1.88

[a] From "Tables of Percentage Points of the Inverted Beta (F) Distribution," *Biometrika*, Vol. 33 (1943), pp. 73–88 by Maxine Merrington and Catherine M. Thompson. Reproduced with the kind permission of E. S. Pearson for the *Biometrika* trustees.

					v_1					d.f. for
10	12	15	20	24	30	40	60	120	∞	v_2
241.9	243.9	245.9	248.0	249.1	250.1	251.1	252.2	253.3	254.3	1
19.40	19.41	19.43	19.45	19.45	19.46	19.47	19.48	19.49	19.50	2
8.79	8.74	8.70	8.66	8.64	8.62	8.59	8.57	8.55	8.53	3
5.96	5.91	5.86	5.80	5.77	5.75	5.72	5.69	5.66	5.63	4
4.74	4.68	4.62	4.56	4.53	4.50	4.46	4.43	4.40	4.36	5
4.06	4.00	3.94	3.87	3.84	3.81	3.77	3.74	3.70	3.67	6
3.64	3.57	3.51	3.44	3.41	3.38	3.34	3.30	3.27	3.23	7
3.35	3.28	3.22	3.15	3.12	3.08	3.04	3.01	2.97	2.93	8
3.14	3.07	3.01	2.94	2.90	2.86	2.83	2.79	2.75	2.71	9
2.98	2.91	2.85	2.77	2.74	2.70	2.66	2.62	2.58	2.54	10
2.85	2.79	2.72	2.65	2.61	2.57	2.53	2.49	2.45	2.40	11
2.75	2.69	2.62	2.54	2.51	2.47	2.43	2.38	2.34	2.30	12
2.67	2.60	2.53	2.46	2.42	2.38	2.34	2.30	2.25	2.21	13
2.60	2.53	2.46	2.39	2.35	2.31	2.27	2.22	2.18	2.13	14
2.54	2.48	2.40	2.33	2.29	2.25	2.20	2.16	2.11	2.07	15
2.49	2.42	2.35	2.28	2.24	2.19	2.15	2.11	2.06	2.01	16
2.45	2.38	2.31	2.23	2.19	2.15	2.10	2.06	2.01	1.96	17
2.41	2.34	2.27	2.19	2.15	2.11	2.06	2.02	1.97	1.92	18
2.38	2.31	2.23	2.16	2.11	2.07	2.03	1.98	1.93	1.88	19
2.35	2.28	2.20	2.12	2.08	2.04	1.99	1.95	1.90	1 84	20
2.32	2.25	2.18	2.10	2.05	2.01	1.96	1.92	1.87	1.81	21
2.30	2.23	2.15	2.07	2.03	1.98	1.94	1.89	1.84	1.78	22
2.27	2.20	2.13	2.05	2.01	1.96	1.91	1.86	1.81	1.76	23
2.25	2.18	2.11	2.03	1.98	1.94	1.89	1.84	1.79	1.73	24
2.24	2.16	2.09	2.01	1.96	1.92	1.87	1.82	1.77	1.71	25
2.22	2.15	2.07	1.99	1.95	1.90	1.85	1.80	1.75	1.69	26
2.20	2.13	2.06	1.97	1.93	1.88	1.84	1.79	1.73	1.67	27
2.19	2.12	2.04	1.96	1.91	1.87	1.82	1.77	1.71	1.65	28
2.18	2.10	2.03	1.94	1.90	1.85	1.81	1.75	1.70	1.64	29
2.16	2.09	2.01	1.93	1.89	1.84	1.79	1.74	1.68	1.62	30
2.08	2.00	1.92	1.84	1.79	1.74	1.69	1.64	1.58	1.51	40
1.99	1.92	1.84	1.75	1.70	1.65	1.59	1.53	1.47	1.39	60
1.91	1.83	1.75	1.66	1.61	1.55	1.50	1.43	1.35	1.25	120
1.83	1.75	1.67	1.57	1.52	1.46	1.39	1.32	1.22	1.00	∞

Continued

TABLE III

The F-Distribution ^a(Continued) α = 0.01

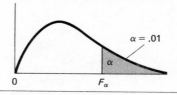

ν_1

d.f. for ν_2	1	2	3	4	5	6	7	8	9
1	4052	4999.5	5403	5625	5764	5859	5928	5982	6022
2	98.50	99.00	99.17	99.25	99.30	99.33	99.36	99.37	99.39
3	34.12	30.82	29.46	28.71	28.24	27.91	27.67	27.49	27.35
4	21.20	18.00	16.69	15.98	15.52	15.21	14.98	14.80	14.66
5	16.26	13.27	12.06	11.39	10.97	10.67	10.46	10.29	10.16
6	13.75	10.92	9.78	9.15	8.75	8.47	8.26	8.10	7.98
7	12.25	9.55	8.45	7.85	7.46	7.19	6.99	6.84	6.72
8	11.26	8.65	7.59	7.01	6.63	6.37	6.18	6.03	5.91
9	10.56	8.02	6.99	6.42	6.06	5.80	5.61	5.47	5.35
10	10.04	7.56	6.55	5.99	5.64	5.39	5.20	5.06	4.94
11	9.65	7.21	6.22	5.67	5.32	5.07	4.89	4.74	4.63
12	9.33	6.93	5.95	5.41	5.06	4.82	4.64	4.50	4.39
13	9.07	6.70	5.74	5.21	4.86	4.62	4.44	4.30	4.19
14	8.86	6.51	5.56	5.04	4.69	4.46	4.28	4.14	4.03
15	8.68	6.36	5.42	4.89	4.56	4.32	4.14	4.00	3.89
16	8.53	6.23	5.29	4.77	4.44	4.20	4.03	3.89	3.78
17	8.40	6.11	5.18	4.67	4.34	4.10	3.93	3.79	3.68
18	8.29	6.01	5.09	4.58	4.25	4.01	3.84	3.71	3.60
19	8.18	5.93	5.01	4.50	4.17	3.94	3.77	3.63	3.52
20	8.10	5.85	4.94	4.43	4.10	3.87	3.70	3.56	3.46
21	8.02	5.78	4.87	4.37	4.04	3.81	3.64	3.51	3.40
22	7.95	5.72	4.82	4.31	3.99	3.76	3.59	3.45	3.35
23	7.88	5.66	4.76	4.26	3.94	3.71	3.54	3.41	3.30
24	7.82	5.61	4.72	4.22	3.90	3.67	3.50	3.36	3.26
25	7.77	5.57	4.68	4.18	3.85	3.63	3.46	3.32	3.22
26	7.72	5.53	4.64	4.14	3.82	3.59	3.42	3.29	3.18
27	7.68	5.49	4.60	4.11	3.78	3.56	3.39	3.26	3.15
28	7.64	5.45	4.57	4.07	3.75	3.53	3.36	3.23	3.12
29	7.60	5.42	4.54	4.04	3.73	3.50	3.33	3.20	3.09
30	7.56	5.39	4.51	4.02	3.70	3.47	3.30	3.17	3.07
40	7.31	5.18	4.31	3.83	3.51	3.29	3.12	2.99	2.89
60	7.08	4.98	4.13	3.65	3.34	3.12	2.95	2.82	2.72
120	6.85	4.79	3.95	3.48	3.17	2.96	2.79	2.66	2.56
∞	6.63	4.61	3.78	3.32	3.02	2.80	2.64	2.51	2.41

										d.f. for v_2
10	12	15	20	24	30	40	60	120	∞	
6056	6106	6157	6209	6235	6261	6287	6313	6339	6366	1
99.40	99.42	99.43	99.45	99.46	99.47	99.47	99.48	99.49	99.50	2
27.23	27.05	26.87	26.69	26.60	26.50	26.41	26.32	26.22	26.13	3
14.55	14.37	14.20	14.02	13.93	13.84	13.75	13.65	13.56	13.46	4
10.05	9.89	9.72	9.55	9.47	9.38	9.29	9.20	9.11	9.02	5
7.87	7.72	7.56	7.40	7.31	7.23	7.14	7.06	6.97	6.88	6
6.62	6.47	6.31	6.16	6.07	5.99	5.91	5.82	5.74	5.65	7
5.81	5.67	5.52	5.36	5.28	5.20	5.12	5.03	4.95	4.86	8
5.26	5.11	4.96	4.81	4.73	4.65	4.57	4.48	4.40	4.31	9
4.85	4.71	4.56	4.41	4.33	4.25	4.17	4.08	4.00	3.91	10
4.54	4.40	4.25	4.10	4.02	3.94	3.86	3.78	3.69	3.60	11
4.30	4.16	4.01	3.86	3.78	3.70	3.62	3.54	3.45	3.36	12
4.10	3.96	3.82	3.66	3.59	3.51	3.43	3.34	3.25	3.17	13
3.94	3.80	3.66	3.51	3.43	3.35	3.27	3.18	3.09	3.00	14
3.80	3.67	3.52	3.37	3.29	3.21	3.13	3.05	2.96	2.37	15
3.69	3.55	3.41	3.26	3.18	3.10	3.02	2.93	2.84	2.75	16
3.59	3.46	3.31	3.16	3.08	3.00	2.92	2.83	2.75	2.65	17
3.51	3.37	3.23	3.08	3.00	2.92	2.84	2.75	2.66	2.57	18
3.43	3.30	3.15	3.00	2.92	2.84	2.76	2.67	2.58	2.49	19
3.37	3.23	3.09	2.94	2.86	2.78	2.69	2.61	2.52	2.42	20
3.31	3.17	3.03	2.88	2.80	2.72	2.64	2.55	2.46	2.36	21
3.26	3.12	2.98	2.83	2.75	2.67	2.58	2.50	2.40	2.31	22
3.21	3.07	2.93	2.78	2.70	2.62	2.54	2.45	2.35	2.26	23
3.17	3.03	2.89	2.74	2.66	2.58	2.49	2.40	2.31	2.21	24
3.13	2.99	2.85	2.70	2.62	2.54	2.45	2.36	2.27	2.17	25
3.09	2.96	2.81	2.66	2.58	2.50	2.42	2.33	2.23	2.13	26
3.06	2.93	2.78	2.63	2.55	2.47	2.38	2.29	2.20	2.10	27
3.03	2.90	2.75	2.60	2.52	2.44	2.35	2.26	2.17	2.06	28
3.00	2.87	2.73	2.57	2.49	2.41	2.33	2.23	2.14	2.03	29
2.98	2.84	2.70	2.55	2.47	2.39	2.30	2.21	2.11	2.01	30
2.80	2.66	2.52	2.37	2.29	2.20	2.11	2.02	1.92	1.80	40
2.63	2.50	2.35	2.20	2.12	2.03	1.94	1.84	1.73	1.60	60
2.47	2.34	2.19	2.03	1.95	1.86	1.76	1.66	1.53	1.38	120
2.32	2.18	2.04	1.88	1.79	1.70	1.59	1.47	1.32	1.00	∞

v_1

TABLE IV

The q-Distribution[a]

r = Number of Steps Between Ordered Means

d.f. for $s_{\bar{x}}$	1 − α	2	3	4	5	6	7	8	9	10	11	12	13	14	15
1	0.95	18.0	27.0	32.8	37.1	40.4	43.1	45.4	47.4	49.1	50.6	52.0	53.2	54.3	55.4
	0.99	90.0	135	164	186	202	216	227	237	246	253	260	266	272	277
2	0.95	6.09	8.3	9.8	10.9	11.7	12.4	13.0	13.5	14.0	14.4	14.7	15.1	15.4	15.7
	0.99	14.0	19.0	22.3	24.7	26.6	28.2	29.5	30.7	31.7	32.6	33.4	34.1	34.8	35.4
3	0.95	4.50	5.91	6.82	7.50	8.04	8.48	8.85	9.18	9.46	9.72	9.95	10.2	10.4	10.5
	0.99	8.26	10.6	12.2	13.3	14.2	15.0	15.6	16.2	16.7	17.1	17.5	17.9	18.2	18.5
4	0.95	3.93	5.04	5.76	6.29	6.71	7.05	7.35	7.60	7.83	8.03	8.21	8.37	8.52	8.66
	0.99	6.51	8.12	9.17	9.96	10.6	11.1	11.5	11.9	12.3	12.6	12.8	13.1	13.3	13.5
5	0.95	3.64	4.60	5.22	5.67	6.03	6.33	6.58	6.80	6.99	7.17	7.32	7.47	7.60	7.72
	0.99	5.70	6.97	7.80	8.42	8.91	9.32	9.67	9.97	10.2	10.5	10.7	10.9	11.1	11.2
6	0.95	3.46	4.34	4.90	5.31	5.63	5.89	6.12	6.32	6.49	6.65	6.79	6.92	7.03	7.14
	0.99	5.24	6.33	7.03	7.56	7.97	8.32	8.61	8.87	9.10	9.30	9.49	9.65	9.81	9.95
7	0.95	3.34	4.16	4.69	5.06	5.36	5.61	5.82	6.00	6.16	6.30	6.43	6.55	6.66	6.76
	0.99	4.95	5.92	6.54	7.01	7.37	7.68	7.94	8.17	8.37	8.55	8.71	8.86	9.00	9.12
8	0.95	3.26	4.04	4.53	4.89	5.17	5.40	5.60	5.77	5.92	6.05	6.18	6.29	6.39	6.48
	0.99	4.74	5.63	6.20	6.63	6.96	7.24	7.47	7.68	7.87	8.03	8.18	8.31	8.44	8.55
9	0.95	3.20	3.95	4.42	4.76	5.02	5.24	5.43	5.60	5.74	5.87	5.98	6.09	6.19	6.28
	0.99	4.60	5.43	5.96	6.35	6.66	6.91	7.13	7.32	7.49	7.65	7.78	7.91	8.03	8.13
10	0.95	3.15	3.88	4.33	4.65	4.91	5.12	5.30	5.46	5.60	5.72	5.83	5.93	6.03	6.11
	0.99	4.48	5.27	5.77	6.14	6.43	6.67	6.87	7.05	7.21	7.36	7.48	7.60	7.71	7.81
11	0.95	3.11	3.82	4.26	4.57	4.82	5.03	5.20	5.35	5.49	5.61	5.71	5.81	5.90	5.99
	0.99	4.39	5.14	5.62	5.97	6.25	6.48	6.67	6.84	6.99	7.13	7.26	7.36	7.46	7.56

12	0.95	3.08	3.77	4.20	4.51	4.75	4.95	5.12	5.27	5.40	5.51	5.62	5.71	5.80	5.88
	0.99	4.32	5.04	5.50	5.84	6.10	6.32	6.51	6.67	6.81	6.94	7.06	7.17	7.26	7.36
13	0.95	3.06	3.73	4.15	4.45	4.69	4.88	5.05	5.19	5.32	5.43	5.53	5.63	5.71	5.79
	0.99	4.26	4.96	5.40	5.73	5.98	6.19	6.37	6.53	6.67	6.79	6.90	7.01	7.10	7.19
14	0.95	3.03	3.70	4.11	4.41	4.64	4.83	4.99	5.13	5.25	5.36	5.46	5.55	5.64	5.72
	0.99	4.21	4.89	5.32	5.63	5.88	6.08	6.26	6.41	6.54	6.66	6.77	6.87	6.96	7.05
16	0.95	3.00	3.65	4.05	4.33	4.56	4.74	4.90	5.03	5.15	5.26	5.35	5.44	5.52	5.59
	0.99	4.13	4.78	5.19	5.49	5.72	5.92	6.08	6.22	6.35	6.46	6.56	6.66	6.74	6.82
18	0.95	2.97	3.61	4.00	4.28	4.49	4.67	4.82	4.96	5.07	5.17	5.27	5.35	5.43	5.50
	0.99	4.07	4.70	5.09	5.38	5.60	5.79	5.94	6.08	6.20	6.31	6.41	6.50	6.58	6.65
20	0.95	2.95	3.58	3.96	4.23	4.45	4.62	4.77	4.90	5.01	5.11	5.20	5.28	5.36	5.43
	0.99	4.02	4.64	5.02	5.29	5.51	5.69	5.84	5.97	6.09	6.19	6.29	6.37	6.45	6.52
24	0.95	2.92	3.53	3.90	4.17	4.37	4.54	4.68	4.81	4.92	5.01	5.10	5.18	5.25	5.32
	0.99	3.96	4.54	4.91	5.17	5.37	5.54	5.69	5.81	5.92	6.02	6.11	6.19	6.26	6.33
30	0.95	2.89	3.49	3.84	4.10	4.30	4.46	4.60	4.72	4.83	4.92	5.00	5.08	5.15	5.21
	0.99	3.89	4.45	4.80	5.05	5.24	5.40	5.54	5.56	5.76	5.85	5.93	6.01	6.08	6.14
40	0.95	2.86	3.44	3.79	4.04	4.23	4.39	4.52	4.63	4.74	4.82	4.91	4.98	5.05	5.11
	0.99	3.82	4.37	4.70	4.93	5.11	5.27	5.39	5.50	5.60	5.69	5.77	5.84	5.90	5.96
60	0.95	2.83	3.40	3.74	3.98	4.16	4.31	4.44	4.55	4.65	4.73	4.81	4.88	4.94	5.00
	0.99	3.76	4.28	4.60	4.82	4.99	5.13	5.25	5.36	5.45	5.53	5.60	5.67	5.73	5.79
120	0.95	2.80	3.36	3.69	3.92	4.10	4.24	4.36	4.48	4.56	4.64	4.72	4.78	4.84	4.90
	0.99	3.70	4.20	4.50	4.71	4.87	5.01	5.12	5.21	5.30	5.38	5.44	5.51	5.56	5.61
∞	0.95	2.77	3.31	3.63	3.86	4.03	4.17	4.29	4.39	4.47	4.55	4.62	4.68	4.74	4.80
	0.99	3.64	4.12	4.40	4.60	4.76	4.88	4.99	5.08	5.16	5.23	5.29	5.35	5.40	5.45

• From "Tables of Range and Studentized Range," *The Annals of Statistics*, Vol. 31 (1960), pp. 1122–1147, by H. Leon Harter. Reproduced with the kind permission of Ingram Olkin, editor of *The Annals of Statistics*.

TABLE V

Sample Size Estimates for Hypothesis Testing[a]

FOR $H_0 : \mu = \mu_1$

D	$\alpha=.10$					$\alpha=.05$					$\alpha=.01$					$\alpha=.001$					D
β	0.50	0.25	0.10	0.05	0.01	0.50	0.25	0.10	0.05	0.01	0.50	0.25	0.10	0.05	0.01	0.50	0.25	0.10	0.05	0.01	β
0.05																					0.05
0.10																					0.10
0.15																					0.15
0.20													1	1	1			1	1	1	0.20
0.25										1			1	1	2		1	1	1	2	0.25
0.30					1				1	1		1	1	2	2		1	2	2	3	0.30
0.35					1			1	1	2		1	2	3	3	1	2	2	3	4	0.35
0.40				1	2			1	2	3	1	2	2	3	3	1	2	3	4	5	0.40
0.45			1	1	2		1	2	2	3	1	2	3	4	4	2	3	4	5	6	0.45
0.50			1	2	3		1	2	3	4	1	3	3	4	5	2	4	5	6	7	0.50
0.55			2	2	3		1	2	3	5	2	3	4	5	6	3	4	6	7	9	0.55
0.60		1	2	3	4		2	3	4	6	2	4	5	6	7	3	5	7	8	11	0.60
0.65		1	3	3	5	1	2	3	4	6	3	4	6	7	8	4	6	8	10	12	0.65
0.70		1	3	4	6	1	3	4	5	7	3	5	6	8	9	5	7	9	11	14	0.70
0.75	1	2	4	5	6	1	3	5	6	8	4	6	7	9	11	5	8	11	13	17	0.75
0.80	1	2	4	5	7	2	4	6	7	9	4	6	8	10	12	6	9	12	14	19	0.80
0.85	1	3	5	6	8	2	4	6	8	11	5	7	9	12	14	7	10	14	16	21	0.85
0.90	1	3	5	7	9	2	5	7	9	13	5	8	11	13	16	8	12	16	18	24	0.90
0.95	2	4	6	8	11	2	6	8	10	14	6	9	12	14	18	9	13	17	20	27	0.95
1.0	2	4	7	9	13	3	6	9	11	16	6	10	13	16	22	10	14	19	22	29	1.0
1.1	2	5	8	10	16	3	7	10	13	19	7	11	16	19	26	12	17	23	27	36	1.1

1.2	2	6	10	12	19	4	8	12	16	23	8	13	19	23	31	14	20	28	32	42	1.2
1.3	3	7	11	15	22	5	9	15	18	27	9	15	22	27	37	16	24	32	38	50	1.3
1.4	3	8	13	17	26	5	11	17	21	31	11	18	26	31	42	19	28	38	44	58	1.4
1.5	4	9	15	19	29	6	12	19	24	36	12	20	29	36	49	22	32	43	50	66	1.5
1.6	4	10	17	22	33	7	14	22	28	40	14	23	33	40	55	24	36	49	57	75	1.6
1.7	5	11	19	25	38	8	16	25	31	46	16	26	38	46	63	28	41	55	65	85	1.7
1.8	5	12	21	28	42	9	17	28	35	51	18	29	42	51	70	31	46	62	73	95	1.8
1.9	6	14	24	31	47	10	19	31	39	57	20	33	47	57	78	35	51	69	81	106	1.9
2.0	7	15	26	34	52	11	22	34	43	63	22	36	52	63	87	38	57	77	90	117	2.0
2.1	7	17	29	38	57	12	24	38	48	70	24	40	57	70	95	42	63	84	99	129	2.1
2.2	8	19	32	42	63	13	26	42	52	76	26	44	63	76	105	46	69	93	109	142	2.2
2.3	9	20	35	45	69	14	29	45	57	83	29	48	69	83	115	51	75	101	119		2.3
2.4	10	22	38	49	75	16	31	49	62	91	31	52	75	91	125	55	82	110	129		2.4
2.5	10	24	41	54	81	17	34	54	68	99	34	56	81	99	135	60	89	120	140		2.5
2.6	11	26	44	58	88	18	36	58	73	107	37	61	88	107	146	65	96	129			2.6
2.7	12	28	48	63	95	20	39	63	79	115	39	66	95	115		70	103	139			2.7
2.8	13	30	52	67	102	21	42	67	85	124	42	71	102	124		75	111	150			2.8
2.9	14	32	55	72	110	23	45	72	91	133	46	76	110	133		80	119				2.9
3.0	15	35	59	77	117	24	48	77	97	143	49	81	117	142		86	128				3.0
3.1	16	37	63	82	125	26	52	82	104		52	87	125			92	136				3.1
3.2	17	39	67	88	133	28	55	88	111		55	92	133			98	145				3.2
3.3	18	42	72	93	142	30	59	93	118		59	98	142			104					3.3
3.4	19	44	76	99	150	31	62	99	125		63	104	151			110					3.4
3.5	20	47	81	105		33	66	105	133		66	110				117					3.5
3.6	21	50	85	111		35	70	111	140		70	117				124					3.6
3.7	23	52	90	117		37	74	117	148		74	123				131					3.7
3.8	24	55	95	124		39	78	124			78	130				138					3.8
3.9	25	58	100	130		41	82	130			82	137				145					3.9
4.0	26	61	105	137		43	86	137			87	144									4.0

Continued

* Tabled values generated by a computer program written by D'Laine Santa Maria, Department of Physical Education, University of Maryland, College Park, Maryland.

TABLE V

Sample Size Estimates for Hypothesis Testing (*Continued*)

FOR $H_0: \mu_1 = \mu_2$

D	α = .10					α = .05					α = .01					α = .001				
β →	0.50	0.25	0.10	0.05	0.01	0.50	0.25	0.10	0.05	0.01	0.50	0.25	0.10	0.05	0.01	0.50	0.25	0.10	0.05	0.01
0.05																				
0.10																				
0.15					1									1	1			1	1	1
0.20					2					1			1	2	2		1	2	2	2
0.25				1	2			1	1	1		1	2	2	3	1	2	2	3	4
0.30				2	3		1	2	1	2	1	2	2	3	4	2	3	3	4	5
0.35			1	2	4		1	2	2	3	1	2	3	4	5	2	4	5	6	7
0.40		1	2	3	5	1	2	3	3	4	2	3	4	5	7	3	5	6	7	9
0.45		1	2	4	6	1	2	4	4	6	2	4	5	6	9	4	6	8	9	12
0.50	1	2	3	4	7	1	3	4	5	8	3	5	7	8	11	5	7	10	11	15
0.55	1	2	3	5	8	2	3	5	7	10	3	5	8	10	13	6	9	12	14	18
0.60	1	3	4	6	9	2	4	6	8	11	4	7	9	11	16	7	10	14	16	21
0.65	2	3	5	7	11	2	5	7	9	13	5	8	11	13	18	8	12	16	19	25
0.70	2	4	6	8	13	3	5	8	11	16	5	9	13	16	21	9	14	19	22	29
0.75	2	4	7	10	15	3	6	10	12	18	6	10	15	18	24	11	16	22	25	33
0.80	2	5	8	11	17	4	7	11	14	20	7	12	17	20	28	12	18	25	29	38
0.85	3	6	10	12	19	4	8	12	16	23	8	13	19	23	31	14	21	28	32	42
0.90	3	6	11	14	21	4	9	14	18	26	9	15	21	26	35	16	23	31	36	48
0.95	3	7	12	16	24	5	10	16	20	29	10	16	24	29	39	17	26	35	41	53
1.0	3	8	13	17	26	5	11	17	22	32	11	18	26	32	43	19	28	38	45	59

1.1	4	9	16	21	32	7	13	21	26	38	13	22	32	38	52	23	34	46	54	71	1.1
1.2	5	11	19	25	38	8	16	25	31	45	16	26	38	45	62	28	41	55	65	85	1.2
1.3	6	13	22	29	44	9	18	29	37	53	18	30	44	53	73	32	48	65	76	99	1.3
1.4	6	15	26	34	51	11	21	34	42	62	21	35	51	62	85	37	56	75	88	115	1.4
1.5	7	17	30	39	59	12	24	39	49	71	24	41	59	71	97	43	64	86	101	132	1.5
1.6	8	20	34	44	67	14	28	44	55	81	28	46	67	81	111	49	73	98	115	150	1.6
1.7	10	22	38	50	75	16	31	50	63	91	31	52	75	91	125	55	82	111	130		1.7
1.8	11	25	43	56	84	18	35	56	70	102	35	58	84	102	140	62	92	124	145		1.8
1.9	12	28	48	62	94	20	39	62	78	114	39	65	94	114		69	102	138			1.9
2.0	13	31	53	69	104	22	43	69	87	126	43	72	104	126		76	113				2.0
2.1	15	34	58	76	115	24	48	76	100	139	48	79	115	139		84	125				2.1
2.2	16	37	64	83	126	26	52	83	105		52	87	126			92	137				2.2
2.3	17	41	70	91	138	29	57	91	115		57	95	138			101	150				2.3
2.4	19	44	76	99	150	31	62	99	125		62	104	150			110					2.4
2.5	21	48	82	107		34	67	107	135		68	113				119					2.5
2.6	22	52	89	116		37	73	116	146		73	122				129					2.6
2.7	24	56	96	125		40	78	125			79	131				139					2.7
2.8	26	60	103	134		42	84	134			85	142				150					2.8
2.9	28	64	111	144		46	91	144			91										2.9
3.0	30	69	118			49	97				97										3.0
3.1	32	74	126			52	103				104										3.1
3.2	34	78	135			55	110				111										3.2
3.3	36	83	143			59	117				118										3.3
3.4	38	89				63	124				125										3.4
3.5	40	94				66	132				133										3.5
3.6	43	99				70	140				140										3.6
3.7	45	105				74	147				148										3.7
3.8	48	111				78															3.8
3.9	50	116				82															3.9
4.0	53	123				87															4.0

TABLE VI

The Chi-Square Distribution[a]

d.f.	$\chi^2_{0.005}$	$\chi^2_{0.005}$	$\chi^2_{0.01}$	$\chi^2_{0.025}$	$\chi^2_{0.05}$	$\chi^2_{0.10}$	$\chi^2_{0.20}$	$\chi^2_{0.30}$	$\chi^2_{0.40}$
1	0.000000393	0.0000393	0.000157	0.000982	0.00393	0.0158	0.0642	0.148	0.275
2	0.00100	0.0100	0.0201	0.0506	0.103	0.211	0.446	0.713	1.022
3	0.0153	0.0717	0.115	0.216	0.352	0.584	1.005	1.424	1.869
4	0.0639	0.207	0.297	0.484	0.711	1.004	1.649	2.195	2.753
5	0.158	0.412	0.554	0.831	1.145	1.610	2.343	3.000	3.655
6	0.299	0.676	0.872	1.237	1.635	2.204	3.070	3.828	4.570
7	0.485	0.989	1.239	1.690	2.167	2.833	3.822	4.671	5.493
8	0.710	1.344	1.646	2.180	2.733	3.490	4.594	5.527	6.423
9	0.972	1.735	2.088	2.700	3.325	4.168	5.380	6.393	7.357
10	1.265	2.156	2.558	3.247	3.940	4.865	6.179	7.267	8.295
11	1.587	2.603	3.053	3.816	4.575	5.578	6.989	8.148	9.237
12	1.934	3.074	3.571	4.404	5.226	6.304	7.807	9.034	10.182
13	2.305	3.565	4.107	5.009	5.892	7.042	8.634	9.926	11.129
14	2.697	4.075	4.660	5.629	6.571	7.790	9.467	10.821	12.079
15	3.108	4.601	5.229	6.262	7.261	8.547	10.307	11.721	13.030
16	3.536	5.142	5.812	6.908	7.962	9.312	11.152	12.624	13.983
17	3.980	5.697	6.408	7.564	8.672	10.085	12.002	13.531	14.937
18	4.439	6.265	7.015	8.231	9.390	10.865	12.857	14.440	15.893
19	4.912	6.844	7.633	8.907	10.117	11.651	13.716	15.352	16.850
20	5.398	7.434	8.260	9.591	10.851	12.443	14.578	16.266	17.809
21	5.896	8.034	8.897	10.283	11.591	13.240	15.445	17.182	18.768
22	6.405	8.643	9.542	10.982	12.338	14.041	16.314	18.101	19.729
23	6.924	9.260	10.196	11.688	13.091	14.848	17.187	19.021	20.690
24	7.453	9.886	10.856	12.401	13.848	15.659	18.062	19.943	21.652
25	7.991	10.520	11.524	13.120	14.611	16.473	18.940	20.867	22.616
26	8.538	11.160	12.198	13.844	15.379	17.292	19.820	21.792	23.579
27	9.093	11.808	12.879	14.573	16.151	18.114	20.703	22.719	24.544
28	9.656	12.461	13.565	15.308	16.928	18.939	21.588	23.647	25.509
29	10.227	13.121	14.256	16.047	17.708	19.768	22.475	24.577	26.475
30	10.804	13.787	14.953	16.791	18.493	20.599	23.364	25.508	27.442
35	13.788	17.192	18.509	20.569	22.465	24.797	27.836	30.178	32.282
40	16.906	20.707	22.164	24.433	26.509	29.051	32.345	34.872	37.134
45	20.136	24.311	25.901	28.366	30.612	33.350	36.884	39.585	41.995
50	23.461	27.991	29.707	32.357	34.764	37.689	41.449	44.313	46.864
60	30.340	35.535	37.485	40.482	43.188	46.459	50.641	53.809	56.620
70	37.467	43.275	45.442	48.758	51.739	55.329	59.898	63.346	66.396
80	44.791	51.172	53.540	57.153	60.391	64.278	69.207	72.915	76.188
90	52.276	59.196	61.754	65.647	69.126	73.291	78.558	82.511	85.993
100	59.897	67.328	70.065	74.222	77.930	82.358	87.945	92.129	95.808
120	75.468	83.852	86.924	91.573	95.705	100.624	106.806	111.419	115.465
140	91.393	100.655	104.035	109.137	113.659	119.029	125.758	130.766	135.149
160	107.598	117.680	121.346	126.870	131.756	137.546	144.783	150.158	154.856
180	124.033	134.885	138.821	144.741	149.969	156.153	163.868	169.588	174.580
200	140.661	152.241	156.432	162.728	168.279	174.835	183.003	189.049	194.319

[a] Reproduced from *Documenta Geigy Scientific Tables*, 7th edition, Basle, Switzerland, 1970. Courtesy CIBA-GEIGY Limited, Basle, Switzerland.

$\chi^2_{0.50}$	$\chi^2_{0.60}$	$\chi^2_{0.70}$	$\chi^2_{0.80}$	$\chi^2_{0.90}$	$\chi^2_{0.95}$	$\chi^2_{0.975}$	$\chi^2_{0.99}$	$\chi^2_{0.995}$	$\chi^2_{0.9995}$	d.f.
0.455	0.708	1.074	1.642	2.706	3.841	5.024	6.635	7.879	12.116	1
1.386	1.833	2.408	3.219	4.605	5.991	7.378	9.210	10.597	15.202	2
2.366	2.946	3.665	4.642	6.251	7.815	9.348	11.345	12.838	17.730	3
3.357	4.045	4.878	5.989	7.779	9.488	11.143	13.277	14.860	19.998	4
4.351	5.132	6.064	7.289	9.236	11.070	12.832	15.086	16.750	22.105	5
5.348	6.211	7.231	8.558	10.645	12.592	14.449	16.812	18.548	24.103	6
6.346	7.283	8.383	9.803	12.017	14.067	16.013	18.475	20.278	26.018	7
7.344	8.351	9.524	11.030	13.362	15.507	17.535	20.090	21.955	27.868	8
8.343	9.414	10.656	12.242	14.684	16.919	19.023	21.666	23.589	29.666	9
9.342	10.473	11.781	13.442	15.987	18.307	20.483	23.209	25.188	31.419	10
10.341	11.530	12.899	14.631	17.275	19.675	21.920	24.725	26.757	33.136	11
11.340	12.584	14.011	15.812	18.549	21.026	23.336	26.217	28.300	34.821	12
12.340	13.636	15.119	16.985	19.812	22.362	24.736	27.688	29.819	36.478	13
13.339	14.685	16.222	18.151	21.064	23.685	26.119	29.141	31.319	38.109	14
14.339	15.733	17.322	19.311	22.307	24.996	27.488	30.578	32.601	39.719	15
15.338	16.780	18.418	20.465	23.542	26.296	28.845	32.000	34.267	41.308	16
16.338	17.824	19.511	21.615	24.769	27.587	30.191	33.409	35.718	42.879	17
17.338	18.868	20.601	22.760	25.989	28.869	31.526	34.805	37.156	44.434	18
18.338	19.910	21.689	23.900	27.204	30.144	32.852	36.191	38.582	45.973	19
19.337	20.951	22.775	25.038	28.412	31.410	34.170	37.566	39.997	47.498	20
20.337	21.991	23.858	26.171	29.615	32.671	35.479	38.932	41.401	49.010	21
21.337	23.031	24.939	27.301	30.813	33.924	36.781	40.289	42.796	50.511	22
22.337	24.069	26.018	28.429	32.007	35.172	38.076	41.638	44.181	52.000	23
23.337	25.106	27.096	29.553	33.196	36.415	39.364	42.980	45.558	53.479	24
24.337	26.143	28.172	30.675	34.382	37.652	40.646	44.314	46.928	54.947	25
25.336	27.179	29.246	31.795	35.563	38.885	41.923	45.642	48.290	56.407	26
26.336	28.214	30.319	32.912	36.741	40.113	43.194	46.963	49.645	57.858	27
27.336	29.249	31.391	34.027	37.916	41.337	44.461	48.278	50.993	59.300	28
28.336	30.283	32.461	35.139	39.087	42.537	45.722	49.588	52.336	60.734	29
29.336	31.316	33.530	36.250	40.256	43.773	46.979	50.892	53.672	62.161	30
34.336	36.475	38.859	41.778	46.059	49.802	53.203	57.342	60.275	69.198	35
39.335	41.622	44.165	47.269	51.805	55.758	59.342	63.691	66.766	76.095	40
44.335	46.761	49.452	52.729	57.505	61.656	65.410	69.957	73.166	82.876	45
49.335	51.892	54.723	58.164	63.167	67.505	71.420	76.154	79.490	89.561	50
59.335	62.135	65.226	68.972	74.397	79.082	83.298	88.379	91.952	102.695	60
69.334	72.358	75.689	79.715	85.527	90.531	95.023	100.425	104.215	115.577	70
79.334	82.566	86.120	90.405	96.578	101.879	106.629	112.329	116.321	128.261	80
89.334	92.761	96.524	101.054	107.565	113.145	118.136	124.116	128.299	140.783	90
99.334	102.946	106.906	111.667	118.498	124.342	129.561	135.806	140.169	153.165	100
119.334	123.289	127.616	132.806	140.233	146.567	152.211	158.950	163.648	177.602	120
139.334	143.604	148.269	153.854	161.827	168.613	174.648	181.840	186.846	201.682	140
159.334	163.898	168.876	174.828	183.311	190.516	196.915	204.530	209.824	225.480	160
179.334	184.173	189.446	195.743	204.704	212.304	219.044	227.056	232.620	249.048	180
199.334	204.434	209.985	216.609	226.021	233.994	241.058	249.445	255.264	272.422	200

TABLE VII

Critical Values of U and U'

FOR A ONE-TAILED TEST, $\alpha = 0.005$
FOR A TWO-TAILED TEST, $\alpha = 0.01$

Values shown as U / U'.

n_1 \ n_2	1	2	3	4	5	6	7	8	9	10	11	12	13	14	15	16	17	18	19	20
1	—[b]	—	—	—	—	—	—	—	—	—	—	—	—	—	—	—	—	—	—	—
2	—	—	—	—	—	—	—	—	—	—	—	—	—	—	—	—	—	—	0/38	0/40
3	—	—	—	—	—	—	—	—	0/27	0/30	0/33	1/35	1/38	1/41	2/43	2/46	2/49	2/52	3/54	3/57
4	—	—	—	—	—	0/24	0/28	1/31	1/35	2/38	2/42	3/45	3/49	4/52	5/55	5/59	6/62	6/66	7/69	8/72
5	—	—	—	—	0/25	1/29	1/34	2/38	3/42	4/46	5/50	6/54	7/58	7/63	8/67	9/71	10/75	11/79	12/83	13/87
6	—	—	—	0/24	1/29	2/34	3/39	4/44	5/49	6/54	7/59	9/63	10/68	11/73	12/78	13/83	15/87	16/92	17/97	18/102
7	—	—	—	0/28	1/34	3/39	4/45	6/50	7/56	9/61	10/67	12/72	13/78	15/83	16/89	18/94	19/100	21/105	22/111	24/116
8	—	—	—	1/31	2/38	4/44	6/50	7/57	9/63	11/69	13/75	15/81	17/87	18/94	20/100	22/106	24/112	26/118	28/124	30/130
9	—	—	0/27	1/35	3/42	5/49	7/56	9/63	11/70	13/77	16/83	18/90	20/97	22/104	24/111	27/117	29/124	31/131	33/138	36/144
10	—	—	0/30	2/38	4/46	6/54	9/61	11/69	13/77	16/84	18/92	21/99	24/106	26/114	29/121	31/129	34/136	37/143	39/151	42/158
11	—	—	0/33	2/42	5/50	7/59	10/67	13/75	16/83	18/92	21/100	24/108	27/116	30/124	33/132	36/140	39/148	42/156	45/164	48/172
12	—	—	1/35	3/45	6/54	9/63	12/72	15/81	18/90	21/99	24/108	27/117	31/125	34/134	37/143	41/151	44/160	47/169	51/177	54/186
13	—	—	1/38	3/49	7/58	10/68	13/78	17/87	20/97	24/106	27/116	31/125	34/135	38/144	42/153	45/163	49/172	53/181	56/191	60/200
14	—	—	1/41	4/52	7/63	11/73	15/83	18/94	22/104	26/114	30/124	34/134	38/144	42/154	46/164	50/174	54/184	58/194	63/203	67/213
15	—	—	2/43	5/55	8/67	12/78	16/89	20/100	24/111	29/121	33/132	37/143	42/153	46/164	51/174	55/185	60/195	64/206	69/216	73/227
16	—	—	2/46	5/59	9/71	13/83	18/94	22/106	27/117	31/129	36/140	41/151	45/163	50/174	55/185	60/196	65/207	70/218	74/230	79/241
17	—	—	2/49	6/62	10/75	15/87	19/100	24/112	29/124	34/136	39/148	44/160	49/172	54/184	60/195	65/207	70/219	75/231	81/242	86/254
18	—	—	2/52	6/66	11/79	16/92	21/105	26/118	31/131	37/143	42/156	47/169	53/181	58/194	64/206	70/218	75/231	81/243	87/255	92/268
19	—	0/38	3/54	7/69	12/83	17/97	22/111	28/124	33/138	39/151	45/164	51/177	56/191	63/203	69/216	74/230	81/242	87/255	93/268	99/281
20	—	0/40	3/57	8/72	13/87	18/102	24/116	30/130	36/144	42/158	48/172	54/186	60/200	67/213	73/227	79/241	86/254	92/268	99/281	105/295

[a] To be significant for any given n_1 and n_2: Obtained U must be equal to or *less than* the value shown in the table. Obtained U' must be equal to or *greater than* the value shown in the table.

[b] Dashes in the body of the table indicate that no decision is possible at the stated level of significance.

From "On a Test of Whether One of Two Random Variables is Stochastically Larger than the Other," *The Annals of Statistics*, Vol. 18 (1947), pp. 52–54, by H. B. Mann and D. R. Whitney. Reproduced with the kind permission of Ingram Olkin, editor of *The Annals of Statistics*.

TABLE VII

Critical Values of U and U' (Continued)

FOR A ONE-TAILED TEST, $\alpha = 0.01$
FOR A TWO-TAILED TEST, $\alpha = 0.02$

n_2\n_1	1	2	3	4	5	6	7	8	9	10	11	12	13	14	15	16	17	18	19	20
1	—	—	—	—	—	—	—	—	—	—	—	—	—	—	—	—	—	—	—	—
2	—	—	—	—	—	—	—	—	—	—	—	—	0 26	0 28	0 30	0 32	0 34	0 36	1 37	1 39
3	—	—	—	—	—	—	0 21	0 24	1 26	1 29	1 32	2 34	2 37	2 40	3 42	3 45	4 47	4 50	4 52	5 55
4	—	—	—	—	0 20	1 23	1 27	2 30	3 33	3 37	4 40	5 43	5 47	6 50	7 53	7 57	8 60	9 63	9 67	10 70
5	—	—	—	0 20	1 24	2 28	3 32	4 36	5 40	6 44	7 48	8 52	9 56	10 60	11 64	12 68	13 72	14 76	15 80	16 84
6	—	—	—	1 23	2 28	3 33	4 38	6 42	7 47	8 52	9 57	11 61	12 66	13 71	15 75	16 80	18 84	19 89	20 94	22 93
7	—	—	0 21	1 27	3 32	4 38	6 43	7 49	9 54	11 59	12 65	14 70	16 75	17 81	19 86	21 91	23 96	24 102	26 107	28 112
8	—	—	0 24	2 30	4 36	6 42	7 49	9 55	11 61	13 67	15 73	17 79	20 84	22 90	24 96	26 102	28 108	30 114	32 120	34 126
9	—	—	1 26	3 33	5 40	7 47	9 54	11 61	14 67	16 74	18 81	21 87	23 94	26 100	28 107	31 113	33 120	36 126	38 133	40 140
10	—	—	1 29	3 37	6 44	8 52	11 59	13 67	16 74	19 81	22 88	24 96	27 103	30 110	33 117	36 124	38 132	41 139	44 146	47 153
11	—	—	1 32	4 40	7 48	9 57	12 65	15 73	18 81	22 88	25 96	28 104	31 112	34 120	37 128	41 135	44 143	47 151	50 159	53 167
12	—	—	2 34	5 43	8 52	11 61	14 70	17 79	21 87	24 96	28 104	31 113	35 121	38 130	42 138	46 146	49 155	53 163	56 172	60 180
13	—	0 26	2 37	5 47	9 56	12 66	16 75	20 84	23 94	27 103	31 112	35 121	39 130	43 139	47 148	51 157	55 166	59 175	63 184	67 193
14	—	0 28	2 40	6 50	10 60	13 71	17 81	22 90	26 100	30 110	34 120	38 130	43 139	47 149	51 159	56 168	60 178	65 187	69 197	73 207
15	—	0 30	3 42	7 53	11 64	15 75	19 86	24 96	28 107	33 117	37 128	42 138	47 148	51 159	56 169	61 179	66 189	70 200	75 210	80 220
16	—	0 32	3 45	7 57	12 68	16 80	21 91	26 102	31 113	36 124	41 135	46 146	51 157	56 168	61 179	66 190	71 201	76 212	82 222	87 233
17	—	0 34	4 47	8 60	13 72	18 84	23 96	28 108	33 120	38 132	44 143	49 155	55 166	60 178	66 189	71 201	77 212	82 224	88 234	93 247
18	—	0 36	4 50	9 63	14 76	19 89	24 102	30 114	36 126	41 139	47 151	53 163	59 175	65 187	70 200	76 212	82 224	88 236	94 248	100 260
19	—	1 37	4 53	9 67	15 80	20 94	26 107	32 120	38 133	44 146	50 159	56 172	63 184	69 197	75 210	82 222	88 235	94 248	101 260	107 273
20	—	1 39	5 55	10 70	16 84	22 98	28 112	34 126	40 140	47 153	53 167	60 180	67 193	73 207	80 220	87 233	93 247	100 260	107 273	114 286

Continued

TABLE VII

Critical Values of U and U' (*Continued*)

FOR A ONE-TAILED TEST, $\alpha = 0.025$
FOR A TWO-TAILED TEST, $\alpha = 0.05$

n_2 \ n_1	1	2	3	4	5	6	7	8	9	10	11	12	13	14	15	16	17	18	19	20
1	—	—	—	—	—	—	—	—	—	—	—	—	—	—	—	—	—	—	—	—
2	—	—	—	—	—	—	—	0 16	0 18	0 20	0 22	1 23	1 25	1 27	1 29	1 31	2 32	2 34	2 36	2 38
3	—	—	—	—	0 15	1 17	1 20	2 22	2 25	3 27	3 30	4 32	4 35	5 37	5 40	6 42	6 45	7 47	7 50	8 52
4	—	—	—	0 16	1 19	2 22	3 25	4 28	4 32	5 35	6 38	7 41	8 44	9 47	10 50	11 53	11 57	12 60	13 63	13 67
5	—	—	0 15	1 19	2 23	3 27	5 30	6 34	7 38	8 42	9 46	11 49	12 53	13 57	14 61	15 65	17 68	18 72	19 76	20 80
6	—	—	1 17	2 22	3 27	5 31	6 36	8 40	10 44	11 49	13 53	14 58	16 62	17 67	19 71	21 75	22 80	24 84	25 89	27 93
7	—	—	1 20	3 25	5 30	6 36	8 41	10 46	12 51	14 56	16 61	18 66	20 71	22 76	24 81	26 86	28 91	30 96	32 101	34 106
8	—	0 16	2 22	4 28	6 34	8 40	10 46	13 51	15 57	17 63	19 69	22 74	24 80	26 86	29 91	31 97	34 102	36 108	38 111	41 119
9	—	0 18	2 25	4 32	7 38	10 44	12 51	15 57	17 64	20 70	23 76	26 82	28 89	31 95	34 101	37 107	39 114	42 120	45 126	48 132
10	—	0 20	3 27	5 35	8 42	11 49	14 56	17 63	20 70	23 77	26 84	29 91	33 97	36 104	39 111	42 118	45 125	48 132	52 138	55 145
11	—	0 22	3 30	6 38	9 46	13 53	16 61	19 69	23 76	26 84	30 91	33 99	37 106	40 114	44 121	47 129	51 136	55 143	58 151	62 158
12	—	1 23	4 32	7 41	11 49	14 58	18 66	22 74	26 82	29 91	33 99	37 107	41 115	45 123	49 131	53 139	57 147	61 155	65 163	69 171
13	—	1 25	4 35	8 44	12 53	16 62	20 71	24 80	28 89	33 97	37 106	41 115	45 124	50 132	54 141	59 149	63 158	67 167	72 175	76 184
14	—	1 27	5 37	9 47	13 51	17 67	22 76	26 86	31 95	36 104	40 114	45 123	50 132	55 141	59 151	64 160	67 171	74 178	78 188	83 197
15	—	1 29	5 40	10 50	14 61	19 71	24 81	29 91	34 101	39 111	44 121	49 131	54 141	59 151	64 161	70 170	75 180	80 190	85 200	90 210
16	—	1 31	6 42	11 53	15 65	21 75	26 86	31 97	37 107	42 118	47 129	53 139	59 149	64 160	70 170	75 181	81 191	86 202	92 212	98 222
17	—	2 32	6 45	11 57	17 68	22 80	28 91	34 102	39 114	45 125	51 136	57 147	63 158	67 171	75 180	81 191	87 202	93 213	99 224	105 235
18	—	2 34	7 47	12 60	18 72	24 84	30 96	36 108	42 120	48 132	55 143	61 155	67 167	74 178	80 190	86 202	93 213	99 225	106 236	112 248
19	—	2 36	7 50	13 63	19 76	25 89	32 101	38 114	45 126	52 138	58 151	65 163	72 175	78 188	85 200	92 212	99 224	106 236	113 248	119 261
20	—	2 38	8 52	13 67	20 80	27 93	34 106	41 119	48 132	55 145	62 158	69 171	76 184	83 197	90 210	98 222	105 235	112 248	119 261	127 273

TABLE VII

Critical Values of U and U' (*Continued*)

FOR A ONE-TAILED TEST, $\alpha = 0.05$
FOR A TWO-TAILED TEST, $\alpha = 0.10$

n_2 \ n_1	1	2	3	4	5	6	7	8	9	10	11	12	13	14	15	16	17	18	19	20
1	—	—	—	—	—	—	—	—	—	—	—	—	—	—	—	—	—	—	0 / 19	0 / 20
2	—	—	—	—	0 / 10	0 / 12	0 / 14	1 / 15	1 / 17	1 / 19	1 / 21	2 / 22	2 / 24	2 / 26	3 / 27	3 / 29	3 / 31	4 / 32	4 / 34	4 / 36
3	—	—	0 / 9	0 / 12	1 / 14	2 / 16	2 / 19	3 / 21	3 / 24	4 / 26	5 / 28	5 / 31	6 / 33	7 / 35	7 / 38	8 / 40	9 / 42	9 / 45	10 / 47	11 / 49
4	—	—	0 / 12	1 / 15	2 / 18	3 / 21	4 / 24	5 / 27	6 / 30	7 / 33	8 / 36	9 / 39	10 / 42	11 / 45	12 / 48	14 / 50	15 / 53	16 / 56	17 / 59	18 / 62
5	—	0 / 10	1 / 14	2 / 18	4 / 21	5 / 25	6 / 29	8 / 32	9 / 36	11 / 39	12 / 43	13 / 47	15 / 50	16 / 54	18 / 57	19 / 61	20 / 65	22 / 68	23 / 72	25 / 75
6	—	0 / 12	2 / 16	3 / 21	5 / 25	7 / 29	8 / 34	10 / 38	12 / 42	14 / 46	16 / 50	17 / 55	19 / 59	21 / 63	23 / 67	25 / 71	26 / 76	28 / 80	30 / 84	32 / 88
7	—	0 / 14	2 / 19	4 / 24	6 / 29	8 / 34	11 / 38	13 / 43	15 / 48	17 / 53	19 / 58	21 / 63	24 / 67	26 / 72	28 / 77	30 / 82	33 / 86	35 / 91	37 / 96	39 / 101
8	—	1 / 15	3 / 21	5 / 27	8 / 32	10 / 38	13 / 43	15 / 49	18 / 54	20 / 60	23 / 65	26 / 70	28 / 76	31 / 81	33 / 87	36 / 92	39 / 97	41 / 103	44 / 108	47 / 113
9	—	1 / 17	3 / 24	6 / 30	9 / 36	12 / 42	15 / 48	18 / 54	21 / 60	24 / 66	27 / 72	30 / 78	33 / 84	36 / 90	39 / 96	42 / 102	45 / 108	48 / 114	51 / 120	54 / 126
10	—	1 / 19	4 / 26	7 / 33	11 / 39	14 / 46	17 / 53	20 / 60	24 / 66	27 / 73	31 / 79	34 / 86	37 / 93	41 / 99	44 / 106	48 / 112	51 / 119	55 / 125	58 / 132	62 / 138
11	—	1 / 21	5 / 28	8 / 36	12 / 43	16 / 50	19 / 58	23 / 65	27 / 72	31 / 79	34 / 87	38 / 94	42 / 101	46 / 108	50 / 115	54 / 122	57 / 130	61 / 137	65 / 144	69 / 151
12	—	2 / 22	5 / 31	9 / 39	13 / 47	17 / 55	21 / 63	26 / 70	30 / 78	34 / 86	38 / 94	42 / 102	47 / 109	51 / 117	55 / 125	60 / 132	64 / 140	68 / 148	72 / 156	77 / 163
13	—	2 / 24	6 / 33	10 / 42	15 / 50	19 / 59	24 / 67	28 / 76	33 / 84	37 / 93	42 / 101	47 / 109	51 / 118	56 / 126	61 / 134	65 / 143	70 / 151	75 / 159	80 / 167	84 / 176
14	—	2 / 26	7 / 35	11 / 45	16 / 54	21 / 63	26 / 72	31 / 81	36 / 90	41 / 99	46 / 108	51 / 117	56 / 126	61 / 135	66 / 144	71 / 153	77 / 161	82 / 170	87 / 179	92 / 188
15	—	3 / 27	7 / 38	12 / 48	18 / 57	23 / 67	28 / 77	33 / 87	39 / 96	44 / 106	50 / 115	55 / 125	61 / 134	66 / 144	72 / 153	77 / 163	83 / 172	88 / 182	94 / 191	100 / 200
16	—	3 / 29	8 / 40	14 / 50	19 / 61	25 / 71	30 / 82	36 / 92	42 / 102	48 / 112	54 / 122	60 / 132	65 / 143	71 / 153	77 / 163	83 / 173	89 / 183	95 / 193	101 / 203	107 / 213
17	—	3 / 31	9 / 42	15 / 53	20 / 65	26 / 76	33 / 86	39 / 97	45 / 108	51 / 119	57 / 130	64 / 140	70 / 151	77 / 161	83 / 172	89 / 183	96 / 193	102 / 204	109 / 214	115 / 225
18	—	4 / 32	9 / 45	16 / 56	22 / 68	28 / 80	35 / 91	41 / 103	48 / 114	55 / 123	61 / 137	68 / 148	75 / 159	82 / 170	88 / 182	95 / 193	102 / 204	109 / 215	116 / 226	123 / 237
19	0 / 19	4 / 34	10 / 47	17 / 59	23 / 72	30 / 84	37 / 96	44 / 108	51 / 120	58 / 132	65 / 144	72 / 156	80 / 167	87 / 179	94 / 191	101 / 203	109 / 214	116 / 226	123 / 238	130 / 250
20	0 / 20	4 / 36	11 / 49	18 / 62	25 / 75	32 / 88	39 / 101	47 / 113	54 / 126	62 / 138	69 / 151	77 / 163	84 / 176	92 / 188	100 / 200	107 / 213	115 / 225	123 / 237	130 / 250	138 / 262

TABLE VIII

The Cumulative Binomial Distribution[a]

$P = 0.50$

x_0 \ N	1	2	3	4	5	6	7	8	9	10
0	0.50000	0.25000	0.12500	0.06250	0.03125	0.01563	0.00781	0.00391	0.00195	0.00098
1	1.00000	0.75000	0.50000	0.31250	0.18750	0.10938	0.06250	0.03516	0.01953	0.01074
2		1.00000	0.87500	0.68750	0.50000	0.34375	0.22656	0.14453	0.08984	0.05469
3			1.00000	0.93750	0.81250	0.65625	0.50000	0.36328	0.25391	0.17188
4				1.00000	0.96875	0.89063	0.77344	0.63672	0.50000	0.37695
5					1.00000	0.98438	0.93750	0.85547	0.74609	0.62305
6						1.00000	0.99219	0.96484	0.91016	0.82813
7							1.00000	0.99609	0.98047	0.94531
8								1.00000	0.99805	0.98926
9									1.00000	0.99902
10										1.00000

X_0 \ N	11	12	13	14	15	16	17	18	19	20
0	0.00049	0.00024	0.00012	0.00006	0.00003	0.00002	0.00001	0.00000	0.00000	0.00000
1	0.00586	0.00317	0.00171	0.00092	0.00049	0.00026	0.00014	0.00007	0.00004	0.00002
2	0.03271	0.01929	0.01123	0.00647	0.00369	0.00209	0.00117	0.00066	0.00036	0.00020
3	0.11328	0.07300	0.04614	0.02869	0.01758	0.01064	0.00636	0.00377	0.00221	0.00129
4	0.27441	0.19385	0.13342	0.08978	0.05923	0.03841	0.02452	0.01544	0.00961	0.00591
5	0.50000	0.38721	0.29053	0.21198	0.15088	0.10506	0.07173	0.04813	0.03178	0.02069
6	0.72559	0.61279	0.50000	0.39526	0.30362	0.22725	0.16615	0.11894	0.08353	0.05766
7	0.88672	0.80615	0.70947	0.60474	0.50000	0.40181	0.31453	0.24034	0.17964	0.13159
8	0.96729	0.92700	0.86658	0.78802	0.69638	0.59819	0.50000	0.40726	0.32380	0.25172
9	0.99414	0.98071	0.95386	0.91022	0.84912	0.77275	0.68547	0.59274	0.50000	0.41190
10	0.99951	0.99683	0.98877	0.97131	0.94077	0.89494	0.83385	0.75966	0.67620	0.58810
11	1.00000	0.99976	0.99829	0.99353	0.98242	0.96159	0.92827	0.88106	0.82036	0.74828
12		1.00000	0.99988	0.99908	0.99631	0.98936	0.97548	0.95187	0.91647	0.86841
13			1.00000	0.99994	0.99951	0.99791	0.99364	0.98456	0.96822	0.94234
14				1.00000	0.99997	0.99974	0.99883	0.99623	0.99039	0.97931
15					1.00000	0.99998	0.99986	0.99934	0.99779	0.99409
16						1.00000	0.99999	0.99993	0.99964	0.99871
17							1.00000	1.00000	0.99996	0.99980
18								1.00000	1.00000	0.99998
19									1.00000	1.00000
20										1.00000

[a] Tabled values generated by a computer program written by D'Laine Santa Maria, Department of Physical Education, University of Maryland, College Park, Maryland. Tabled values are given for $P(X \leq X_0)$.

TABLE IX

Wilcoxon Signed-Rank Test[a]

n = number of pairs

n	Critical Values $\alpha \leq 0.10$	$\alpha \leq 0.05$	$\alpha \leq 0.02$	$\alpha \leq 0.01$
1				
2				
3				
4				
5	0, 15			
6	2, 19	0, 21		
7	3, 25	2, 26	0, 28	
8	5, 31	3, 33	1, 35	0, 36
9	8, 37	5, 40	3, 42	1, 44
10	10, 45	8, 47	5, 50	3, 52
11	13, 53	10, 56	7, 59	5, 61
12	17, 61	13, 65	9, 69	7, 71
13	21, 70	17, 74	12, 79	9, 82
14	25, 80	21, 84	15, 90	12, 93
15	30, 90	25, 95	19, 101	15, 105
16	35, 101	29, 107	23, 113	19, 117
17	41, 112	34, 119	28, 125	23, 130
18	47, 124	40, 131	32, 139	27, 144
19	53, 137	46, 144	37, 153	33, 158
20	60, 150	52, 158	43, 167	37, 173
21	67, 164	58, 173	49, 182	42, 189
22	75, 178	66, 187	55, 198	48, 205
23	83, 193	73, 203	62, 214	54, 222
24	91, 209	81, 210	69, 231	61, 239
25	100, 225	89, 236	76, 249	68, 257

[a] Reproduced from *Documenta Geigy Scientific Tables*, 7th edition, Basle, Switzerland, 1970. Courtesy CIBA-GEIGY Limited, Basle, Switzerland.

Appendix C

Glossary of Symbols
Used in the Text

This Glossary is designed to be used when a preview of unfamiliar notation becomes desirable or when a handy review of previously encountered notation is in order. Given the brief description in the Glossary, the reader can then turn to the chapter and section in the text where the term is explained in greater detail.

Chapter and Section	Mathematical Symbols	
2.2	$a < b$	a is less than b
2.2	$a > b$	a is greater than b
2.2	$a \leqslant b$	a is equal to or less than b
2.2	$a \geqslant b$	a is equal to or greater than b
2.2	P_a	percentile rank of a score or the percentage of cases below the given score
2.2	$Q_1 = P_{25}$	twenty-fifth percentile or first quartile
3.2	Σ	sum of something
3.2	Mdn	median, the middle point in a distribution
3.2	$\bar{X}$	mean or average score of a sample
3.2	M_0	mode or most frequently occurring score in a distribution
3.3	C	coefficient of variation $= \dfrac{s}{X}$
3.3	s	standard deviation for a sample of data
3.3	s^2	variance for a sample of data
3.4	$6\text{-}\sigma_i$	standard score with a mean of 50 and standard deviation of 16.67
3.4	$T\text{-score}_{(i)}$	standard score with a mean of 50 and standard deviation of 10

Chapter and Section	Mathematical Symbols	
3.4	Z_i	standard score with a mean of 0 and standard deviation of 1
4.1	μ	mean or average score of a population
4.3	$\mu_{\overline{x}}$	mean of sample means in a population
4.3	N	total number of observations or scores in a population
4.3	n	total number of observations or scores in a sample
4.3	$\mu_s{}^2$	mean of sample variances in a population
4.3	$s_{\overline{x}}$	standard error of the mean (estimated standard deviation of sample means in a population)
4.3	$s_{\overline{X}}{}^2$	estimated variance of sample means in a population
4.3	σ	population standard deviation
4.3	σ^2	population variance
4.3	$\sigma_{\overline{x}}$	standard deviation of sample means
4.3	$\sigma_{\overline{X}}{}^2$	variance of sample means
5.1	$P(A)$	probability of event A occurring
5.1	$\bar{A}$	collection of outcomes not favorable to the event A
5.2	$(A \text{ or } B)$	composite event "either A or B"; the composite event is said to have occurred only if an outcome favorable to either A or B or both occurs
5.2	(AB)	composite event "A and B"; the composite event is said to have occurred if an outcome favorable to both A and B occurs
5.3	$_nP_n$	number of permutations of a set of n different objects taken all together
5.3	$n!$	"n factorial"; the product of all integers from one to n, inclusive

Chapter and Section	Mathematical Symbols	
5.3	$\cdots$	dot notation employed to represent a series of numerals and/or mathematical operations omitted from a mathematical formula for convenience when the series meaning is understood
5.3	$_nP_r$	number of permutations of n objects, taken r at a time
5.3	$_NP_{n_1,n_2}$	number of permutations of n things, taken all together, when n_1 objects are alike and n_2 objects are alike of another kind
5.3	$\binom{n}{r}$	number of combinations of a set of n different objects, taken r at a time
6.2	X	random variable observed during the conduct of an experiment
6.2	X_i	one of the outcomes for the random variable X
6.3	$E(X)$	expected value for the random variable X
6.3	$\mathrm{Var}(X)$	variance for the random variable X
6.4	p	probability of the event "success" occurring on a single trial of a binomial experiment
6.4	q	probability of the event "failure" occurring on a single trial of a binomial experiment
7.3	Z	standard normal unit
7.4	π	constant term approximately equal to 3.14159
7.4	$f(X)$	frequency of a discrete random variable and the density function of a continuous random variable
7.4	e	constant term approximately equal to 2.71828
7.4	$A(Z)$	area under the standard normal curve between 0 and Z

Chapter and Section	Mathematical Symbols	
8.2	$\hat{\Theta}$	estimator of a population parameter
8.6	$\sigma^2_{\bar{X}_1 - \bar{X}_2}$	variance of the sampling distribution $\bar{X}_1 - \bar{X}_2$
8.7	d.f.	degrees of freedom
8.7	t	random variable following a distribution similar to the normal distribution but dependent upon sample size
8.7	$t_{p,v}$	value of t in a distribution with v degrees of freedom and probability level p
8.9	$s^2_{\bar{X}_1 - \bar{X}_2}$	unbiased estimate of $\sigma^2_{\bar{X}_1 - \bar{X}_2}$
8.9	$s_p{}^2$	pooled estimate of the population variance
8.9	s_p	pooled estimate of the population standard deviation
8.10	d_i	difference between paired observations, $X_{1i} - X_{2i}$
8.10	$\bar{d}$	difference between the means of related groups, $\bar{X}_1 - \bar{X}_2$
9.1	α	probability of rejecting H_0 when H_0 is true
9.1	$1 - \alpha$	probability of accepting H_0 when H_0 is true
9.1	β	probability of accepting H_0 when H_0 is false
9.1	$1 - \beta$	power of a statistical test or the probability of rejecting H_0 when H_0 is false
9.2	H_0	hypothesis which is being tested
9.2	H_A	alternative hypothesis when H_0 is rejected
9.2	μ_0	hypothesized mean of a population
10.2	A	Y-intercept term in the equation identifying the linear relationship between two variables

Chapter and Section		Mathematical Symbols
10.2	B	amount of change in one variable for a corresponding unit change in a second variable; the slope of a straight line
10.2	a	unbiased estimate of the Y-intercept A
10.2	b	unbiased estimate of the slope B
10.2	e_i	error produced when one uses a linear equation to estimate the ith individual's score on one variable knowing his score on a second variable
10.2	Y_i	observed value for the variable Y
10.3	SSE	sum of squares due to error; represents the sum of squared deviations (e_i) from the regression line nearest every (X, Y) point
10.3	SST	total sum of squares; represents the sum of squared deviations from the mean
10.3	SSR	sum of squares for regression; represents that part of the total sum of squares of the random variable that can be explained by a linear relationship between Y and X
10.4	x	deviations from the mean for the random variable X; that is $x = X - \bar{X}$
10.4	y	deviations from the mean for the random variable Y; that is, $y = Y - \bar{Y}$
10.4	$\sigma^2_{Y\mid X}$	standard error of estimate for predicting Y from a known value of X
10.4	$s^2_{Y\mid X}$	unbiased estimate of $\sigma^2_{Y\mid X}$
10.4	$s_a{}^2$	unbiased estimate of the variance for the sample Y-intercept a
10.4	$s_b{}^2$	unbiased estimate of the variance for the sample slope b
10.6	ρ	the coefficient of linear correlation between Y and X
10.6	r	estimate of the coefficient of linear correlation between Y and X

Chapter and Section	Mathematical Symbols	
10.6	r^2	square of the coefficient of linear correlation; represents the amount of variation in the variable Y that can be explained by the linear relationship between the variable Y and the variable X
11.2	SSA	sum of squares among means or among groups; often interpreted as the treatment sum of squares
11.2	SSW	sum of squares within groups often interpreted as the experimental error sum of squares
11.2	MSA	mean square among groups or treatments in the terminology of analysis of variance; represents the variance estimate of the variability among groups or treatments
11.2	MSW	mean square within groups of experimental error in the terminology of analysis of variance; represents the variance estimate of the variability within groups or experimental error
11.3	F	ratio of two variances; random variable describing the random behavior of the ratio of two independent (χ^2) statistics under a stated null hypothesis
11.4	n_i	total number of observations or scores in sample i
11.4	SSG	correction factor for the mean employed in analysis of variance for CR and RCB designed experiments
11.4	G_i	sum of criterion measurements for the ith group
11.4	G	grand total of all observations in the experiment
11.4	k	number of treatments or groups included in the experiment
11.4	T_i	true effect of the ith treatment

Chapter and Section	Mathematical Symbols	
11.4	E	experimental error; defined as the failure of two identically treated experimental units (subjects or objects) to yield identical responses.
11.4	K	total number of treatments or population potentially available for inclusion in an experiment
11.5	q_r	studentized range statistic used to test for the significant difference between sets of ranked treatment means
11.5	$\bar{n}$	harmonic mean of unequal sample sizes
11.6	SSB	sum of squares among blocks
11.6	MSB	mean square among blocks in the terminology of analysis of variance; represents the variance estimate of the variability among blocks
11.6	B_i	sum of criterion measurements for the ith block
11.6	$\bar{Y}._j$	mean value for the jth treatment
11.6	$\bar{Y}_i.$	mean value for the ith block
11.6	$\bar{Y}..$	grand mean for all observations in a RCB designed experiment
11.6	β_i	represents the true effect of the ith block
11.6	m	number of blocks included in an RCB designed experiment
12.2	χ^2	statistic in a test of goodness of fit
12.3	U	statistic used in the Mann-Whitney U-test of equality of distribution of ranks
12.4	T	statistic used in the Wilcoxon Matched-Pairs Signed-Ranked Test of equality of ranks
12.5	r_{rho}	Spearman rank-order correlation coefficient

The Greek Alphabet		
Lowercase	Name of Letter	Capital
α	alpha	A
β	beta	B
γ	gamma	Γ
δ	delta	Δ
ϵ	epsilon	E
ζ	zeta	Z
η	eta	H
θ	theta	Θ
ι	iota	I
κ	kappa	K
λ	lambda	Λ
μ	mu	M
ν	nu	N
ξ	xi	Ξ
o	omicron	O
π	pi	Π
ρ	rho	P
σ	sigma	Σ
τ	tau	T
υ	upsilon	Υ
ϕ	phi	Φ
χ	chi	X
ψ	psi	Ψ
ω	omega	Ω

Index